D1236458

TRIAL OF FAITH

DR. A. STEWART ALLEN (1947)

TRIAL OF FAITH

The Imprisonment of a Medical Missionary

under Chinese Communism, 1950-1951

Dr. A. Stewart Allen

Published by the Estate of Dr. A. Stewart Allen

c/o Barry David Laushway
Beaumont and Laushway
214 King Street West
P.O. Box 190
Prescott, Ontario K0E 1T0
Canada

© 1995 by Dr. A. Stewart Allen

All rights reserved. No part of this book may be reproduced or transmitted in any form by any means without permission in writing from the publisher, except by a reviewer, who may quote brief passages in a review.

Editing, book design, covers, maps and typesetting by Frontenac Wordsmiths, R.R. #5, Brockville, Ontario K6V 5T5

Printed in Canada by Henderson Printing Inc., 23 Abbott Street, Brockville, Ontario K6V 4A5

Canadian Cataloguing in Publication Data

Allen, A. Stewart (Alexander Stewart), 1899-1992

 Trial of faith : the imprisonment of a medical missionary under Chinese communism, 1950-1951

Includes index.
ISBN 0-9698978-0-4

 1. Allen, A. Stewart (Alexander Stewart), 1899-1992— Imprisonment. 2. Missionaries, Medical—China— Biography. 3. United Church of Canada—Missions— China. I. Title.

BV3427.A44A44 1995   266'.792   C95-900009-7

ISBN   0-9698978-0-4

To My Dearest Win

Contents

Preface

WHEN I REACHED Hong Kong at the close of 1951, I had no thought of putting my experiences as a deported Canadian missionary doctor in writing. I still felt my one-year imprisonment by the Chinese Communists was simply the result of a few people's violent animosity toward me.

Before returning to Canada, while I was being briefed on the events of 1951 under the Communists in China, well-meaning Hong Kong friends sheltered me from many representatives of the press. Christian organizations and the Canadian government wisely hesitated to publicize the fate and experiences of many of their imprisoned or released missionaries. They believed that glaring headlines might make the lot of those still in China more difficult.

A few brief news items and one short, moderately-written story, "I Was a Prisoner of the Chinese Reds," published in *Maclean's* magazine on April 15, 1952, seemed to satisfy the public demand for a full, factual statement about my experiences.

Since that time, however, other facts have come to light that considerably alter some aspects of earlier written and verbal statements.

I have delivered some two hundred sermons, talks and lectures on my experience. I also prepared a series of thirteen lectures on China and the Communist movement, which I gave at the Leadership Training School in Naramata, British Columbia. I have answered the eager questions of many hundreds who in varying degrees failed to understand fully the devious methods used by the Communists to make inroads on an unsuspecting public. All these efforts to tell my story convinced me that I could fill a specific need in democratic countries if I were to write the experiences down. Friends have urged me to write as a duty to humanity at large. *Trial of Faith* is the result.

The experiences contained in this memoir span the period from 1949 to 1952. The bulk of the story relates to my experiences in solitary confinement under investigation by the Chinese Communists (December 20, 1950, to August 27, 1951) and later in a Communist prison (August 27 to October 23, 1951), followed by a period under house arrest until my deportation from China on December 28, 1951. From my posts at mission hospitals operated by the United Church of Canada through the Szechuan Synod of the Church of Christ in China, I had watched Communist activities at close range since 1935. I was in China during the Long March,[1] when the mission field of the synod had fallen victim to Communist plundering. Some known Communists were patients in our mission hospital on the south side of the Yangtze River, opposite Chungking, during the Sino-Japanese war from 1938 to 1945. In 1946 I spent a short period as a guest of the Communists while on medical relief investigations in Kalgan, Inner Mongolia, and the surrounding regions, as well as in the Shensi, Honan, Hopei and Shantung border region. Finally, following the Communist takeover of Chungking in late November 1949, I had thirteen months of freedom to work in our hospital, adapting to the new government's changes, before beginning my 373 days as a prisoner of the Chinese Communists.

In preparing *Trial of Faith* I have used the materials I was able to bring or send out of China, along with letters to friends and relatives that I wrote while I was still free to observe changing conditions. I have not always used the real names of those characters who play a part in my story, especially where I have felt any reference to them might lead to personal difficulties for them. Where it seems safe and desirable, full names are given. I have reason to believe that reference to missionaries, even if they are still in Chinese prisons, will cause them no undue harm, since none can be classed as criminals and so do not risk death.

In this book I attempt to show, without exaggeration, how communism works in actual daily practice. The book is a personal one, in which I illustrate my points as I proceed to give in full detail the story of my

---

1 The Long March was the tactical retreat in 1934-35 of the Chinese Communist forces, captained by Mao Tse-tung, Chu Teh, Chou En-lai and Lin Piao. Some 90,000 Communist troops went from Kiangsi province, where they were threatened by Chiang Kai-shek, to sanctuary in Yenan, Shensi province, a journey of some six thousand miles.

accusation, my investigation and my living conditions in prison. I describe the use Communists made of missionaries to extract what they considered valuable information—mostly about other people or organizations suspected of disloyalty—that would contribute to the success of their government. I tell of their attempts to secure information from me concerning my medical services for the U.S. embassy. They intended to use it to build up a criminal case against the United States, considered to be the archenemy of the Soviet Union and her satellites, including China. I explain the Communist methods of indoctrination through "brainwashing," which I, like every other prisoner in similar conditions, was forced to undergo. Through it all, it will become clear just why and how the People's Government, led by Mao Tse-tung and the Communist Party, was able to persuade the five hundred million Chinese to accept without gross reservation their complete subjugation to communist ideologies.

If I have succeeded in providing a readable book which helps ordinary people to understand communism's methods and dangers, I shall feel I have accomplished my aim.

The experiences contained in this book are autobiographical. It has not been an easy task to reveal enough subjective material for the purposes of the book and still deal with it objectively. I have tried to present the facts irrespective of any personal prejudice, giving due credit where that is demanded or condemnation where that seems justified. The degree to which I have succeeded will determine the value of the book.

DR. A. STEWART ALLEN
(1954)

Acknowledgments

M Y THANKS go to my sister Phyllis Donaghy, who left China six years later than I, for her assistance in clarifying some details in our father's book; for providing some photographs from her collection; for copies of the Chinese original of our father's court judgment and deportation order, which was in her possession and appears in the photograph section; for her research into the Allen family history, which appears on page xvii; and for her memories of the Mission Hospital and residence compound, which enabled her to produce the map on the inside back cover. She also drew the Chinese characters for his name, which appeared on his hospital business card and are shown on the front cover.

My sister Gwyneth Smith read through the manuscript and her comments were gratefully received and helped improve the accuracy of the book.

I have appreciated the helpful criticism of my writing by my daughter-in-law Jennifer Gibson. Her literary knowledge helped guide us in selecting titles that expressed the essence of the chapters and the book itself.

Olin Stockwell's son, Foster Stockwell, was able to provide some background history of his father, for which I thank him.

Much credit is due to Evelyn Markell of Busy B Typing Service in Brockville. It was she who initially typed Dr. Allen's original manuscript chapters and transcribed later voice tapes to the written page. She did a remarkable job in view of the many Chinese words and names of places and people contained in his narrative.

I wish to extend my particular thanks to the editor of *Trial of Faith*, Christine Simons Stesky, of Frontenac Wordsmiths in Brockville, Ontario. Although she met with my father only a few times before his final illness, she was able to hear in his own words about some of his experiences during his China years and understood what he wished to convey in the completed book. She told me she wanted his voice to shine through in this account of his imprisonment, and she has been successful in accomplishing this while kindly cutting and condensing the manuscript.

Robert Stesky, also of Frontenac Wordsmiths, has used his artistic expertise in designing the book's covers and drawing the maps on the inside covers. I wish to thank him for his advice on laying out the book and getting it on disk for the printer.

Finally, I am forever grateful to my father for saving all his notes and correspondence, which made it possible to produce this book after he was gone. We have striven for accuracy and readability. Ultimately, I take responsibility for any errors or omissions in the book.

MARGARET (ALLEN) WILLIAMSON

Introduction

D R. STEWART ALLEN went to China as a medical missionary under the auspices of the United Church of Canada in the year 1929, just a few months after his graduation with a degree in Medicine from McGill University in Montreal. He served the Chinese people in the province of Sichuan (then Szechuan) for more than twenty years. His first term in China, from 1929 to 1936, was spent in the city of Leshan (then Kiating) where he was in charge of the medical work at the Canadian (United Church) Mission Hospital. When he returned to Canada on furlough in 1936, he pursued graduate studies and obtained his degree in surgery. He was superintendent of the Mission Hospital in Chongqing (Chungking, as he knew it) from 1938 to 1945 and started a second term there early in 1948. The hospital was located on the south bank of the Yangtze River across from the city proper, which is at the confluence of the Yangtze and Kialing Rivers. After the Communist takeover of the city in late 1949, he decided to continue working at the hospital, although many missionaries chose to leave the country and return to their homelands at that time. In December 1950, just before Christmas, he was led to an accusation meeting in the hall of the Mission Hospital Nursing School adjoining the hospital. At this moment his medical career in China came to an abrupt end and for a year he was no longer a free man. This book describes the events of 1951, when he was held in captivity and eventually deported from the country he had loved so dearly.

I am Dr. Allen's eldest daughter and live with my husband, Don, in the state of Maryland in the United States. I became involved in the work of preparing my father's book for publication after his death at the age of 92 in September 1992. In late June of that year, the last time I saw him well, he introduced me to his editor, Christine Stesky of Brockville, Ontario, to whom he had given his manuscript some weeks earlier. This introduction has led to a close association between the two of us as the project has progressed. Because the manuscript has been edited posthumously, we have had many moments of frustration when we longed to have my father present to clarify a passage. Sometimes we have had to make assumptions based on my family's experiences in China and memories of many conversations with him over the years since 1951. However, it has been our aim to preserve his words, as he wrote them, as much as possible.

From a letter to him and from certain references in the manuscript, we think he had most of his story written by 1954. In a letter dated September 1954, his colleague, Howard Veals, reviews the manuscript, which my father had sent him earlier in the year. As well, in his preface, my father refers to missionaries who might still be in prison in China, which indicates he was writing in the early 1950s, before all missionaries had left the country. For many years, however, the manuscript lay unpublished. My father did not again find time for serious composition until 1987, when he moved into a retirement home with my mother, Winnifred. Using his first draft, handwritten notes and his very detailed recollections, he dictated the account into a tape recorder. The resultant tapes were transcribed by Busy B Typing of Brockville onto the printed page via computer, and it was this word-processed text that he passed on to his editor. We are not sure if he completed what he wished to include in the manuscript. To fill in some of the details we thought would add to his story, we have taken the liberty of writing a new first chapter and an epilogue, both based heavily on his own notes. Also, his original Chapters 11-13 (now Chapters 12-14) have been extensively rewritten and expanded. The material for these additions has been taken from his and my mother's personal letters, written before his incarceration and later after his deportation from China.

Chapter 1, which I compiled from his letters and notes, describes the liberation of Chongqing by the Communists and should help the reader to understand something about life under the new regime, how it affected Dr. Allen personally and also his work at the hospital. Chapter 2 begins with a description of a normal day for Dr. Allen, a day like so many he had spent over the years, with no inkling that it would be the last day he would spend in an operating room in China. Chapter 3 describes the Communists' methods of disposing of their enemies and Chapter 4 details how one of those methods—the accusation meeting—was used against Dr. Allen. The following day he was taken to a place of solitary confinement where he was held for eight months. For the first three months he endured endless days of interrogation and accusation. The meetings with his interrogators are covered in Chapters 5-9. Chapters 10 and 11 are more personal, describing the days in solitary confinement, his secret communication with an American missionary, Rev. F. Olin Stockwell, held in the same prison, and the effects of imprisonment on his Christian faith. Dr. Allen also included a chapter (Chapter 12) about the Rotary Club of Chongqing, of which he was the last president before the Communists outlawed all service clubs with foreign connections. (He was a member of Rotary International for over fifty years and this organization played a very important part in his life. He rarely missed a meeting, even when he was travelling in a foreign country, and he truly lived according to the Rotary motto: "Service above Self." When he eventually entered private practice, after his return from China, he was always deeply involved in church and community affairs.) Chapter 12 was retained for all those Rotarians who will be readers of this book. A chapter on the Communist brainwashing he endured for two months in a typical Chinese prison and another on his house arrest in Chongqing and eventual deportation to Hong Kong and true freedom conclude the account of his imprisonment. Finally, an epilogue, compiled from a rough draft he had written and from correspondence, touches on what he did in Hong Kong before returning home to Canada, where he was debriefed by officials in the Louis St. Laurent government and gave speeches and interviews about his experience. It also summarizes highlights of the Chongqing portion of his nephew's trip to the People's Republic of China in 1993 and his daughters' trip in 1994, showing how China has changed since the liberation of 1949.

Stewart Allen was born into a Wesleyan Methodist family. His paternal ancestors were very strong, talented, well-educated people. He was a tall, broad-shouldered, active man who was rarely sick. His only disability was a hearing impediment, acquired as a young boy. The first turning point in his life came at the age of twenty, when he decided to become a doctor. After obtaining his degree in medicine, he chose to become a missionary, instead of entering a private practice as his classmates did. India was the country of his choice, but, as fate would have it, there were no positions open there and he agreed to be posted to China.

Another turning point came during the long days of imprisonment while he considered what course his life should take if he were to be released and returned to Canada. He dreamed of being a physician in a small community, and ultimately this dream was realized in 1959 when he settled in the town of Cardinal, Ontario, where he and my mother lived until his retirement at the age of seventy-eight. In his spare time he loved to garden and grew a huge variety of vegetables. He also pursued a very time-consuming hobby, stamp-collecting, his Chinese collection being particularly notable. When he retired to the village of Lyn, near Brockville, in 1978, he remained active in medical organizations and occasionally assisted in surgical operations at the Brockville hospitals. In 1981 he returned to China as a tourist with a group of former missionaries and their children and grandchildren. He was fortunate to be able to visit and be remembered at the two hospitals where he had worked. Several years later he developed Parkinson's disease. This illness finally forced him to give up his house and he and my mother moved to a retirement home where he spent four busy years working on his manuscript and his stamps until he was hospitalized six weeks before his death.

One might think as one reads all the accusations and interrogations to which my father was subjected that his presence and work in China were not appreciated. It would be wrong to leave this impression. Among his papers I found the translation of a tribute to him written by his Chinese colleagues in the hospital as he left his first posting in Leshan (Kiating) to return to Canada on furlough in 1936. An excerpt from this tribute follows:

> Fortunately in the eighteenth year of the Republic (of China) the Church sent Dr. Allen to Kiating to improve the medical practices and develop the work of public health in the community. From the time he came he has been diligent day and night without weariness building up the declining work of the hospital and fully equipping it in order to help the sick and suffering of the City and save their lives.

> In the dispensing of medicine he has made no distinction between rich and poor, being faithful alike to all. Again, Dr. Allen was different from the ordinary man in that whenever he met hard cases, where the hope of life was small, he was not discouraged by the difficulties of the situation. Consequently the number of lives saved by him in our Kiating cannot be counted. And his help to the poor and the distressed, so freely bestowed from an open purse cannot be estimated. Last year during the two civil wars which affected us, the sick and wounded in the war area depended on his compassion and skill.

> Dr. Allen has spent much energy in travelling back and forth to see distant patients, disregarding the heat of the burning summer sun. He has gone about extensively to do medical and preventive work. As we observe this we are aware that in his devotion he in no way falls below the high spirit of our own sages of the past.

Since Dr. Allen has observed the prevalence of tuberculosis in our country and the lack of adequate provision for those affected, he has determined to go to his own country to prepare himself to bring restored health to these sufferers.

At this time of his departure we wish to express our appreciation of his love and unstinted devotion and his happy co-operation with his associates, giving tribute to his unusual spirit and skill.

This tribute offers a more accurate summary of Dr. Allen's contribution to the welfare of the Chinese people and how it was perceived by them.

As I write this introduction, in November 1994, my three sisters—Gwyneth, Phyllis and Marion—and I have just returned from a month-long tour of China with a group sponsored by the West China Club of Toronto. The highlight for me was our visit to the former Canadian Mission Hospital, now called the 5th People's Hospital of Chongqing. We were met by the vice-principal (superintendent), a surgeon named Dr. Chen, who was delighted to greet the "Allen sisters." Through our National guide, Peter Li, who acted as interpreter, we had a long conversation. Dr. Chen informed us that the hospital will be celebrating its centenary in 1996. In 1896 the London Preaching Association of England sent a representative to set up a private hospital and in 1910 ownership of the hospital was transferred to the United Church of Canada Mission. At that time it was named the Canadian Mission Hospital. In January 1951, about a year after the Communist liberation, the hospital came into the custody of the People's Government of China and was officially taken over by the Government in June 1951.

Dr. Chen told us the staff are searching the hospital archives for photographs of Dr. Allen, his office and the operating room. They are also looking for his writings. He said they would be happy if the four Allen sisters could join in the centennial celebration.

If our father were still alive, he would be proud to know he is remembered with such appreciation for the service he gave to the people of Chongqing and the surrounding area. As the Chinese people say so often now, "The bad things are forgotten. We want to remember only the good things. Let us forget the bad times of 1950-1951 and remember the good things that happened before." That seems a good philosophy for all of us to follow.

MARGARET (ALLEN) WILLIAMSON

Allen Family History

M Y FATHER felt his book ought to begin with his grandfather, the Rev. John Salter Allen, born in 1842, the eleventh of twelve children. He was a Wesleyan Methodist minister in New Brunswick for many years. After retiring in about 1905, he moved to British Columbia, where he founded a number of churches in the interior. He married Charlotte M. N. Tuttle of Pugwash, Nova Scotia, and eight children were born to them. Their fourth child (and third son) was Alexander Beveridge Allen, who was my father's father. He married Mary Margaret Hall, daughter of a sea captain and owner of a general store in New Brunswick. The Allen family were well educated and well respected and it was said that Margaret had married "well above her station" and was very fortunate indeed. They moved to Montreal, where Alexander worked as an accountant.

My father, Alexander Stewart Allen, was born on November 26, 1899, the eldest of four children, followed by Harold, Margaret and Stanley. He was named Alexander for his father and Stewart after a physician in New Brunswick who was much admired and respected by the family. Around 1910, A. B. Allen contracted tuberculosis from a fellow employee. Following treatment at the TB Sanitarium in Saranac Lake, New York State, the family was advised to move to a warmer and drier climate for the father's health.

They went to Naramata, in the Okanagan Valley of British Columbia, where they purchased an orchard. Stewart was not quite fourteen when his father died, and he became the head of the household and his mother's mainstay. He dropped out of school to run the orchard, returning at the age of twenty to complete high school in eighteen months. He entered the University of British Columbia with the intention of becoming a doctor. In those days, U.B.C. was affiliated with McGill University in Montreal where he proceeded to complete his studies in medicine. He graduated in 1929, married Winnifred Griffin in August of that year and embarked on his career as a medical missionary to China.

After Chinese language study in Leshan (then Kiating), Sichuan (then Szechuan) Province, he became responsible for the Mission Hospital there. In spite of civil war and uprisings between opposing warlords, he built up both the size of the hospital and its reputation. Two daughters, Margaret and Catharine, were born in Leshan. Unfortunately, Catharine succumbed to encephalitis in infancy. A third daughter, Gwyneth, was born in Chengdu (then Chengtu), Sichuan's capital. Shortly after the family's return to Canada on their first furlough, Phyllis was born in Vancouver. In 1938, after completing a surgical residency at the Royal Victoria Hospital in Montreal, he sailed with his family across the Pacific Ocean to return to China—this time to the wartime capital of China, Chongqing (then Chungking).

War with the Japanese raged for most of their second term, with many bombings of the city and surrounding hills, where the family spent several summers. Stewart spent long hours tending the wounded, in addition to his regular work as hospital superintendent. Near the end of his second term in China, a fifth daughter, Marion, was born. By 1944, it appeared that the Japanese would invade Sichuan, so most missionary families chose to leave the country by air to India, including Stewart's wife and daughters. Stewart returned to Canada in 1945.

The family returned to Chongqing in 1948, this time without Margaret, who had by now entered McGill University. Gwyneth returned to Canada in 1949 to complete high school, followed by Winnifred, Marion and Phyllis in the summer of 1950.

My father's "darkest days" began less than six months later, with an accusation meeting in December 1950. After imprisonment and deportation to Hong Kong, he returned to Montreal, arriving on February 6, 1952. Shortly thereafter, he began his Canadian medical career. He served on the staff of the Royal Edward Laurentian Hospital for the treatment of lung disease, and later became the medical director of the Grace Dart Hospital, where tuberculosis patients were treated. In 1959, he took up private practice in Cardinal, Ontario, where he was the town doctor until his retirement in 1978.

The four Allen daughters married, ultimately presenting Winnifred and Stewart with sixteen grandchildren. At the time of his death, the family had grown to include seventeen great-grandchildren as well. Stewart and Winnifred had their sixty-third wedding anniversary in August 1992. He died on September 3, 1992, in his 93rd year.

PHYLLIS ALLEN DONAGHY

Chronology of Events

1938-1945

Dr. Allen and his family return to China, this time not to Kiating but to Chungking, where he becomes superintendent of the Canadian (United Church) Mission Hospital on the south bank of the Yangtze. When war forces them to return to Canada, Dr. William Service takes over as superintendent.

May and June **1946**

At the invitation of the Communist government of northern China, Dr. Allen visits hospitals in Kalgan, Inner Mongolia, and in the border regions of Shensi, Honan, Hopei and Shantung provinces to see what they need in the way of medical supplies and help. Communists tell him foreign medical personnel would be welcome to remain in a Communist China.

Early **1948**

Dr. Allen begins second term as superintendent and chief surgeon of the Jen Chi Mission Hospital in Chungking. His eldest daughter, Margaret, remains in Canada to study at McGill.

1949

Nov. 16 — International Relief Committee of China medical supplies are divided, half to mission hospitals, half to be reserved for government hospitals; missionary supplies are held for later distribution; those for the government are stored in Peipeh for safekeeping until liberation takes place. Dr. Allen makes sure there is full documentation of the supplies, their location and their distribution.

Nov. 30 — Communists take over the mission hospital. On Dec. 1 they "liberate" Chungking. Communists immediately restrict movement of foreigners and require vehicle registration; confiscate arms and ammunition; limit exchange of currency; secretly censor mail and monitor speech of foreigners; require personal registration and, for those being intensively investigated (such as Dr. Allen), a detailed life history.

Dec. 5 — Dr. Allen personally goes to report to the Communist authorities on the location of the medical supplies and to arrange to turn them over. His Chinese companion is told Dr. Allen will have to wait until the Foreign Affairs Bureau is officially set up.

Dec. 20 — At Dr. Allen's request, Dr. C. C. Chen, also on the I.R.C., makes sure the government receives its share of the supplies.

1950

Early Jan. — Communists form a preparatory committee to set up a labour union at the hospital. By late February the union has been formed and a representative committee (the executive body) elected. It comes in conflict with and ultimately replaces the hospital executive (or services) committee which had been composed of department heads.

February — Land and building taxes are assessed against the mission hospital for the first time in the history of medical missions in China. Late this month, Chang Tsen-hwa, the hospital business manager, is arrested.

March — New taxes are promulgated on all hospital purchases, except food. Evasion of taxes is regarded as a very serious offence. Notice of these new taxes appears for one day in the newspaper. Person at hospital delegated to watch for these announcements misses reading the paper that day, so Dr. Allen and the staff are unaware of the change. Repercussions from the failure to pay tax on some small items eventually become one of the official reasons for Dr. Allen's deportation. Late in March the hospital accountant, Djang Gwei-han, is ousted by the labour union.

April — Distribution of the missionary hospitals' share of the medical supplies is begun by Dr. Allen, Brother Pretat, Rev. Olin Stockwell and Dr. Yu Enmei; completed sometime in August.

May — The initial draft of the "Christian Manifesto" appears.

July — Winnifred, Marion and Phyllis return to Canada; their departure is sudden because of a flood on the Yangtze and the need to catch the last ferry boat to Chungking in order to board the steamer to Hankow. Also this month, Bob Edwards, the missionary electrical engineer stationed in Chengtu writes the fateful letter to Dr. Allen, asking about the "financial set-up respecting the arsenal," whose X-ray machine he was going to repair. The letter becomes the source of serious spying charges levelled at Dr. Allen after his arrest.

Aug. or Sep. — The Communist government makes Dr. Allen retrieve all medical supplies and give them to the government instead, claiming they rightfully belong to the government and Dr. Allen has been concealing them.

Sept./Oct. — Makes his decision to leave China at end of six more months, realizing the Communists in the hospital are bent on replacing him with one of their own.

Nov. 28 — Celebrates his birthday by inviting some friends and a visiting missionary, Lizzie Toft, to his home for dinner.

Dec. 20 — Last normal day of work, although he is unaware of the fact; accusation meeting takes place in the evening, in the auditorium of the hospital nursing school.

Dec. 21 — Dr. Allen is confined in the hospital.

Dec. 22 — He is transferred to the Political Section of the Public Safety Department in Chungking. That night he is taken before the Political Court for an official hearing. Comrade Lan is the judge.

Dec. 25 — Christmas Day; he receives oranges, which he thinks come from fellow doctor Ian Robb. Feels depressed until he begins singing Christmas carols and a favourite solo, "The Star of Bethlehem."

Dec. 26 — He is interrogated by the intelligent Comrade Wu, most feared of his investigators.

Dec. 27 or 28 — He has a frank discussion with the Political Section's translator, but it is cut short by Wu.

1951

Jan. 1 — He sees Rev. Olin Stockwell and Brother Pretat in same prison.

Jan. 2 or 3 — Interrogated by Wu.

Jan. 4 or 5 — Dr. Allen is moved to a room on the fourth floor; it is cold, but at least he can see the sky and a little sunlight.

Jan. (2nd week) — Interrogated by Chu.

Mid-Jan. — Moved to third floor room between Olin Stockwell and Brother Pretat.

Rest of Jan. — Frequently interrogated by Wu, Chu or both; late in the third week, Wu accuses him of being a spy. About the same time, Dr. Allen begins his secret communications with Olin Stockwell.

February — Chu handles all interrogations this month; late in the month, Brother Pretat is taken away. Dr. Allen is weakened by lack of food and breaks down at end of month, wondering whether to make a false confession. He asks permission to write his wife but is told to wait and write when he is freed.

Early March — Wu realizes Dr. Allen is being undernourished; next day sufficient food begins to be provided. Wu details the main charges being leveled against him, including one that actually appears in the final court judgment: concealment of medical supplies belonging to the government.

Late May — Dr. Allen is moved to a cooler room below ground level on main floor. Further interrogations, now conducted by Liu, about Red Cross, Rotary Club and Rev. George Rackham. Then he writes his "confession."

July — In this month Brother Pretat is deported; Dr. Allen finds a way to let his family know—indirectly—that he is alive: he writes a note advising the mission to use medicines in his residence attic before they reach their expiry date.

August 27 — Dr. Allen is removed from the Political Section to the Chungking court prison.

August 28 — He attends his official court trial where he is charged with concealing medical supplies and evading sales tax.

Sep.-Oct. 14 — He undergoes re-education (indoctrination or brainwashing) in prison.

Oct. 15— He receives the sentence of the court along with the written court judgment. He waives right of appeal because he is too eager to be free.

Oct. 23 — He is released to a Chungking inn for deportees; his movements are restricted.

Dec. 17— Dr. Allen begins his ten-day journey to Hong Kong and freedom.

Dec. 28 — He crosses the border into Hong Kong.

1952

Jan. 18— Dr. Allen takes a flight from Hong Kong to Vancouver; vacations with Winnifred.

Early Feb. — In Toronto, he is debriefed by the United Church's Board of Overseas Missions. With Winnifred, he attends the annual Chinese dinner meeting of the West China Club.

Feb. 6— He and Winnifred return to Montreal.

Late February — In Ottawa, he meets with Lester Pearson, then minister of external affairs, and others in the department, describing his experience.

Mid-April— He speaks to the Montreal Rotary Club.

April 15— His story appears in *Maclean's* magazine.

July— He lectures on Communist China in Naramata, B.C.

Chapter 1

Liberation

THE PEOPLE'S LIBERATION ARMY marched into the city of Chungking in the province of Szechuan, China, on December 1, 1949. The day before, the troops had "liberated" the area where our Canadian (United Church) Mission Hospital stood, on the south bank of the Yangtze River, across from Chungking. Chengtu, Szechuan's capital, was liberated on Christmas Day. Thus ended the rule of the Kuomintang or Nationalist government under Generalissimo Chiang Kai-shek, who fled the mainland by April 1950 and set up his government on the island of Formosa, now Taiwan.

The liberation occurred quite smoothly. There were some gunshots across the river, south of the city of Chungking. The Nationalist troops marched out with a lot of firing for effect. They trudged in endless lines from the Chungking Hills, south of the city, past our mission property. As they crossed the Yangtze and passed through the city, they themselves blew up their munitions arsenal. We found out later that none in the area had been forewarned and there were about two thousand dead, including sleeping employees. Another act of atrocity was committed at a concentration camp just outside Chungking, where local Communists and sympathizers had been interned by the Nationalists, some without proof of their political affiliations. It seems Generalissimo Chiang, as his troops retreated, gave the order for all to be destroyed. Machine guns were turned on several hundred people, including babies who had been born in the camp. Those who escaped did so because one of the guards threw the keys of the place into a small room and told the thirty people within to run for their lives. It is believed such cases of mass murder by the Nationalists occurred in other places.

As the Communist officials took charge, they crossed the river by ferry and were welcomed into Chungking with firecrackers and factory whistles. The Nationalist troops, estimated at 100,000, fled toward Chengtu, to be replaced by only five thousand Communist troops. On the day of liberation there was a huge parade in the city, which was filled with enthusiastic cheering crowds. Military leaders took part, as well as dancers who demonstrated for the first time the new *yang go*, a popular dance introduced by the Communists.

The Communist soldiers were not like any of the Nationalist soldiers we had seen before. They paid for all their needs and were the essence of politeness. During a trip to their areas in 1946, I had noted that their food and discipline were much superior to that of the Nationalist troops. The soldiers ate the best food available, with a good meat allowance, so they were strong and healthy. One group with full equipment marched a distance of about nine hundred miles in twenty-two days, a trip on which Nationalist troops would have foundered. The Nationalist troops actually suffered from malnutrition and many died from starvation. They plundered farms for food and were feared by the general populace. It was obvious to us why the Communist armies had been so victorious. They marched through the countryside after the Nationalist troops, who were in full flight ahead. Once the Communists overtook the Nationalists, the latter simply surrendered. Generalissimo Chiang talked of fighting the Communists to the bitter end, but there were none left to fight for him.

Meanwhile as we awaited liberation, we at the hospital had been without electricity and so had not been in touch with the outside world for several days. We were aware the Communist armies were within striking distance of the city, but I did not know how close they were until the afternoon of November 29. I made certain the hospital and the compound where the three mission homes were located were in order and told the other missionaries what was happening, and then we waited. The hospital staff were aware of the situation the next day when they heard the sound of distant firing. All were rather tense, but I had prepared them for any emergency that might conceivably occur. Many were fearful of what might happen at the hands of the retreating troops or unruly civilians during the entry of the Communist army. Our nurses in training had piled up loads of broken brick at their quarters with which to greet any intruders. We put special guards on the gates. In the next few hours, we had only about ten wounded patients in the hospital from all causes, including a gravedigger who had hit a hand grenade while digging. At home we had been laying in supplies, as there had been persistent rumours of a last stand in Chungking and we did not want to be without food.

On the morning of December 1, the day Chungking was liberated, we found the outside of the hospital and the walls of the hospital compound plastered with numerous placards welcoming the Communists and condemning the previous government and its supporters. These signs could be considered mildly anti-American and certainly anti-imperialist as well as anti-feudalistic in nature, but not particularly anti-foreign. The papers of the day instructed the people to protect foreigners and their property. When I asked about the source of these posters, I learned they had been prepared in the room of the hospital electrician, Tsui Tien-min, and also in the hospital laboratory and nursing school. The electrician turned out to be the leading Communist on the staff. He and his sister had been strong members of the Christian church, so his change of heart and attitude was a cause for disappointment among members of the staff. He was criticized for doing the least around the hospital, and taking the most time, when it became evident that he had spent many hours attending classes in communism. The laboratory technician, Whang Dung-min, another Christian, also turned out to be a Communist by inclination. In the nursing school, at least four of the students, two of them without doubt planted in the probation class, were found to be Communists. Some doctors and others were likewise found to have radical views. It had been intimated by the previous Nationalist government that almost all Christian organizations, churches, schools and hospitals had Communist plants within them. Their true colours were only evident after liberation, which proved especially disheartening in those cases where missionaries had looked to these very people to lead the future Chinese Christian church.

Shortly after liberation, I discovered that this Communist group in the hospital had in fact selected a new superintendent and managerial staff to replace me and my staff, since they had expected to seize the hospital either for their own benefit or for that of the new government. They were thwarted in this action by the government's instructions to protect foreigners and their property. Initially this group did not take particularly offensive action. There were a few minor requests for changes in the quality of food being served to the workmen. In particular they asked for more seasonings such as red peppers, ginger, various sauces and salted vegetables which play an important part in the Szechuanese diet. Since this was a reasonable request, it was granted. But a few staff members kept up their criticisms of the food, the dietitian and the head cook. Then the chief accountant was criticized for the way he kept his books. Nothing personal or disagreeable was brought against me except an intimation that I should have been more strict with those handling money. In the past there were a thousand and one ways that an adept Chinese person could make a few pennies for himself when money passed through his hands. This was a fact of life, both in business and in the home.

A few days after liberation the first representative of the military command came to check on patients in the hospital. During the period of liberation, and just prior to it, I had introduced rules that no persons except bona fide patients would be admitted to our hospitals. Otherwise we might have harboured people wishing to protect their wealth, or Nationalists who wanted to escape the search of their houses. Likewise, no special parcels or baggage coming from outside were permitted entrance without my personal checking and permission. I feared that the hospital property might be used as a place of safety for goods belonging to the Nationalists in the period between their exit and the entrance of the People's Liberation Army (P.L.A.).

When this first P.L.A. official came to the hospital, we showed him through the building and told him what we were doing. He made personal contact with every in-patient, enquiring about his complaint, his status and other relevant points and was finally convinced that all were bona fide patients. He checked on all the wounded soldiers. Just before liberation we had received three injured Nationalist soldiers. One of these had a perforated intestine and he was taken to the operating room immediately. While this successful operation was in progress, the other two soldiers were removed by their fellow Nationalists, who did not want to leave any of their numbers behind. On the day of liberation a Communist soldier with a superficial bullet wound in the arm was admittted. In the following days we received three other soldiers, one a Nationalist with a gunshot fracture of the thigh, and two other Communists wounded when the retreating Nationalists blew up the arsenal without warning. These soldiers had all been treated free of charge.

After the official's tour of the hospital, we went to the library. While tea was served, two or three staff members stayed to chat with him. He volunteered the information that he was a Christian, baptized by a China Inland Mission pastor well known to us, and that there were seven hundred Christians in his group. (Later on, Christians who joined the P.L.A. were not allowed to take their Bibles with them.) He stated that he still had intact the bullet issue given to him nearly one thousand miles away, which indicated to me that there had been no fighting along the way.

About ten days after liberation, we received a local delegate of the P.L.A., who spoke to all the staff of the hospital, from me down to the most humble coolie. I presided over the meeting, which was conducted in a very pleasant atmosphere, and the official was most courteous. He urged the students present to continue with their studies so they might take part in the changes which the new government was to put into effect. He gave a short outline of the hopes of the Communists, saying they would build a new China, clear the country of the Nationalists and keep American imperialism out of China. The United States was cited as "Imperialist Number One." I stated that we looked for the development of a better China, and outlined the church's fifty years of missionary work in the field of medicine. I told him the missionaries had come to China to help her and hoped it would be possible to assist her in the future, as we had tried to do in the past. After the meeting he sat with several of us and was offered refreshments, which he accepted after some urging. A short time after this encounter he came to us requesting our medical assistance in curing a chronic osteomyelitis of the leg, the result of an old gunshot would. His wound healed rapidly after surgery to remove the affected bone. During this initial period we treated many P.L.A. personnel, but some, on finding that an occidental was in charge of the hospital, went elsewhere for treatment.

Within a surprisingly short time we were asked to make a series of reports on all aspects of the hospital work. Initially, they dealt with the kind of patients seen in the hospital and outpatient clinics; there was particular interest in cases that were infectious in character. Later, minutely detailed reports on the hospital, its origin, the auspices under which it operated, both capital and maintenance expenditures, staff personnel and salary scales were required. We were told they were for purposes of taxation and registration. In order to keep up with the number of forms demanded, we had to employ a special secretary.

The first Christmas, less than a month after liberation, was celebrated at the hospital just as it had been since I arrived in 1938. It was a truly Christian holy day, and a full holiday for the staff. At two o'clock in the morning, Winnifred, the children and I were awakened from our slumber and entertained by some of the nurses who each year came carolling to our family home in the compound across from the hospital. Everywhere there was an air of festivity, with decorations throughout the hospital. The staff, servants and nursing students—some four hundred people—partook of a huge feast at noontime. There were extras for the patients, including gifts of oranges, which were not regularly part of the hospital diet. As we distributed these, over one hundred staff members and friends sang Christmas carols and stopped a few moments to tell each Chinese patient the meaning of Christmas. Members of the People's Liberation Army were present. Since the day was a Sunday, the usual morning service was held and well attended. Then the missionary people present were treated to a rendition of the *yang go* dance and "Song of the Sower," a feature of the Communist regime, performed by the hospital servants and coolies. In the evening the nursing students conducted another service with prayers and hymns. A story was read that was not only very fitting from a Christian point of view but also suitable under the new political condition. The service was followed by a program which included a traditional pageant of the manger scene and the Christ Child, skits and acrobatics. This celebration of Christmas showed us the strength of the Christian body in our midst.

I should emphasize that orderlies and labourers took an active part in the festivities of the season. This is important because, for the first time in their lives, this group now attained social position. They had truly been "liberated," as the new regime stated. Although these men had been working in a Christian hospital, they had always been looked down upon to some degree by those of higher social strata. The boundaries were very sharply marked. I had always tried to give them a square deal, but a handful of missionaries can only be leaven, working slowly to bring the Chinese masses something of the meaning of the dignity of labour, even though it may be done by people who are illiterate. Our workmen had given us no trouble in the past. They had all seen I was not afraid to soil my hands with manual labour when necessary, although I was rebuked by more senior staff for doing tasks they felt were the duty of nurses.

One Thursday in early January I returned from the city clinic on the north side of the river earlier than was my habit. I found my secretary, Chang Chi, in the midst of preparing a document calling for signatures of those who would like to form a labour union. He had been asked to act as temporary secretary of the preparatory committee. He was taken aback by my arrival in the office and hastened to explain what he was doing and said that he had been asked to take the position because of his facility with writing. He hoped I had no objections and finally stated that he would continue to act with this body only as long as they did things in an orderly manner and did not take action against me. In spite of his protestations, several other staff members warned me that he was no longer to be trusted. From that time onward it was difficult to know just whom I could trust completely. Within two months, this temporary, self-appointed committee put up a slate of officers for the union upon which the staff and employees were asked to vote. The slate consisted of all their own names and two others, all of whom would form a representative committee for the hospital labour union to speak for all on the payroll of the hospital. By late February, all were elected and went into action.

Previously, hospital administration problems had been handled by a hospital executive committee composed of the heads of departments and representatives from the medical and nursing staff. Shortly before liberation I made a move to have representatives of the workmen on the committee, but this was voted down on the grounds that it would slow down the handling of business. The committee also felt that the workmen had not shown much interest in meetings to which they had been invited. When the union's representative committee (or executive) was elected, it became apparent that it and the old committee, now called the hospital services committee, would come in conflict and the latter was disbanded.

At this time, I found we had to alter many of our methods of dealing with hospital matters. One little incident that happened, of small significance really, is an example of what I mean. A ward coolie was discovered surreptitiously taking away food that should have gone to the patients. He also took leftovers intended for our pigs and gave them to his own. For personal reasons the man in charge of the workers did not want to take any action, fearing repercussions on himself. The coolies' representative on the representative committee was called in and, after a meeting to study the evidence, the committee referred the matter back to me for action, indicating they did not want such a person working in the hospital. Of course, I could have acted in the first place, but with the support of the committee I was able to avoid what could have been a nasty situation.

Soon after the liberation, Mao Tse-tung (Mao Zedong)[1] and other Communist authorities gradually promulgated certain regulations. Instruc-

---

1 The spellings of Chinese proper names are those the author used in the early 1950s; sometimes the current Pinyin spelling appears in parentheses. For old and new spellings of place names, see the map on the inside front cover.

tions were issued that foreign life and property were to be protected; foreigners were to be allowed to continue their work as in the past, but under no condition were they to harbour in their homes, or assist in the escape of, any enemies of the people or counter-revolutionaries. We were to obey the law. The missionaries in our area were registered with the local *bao* (hundred-family group) where our home was located. Instructions from the Foreign Registration Bureau were in process.

New stamps were issued and money was changed into People's currency within five days. Previous Nationalist Government paper currency was worthless immediately after liberation. Currency of the new government was limited in quantity to that brought in by members of the P.L.A. The rapid inflation and falling purchasing power of Nationalist paper currency before the liberation had made everyone suspect that the new People's currency, also a paper currency, would become inflated, too. A certain amount of People's currency was exchanged for silver dollars and vice versa, since silver was considered to have a reliable and relatively constant market value. Black market buying and selling of silver increased rapidly and black market prices for silver rose sixty-six percent. Finally, to stabilize their currency, the new authorities called out the students of all the high schools to parade with banners and slogans urging the populace to have faith in the new currency, denouncing black marketeers and urging everyone to refuse to use silver coins. Within three days these were off the market, never to return.

Since liberation there had been a complete stagnation of business of all kinds. A violent upset occurred, caused by large losses in the value of currency. The new government was investigating all businesses and new taxation programs were being devised. The normal lives of the populace were completely disrupted, except in those areas which were devoted to meeting their daily needs. The shortage of ready cash forced those with commodities to use them in lieu of money. Those not so fortunate had to use their cash sparingly and credits to the limit in order to prevent deprivation or even starvation.

We at the hospital also had financial difficulties. With cash at a premium, illness became secondary and people put off treatment. Our in-patient numbers decreased, and many who remained in hospital could not even meet their expenses for food. As a result, the hospital's income was so limited that, even under the best management, all we could do was guarantee food for our staff and employees and their families. Other hospitals and businesses were reduced to the same low financial level.

Some were able to make token monthly salary payments, which for doctors amounted to the equivalent of $3 in U.S. currency. In the new regime, people who had been privileged in the past had to give way to those who had been less privileged so that all could be equal. In reality, everyone was being reduced to a mere subsistence level. Many of our hospital staff thought that I, personally, or the mission, should make up the difference.

In fact, our staff fared better than many other employees in the city. Before liberation our hospital had had the foresight to purchase enough food for one month, in case serious fighting interfered with deliveries. This extra supply eased our food problem. But lack of ready cash meant we could not pay salaries, and by the middle of February staff salaries were six weeks behind and wages of the lower level employees were one month in arrears. In November, when a liberation war had threatened, we had advanced a month's salary to all employees to help them lay in supplies against possible shortages. In December we cancelled this as a debt and ruled it as a bonus instead, for a year of good work. In all the city there was no institution that treated its staff so well in the matter of salary payments. However, the preparatory committee for the hospital labour union was looking for a way to show its new authority. Logically, as will be told in more detail in Chapter 3, it chose the matter of unpaid salaries as a talking point. Our cash flow problems continued and I was unable to win the co-operation of either the preparatory committee or the later representative committee, even in light of the "new democratic" thinking being promoted by the government. They continued to demand full payment of salaries and we had to borrow heavily from a building fund in New York.

With changing thoughts and ideas on the part of both management and labour, there were many exasperating problems for me to solve at the hospital. I had to keep a cool head and use much patience in trying to find solutions. Under the new regime, people were allowed—even encouraged—to vent their feelings about past injustices. This in turn led others to express much repentance—sometimes real, sometimes hypocritical—for supposed or actual wrongdoing, and the hospital atmosphere was often tense. Nevertheless, sometimes there was a show of co-operation such as I had never seen before. In mid-winter the lower hospital water reservoir went dry and we had to use the auxiliary one behind our home. When it was decided to clean out the hospital reservoir but no workmen could be found to do it, the entire hospital staff offered to do the job, if they would be paid for it. Every lunch hour for ten days they came out—coolies, nurses, laboratory and pharmacy technicians, students and doctors—in the common cause. There was much laughter and singing as they pulled weeds and threw out big lumps of mud. It was a heartening sight for me to see in an otherwise difficult time.

One of the first restrictions we felt was lack of freedom of movement. Motor vehicles could not be used until there had been a re-registration. Leaving the city of Chungking was completely forbidden. Since I had brought a vehicle with me from Canada in 1948, I was affected by this regulation. It applied to other missionaries as well and also to the Friends' (Quakers) Service Unit, which had undertaken to distribute certain medical supplies in the hands of the International Relief Committee (see Appendix B). In addition, all persons were searched when boarding public conveyances, whether leaving the city or crossing the river. We who lived on the south side of the river had parcels searched and often were subjected to personal frisking. This continued for about three months. The searches seemed to be directed toward finding silver or gold currency or other valuables, as well as other contraband such as radios, small arms and ammunition. All arms and ammunition had to be turned in to the nearest police station. I did not own a rifle, but a friend of mine who did turned it over to the authorities and received a receipt for it. It was never returned and he received no compensation for it.

Before two months had passed, it was clear to me that we had to be very cautious about the subjects of our conversations, especially when speaking to known Communists or those associated with them. We had to be very careful about reporting news heard on the radio, particularly over the Voice of America. The Chinese were forbidden to have short-wave radios, but we foreigners were told we could keep our radios, for personal use only, as long as we did not spread news among Chinese friends.

During this period it became evident that organizations that included both foreigners and Chinese—with foreigners in executive positions—were being especially investigated with regard to the activities of the foreign members. We were quick to sense this, and I made the decision to sever my connections with these groups. I had been president of the Chungking Rotary Club and thus automatically chairman of the board of the Chungking School of the Blind, which was sponsored jointly by Rotary and the Y.M.C.A. Men's Club. Other foreigners also resigned their memberships to prevent difficulties for the Chinese who desired to continue these organizations, if permitted to do so by the government. As it happened, the Rotary Club ceased to function in February, as I will relate in Chapter 12.

Personal registration was required when the Foreign Affairs Bureau came into being in February 1950. Each foreigner had to fill out forms detailing everything he had done from the time of birth to the present. This included all schooling; occupation of parents; political, social and public activities in the land of birth; one's occupation and salary; funds held in banks abroad and in China; and properties owned. On receiving these forms, the authorities thoroughly questioned the applicant. For me this examination was very comprehensive since, in addition to my normal hospital activities, I had been active for years in relief work that included positions on voluntary agencies, particularly the American, British and Canadian Red Cross China committees. I was chairman of the latter committee and of the Canadian Aid to China committee. These two organizations had a joint committee in China. I was also chairman of the China Relief Agencies Co-ordinating Committee and the International Relief Committee. In medical circles I was for several years chairman of the Council on Christian Medical Work of the Chinese Medical Association and was its vice-chairman at the time of liberation. Because of all these associations and the fact that I had made a special trip to China in 1946 on relief activities investigating the medical situation in the Tsinan region of North China, I was investigated very carefully and at length. After the questioning the interrogators apologized for taking so much time, but they had felt it necessary to check on my many activities. The questions that seemed to loom large in their minds were: Why was I interested in so many activities and organizations? Who was paying for my travel all over China? To whom was I making reports after my trips? They intimated that they wondered if I were a spy or merely indulging in innocent activities that were helpful to China. I responded that any information they desired would be made available to them. Within ten days I discovered that two of my intimate Chinese friends had also been questioned about me in order to gain further information and confirm my statements. This convinced me that it was wise to have as few contacts as possible with Chinese friends. I subsequently resigned all official positions except the hospital superintendency, which I could not find anyone willing to accept.

About three weeks later I was required to write out in detail a complete life history. This was required of only a few people, those who were being investigated in most detail. The final questioning lasted an entire afternoon. Again, apologies were profuse, following which the investigators were quite informal and we had a conversation in a more relaxed atmosphere. I should mention that during these question periods there was no unfriendliness, but neither was there any warmth. Both of my investigators kept their countenances blank.

On the other hand, my wife found her last examination quite difficult, especially on the matter of the joint ownership of our summer home at the Chungking Hills. I surmised that they might have been trying to learn my attitude toward women and whether we recognized the equality of women with men. Winnifred was also questioned at length about how she used her time. Part of this was spent in helping me correct business correspondence. She also was in charge of the hospital linen supplies and sewing room. Winnifred felt that the investigator pressed her quite strongly to tell information he thought she should know about my work.

In these first few months I had a number of visits from people who wanted help financially to move to other parts of China. In view of later developments, one of these was of special interest. One Sunday a man dressed as a civilian came to ask for help to go to Hong Kong. He claimed to have known me in Kiating, though I did not recognize him. He lifted his shirt to reveal a uniform of the Nationalist army. Since we had been instructed not to give aid to a member of this army, I knew I must be more careful than usual. Occasionally in the past I had given money to people coming to my door after I determined that they were seriously in need. This man assured me he was not begging, but would repay me when he was able to send his money from Hong Kong. Then I worked out a plan whereby he could secure his own money in advance and was about to have my own secretary arrange to send a telegram to Hong Kong. At this point he said it appeared he was causing too much trouble and he promptly left. I have never been sure that this man was not the first of several imposters who were trying to trick me and get me in trouble with the new government.

In February 1950, for the first time in the history of medical work in China, land and building taxes were assessed against hospitals, both government and private. The latter hospitals were taxed considerably higher than the others, and, as far as I could determine, our hospital was assessed proportionately more than any other mission or church hospital in the province. The initial land and building tax was almost exactly equivalent to U.S. $1,000. A week was allowed for payment of this sum. We paid it immediately. We had been led to believe we might receive a refund if it was found that the institution was doing considerable charity work. In our case, there were no rebates.

In addition to these taxes, other taxes were promulgated on March 1. They covered all receipts by the hospital except those for in-patient food. These, like all other new regulations, were published for one day only in the *New China Daily*. In our case, we missed seeing this regulation because the person delegated to watch for these new rules in the newspaper became so involved with the activities of the union's representative committee that he considered his other tasks unimportant. This negligence had serious consequences for the hospital and for me later on.

Nearly all the missionaries who decided to remain in China in 1949 eventually left, were put in prison or under house arrest, or had difficulty securing exit permits to leave China. The persecution of the church went back as far as 1925, when an anti-British, anti-Christian movement was organized. This was directed toward both the foreign missions and the Chinese Christian church. Christian schools and hospitals were forcibly closed, Christian services were interrupted and Chinese Christians and missionaries were put to death. After 1935 the church seemed to function without interference. In the period immediately following World War II, missionaries who had been located in North China—where the Communists had established their headquarters and used guerrilla warfare so effectively against the Japanese—moved to Chengtu because of the situation developing in the North. It became difficult working under Communist controls, and they hoped their work would be permitted to continue in West China. Some two thousand Protestant missionaries decided to remain in China, for better or worse. But after December 1, 1949, it became quite clear that definite restraints were being imposed. In the Chungking–Chengtu area, foreigners who were given permission to leave small towns to go to larger ones for legitimate reasons were often not allowed to return to their homes. When they decided to leave the country, they often had to entrust the packing of their belongings to Chinese friends. Travel for everyone was by permit only and very few foreigners ever received that privilege.

Early in May 1950 a much more serious situation developed respecting missionaries and their relationship to the Chinese Christian church. A group of Chinese Christian leaders, alarmed at what had been happening to the Christian church in many parts of China, decided to investigate and then go to Peking for official consultations. They met with Chou En-lai, foreign minister of the People's Republic. The spokesman for the group

was not a church official but the secretary of the Shanghai Y.M.C.A., Y. T.
Wu, a man trusted by the Communists. Out of this conference came a
statement from Chou which appeared moderate on the surface but
indicated in very definite terms that there was no intention of letting
missionaries remain at their posts indefinitely. His statement was incorpo-
rated in a letter that was sent to the Chinese churches. Its contents were
later adapted into what was popularly called the "Christian Manifesto"
(see Appendix C). Briefly, this document stated that, as a principle, the
Chinese church should use no foreign personnel; as a principle, there
should be no use of foreign funds; the church should guard against
imperialism, especially the American type which uses religion to nurture
reactionary forces and plots. This "Christian Manifesto" was crafted by Y.
T. Wu. Chou En-lai added the statement that "any foreigner who consciously or unconsciously contravenes the law of the land will be deported
from China." This subtly implied that missionaries and other foreigners
would be tolerated only until the time their visas expired. When this
statement was published, a mass exodus of missionaries from China
started, as soon as the government chose to provide them with exit
permits. Various missions issued instructions for their missionaries to come
home as soon as possible, for by this time it had become obvious it was
no longer possible to work in China. Missionaries were refused the
opportunity to work or withdrew from it in order to save their Chinese
co-workers from inconvenience and investigation by the authorities. The
mere request for an exit permit did not mean that it would be approved.
It took more than a month to secure one for my wife and daughters to
leave Chungking. For others it took much longer.

In the early days of liberation I felt I was passing through the crisis
with the complete backing of the hospital staff and nursing students.
Several years earlier I had decided I would stay in China, even if the
Communists took over the country. I had based this decision on a
conversation I had had in 1946 with Dr. Su Ching-kuan, head of the
Medical Department in Yenan in Shensi province. During May and June,
Dr. Su and I toured a considerable area then under Communist control.
He assured me that any medical and nursing personnel truly interested in
the welfare of the people would be welcomed when Mao Tse-tung gained
control of China. Mission hospitals would be expected to be helpful and
make their facilities available for the training of medical and nursing
personnel, and no Christian teaching could be given in mission schools
or hospitals. Pastoral and evangelical workers could continue their work,

but they would find they would not make much progress. I thought this was a fair and reasonable attitude and I kept our conversation in mind after the entry of the People's Liberation Army. I had tried to guide the Chinese I met toward a better and fuller life, with the hope that my words and deeds would be identified with a Christian philosophy. Now that the Communists had indeed taken over, I felt I could carry on without serious conflict with the authorities. I wanted to show them that all the world was not completely against China because of the change she had undergone.

The first time I questioned my decision to stay in China was in mid-February 1950, when the labour union was being formed at the hospital. At a meeting at which I tried to explain how Dr. Su's comments had reassured me that missionaries could continue to work under communism, members of the labour union held their hands to their mouths to try to hide their smiles. It was enough to leave me with the feeling that, like cats toying with mice, the Communists were merely tolerating us missionaries for the time being.

From the outbreak of the Korean conflict in late June 1950, tensions increased. The Chinese people with whom we had contacts had not shown animosity toward us, but they were deluged with government propaganda in posters, bulletin board notices and press reports. Communist servants were planted in our homes to report on our visitors and our activities. Although we could move freely during the day, we had to return home at night unless we went personally to inconveniently located authorities to obtain permission to do otherwise.

In the early months after liberation, I had felt that, with hard work, right would win out in the end, that the authorities would eventually accept a limited role for missionaries in the new China. But by September 1950 I knew the game of cat and mouse could not go on. I decided to leave at the end of another six months.

I did not dream that before I could follow through on that decision the cat would pounce on me.

Chapter 2

Date with Destiny

D ECEMBER 20, 1950, broke cheerlessly over the hospital grounds and Chungking. Cold, grey, low-lying clouds hung heavily in the sky. From my bedroom window the hills surrounding Chungking, only a few thousand yards away, were dimly outlined in the haziness of the opening day, peaceful and serene.

As I calmly shaved, dressed, and went down to breakfast, there was nothing to suggest that this Wednesday was to be one of the turning points in my life. The first had been my decision, at twenty, to enter the field of medicine, which had led to my present life as superintendent of the Mission Hospital—a life fraught with some perils, but also filled with much interest and a happy sense that it had been eminently worthwhile. The second turning point had still to come that evening. Unlike the happiness of the first experience, this was to be a bitter one.

I sat down to breakfast with Constance Ward and Dr. Ian Robb, the other members of the household. Constance was our greying, lovable missionary-associate. When Winnifred had decided to return to Canada with Phyllis and Marion, five months earlier, Constance had willingly agreed to add to her other duties that of housekeeper. Ian, my medical associate, was adjusting his radio. Like me, he was a grass-widower. Witty and always smiling, he had a twinkle in his eyes that made one wonder what new joke was coming.

We listened to the morning radio program from San Francisco, as we ate a plain breakfast of fruit, hot home-ground wheat cereal, toast, jam and ersatz coffee. We were just finishing, when a knock sounded on the door. Before we could answer, a closely shaved head bound with a wool scarf was thrust through the partially opened door.

"*E Sen, yao kai dao.*" (Doctor, they want you to operate.) This was the hospital coolie's usual way of telling me the day's work at the hospital was about to begin.

The Canadian Mission Hospital, founded in 1896 by the London Preaching Association, of England, and transferred to the Canadian United Church in 1910, was by this time a large complex including the main hospital building, doctors' and nurses' residences, a nursing school and the tuberculosis wing, constructed in 1943 under my guidance. I succeeded Dr. Cecil Hoffman as director of the hospital from 1939 to 1945, when it was the main hospital for treating those severely wounded by Japanese bombings. I returned from furlough in 1948, taking over as director from Dr. William Service. Canadian missionaries posted to the hospital lived with their families in a walled compound of houses opposite the hospital, separated by a small valley.

At the hospital, a three minutes' walk from my home, the patient had already been brought into the operating room. My hand-scrubbing was the signal for the anaesthesia to be given. One more appendix was removed and added to the hundreds from which patients had been separated during my twenty years of willing service among the Chinese. A gall bladder removal followed. These two operations were usual in the almost daily round of surgery. The surgical wards were always filled with elective or emergency cases. But now Christmas was only five days away and the number of operations had eased somewhat. My schedule was not heavily filled with other duties either.

So I descended to the new basement radiology room where several opened cases filled with parts of a yet-to-be-assembled deep-therapy X-ray unit were stacked near the walls. Other cases, unopened, filled the middle of the room. In the "pit," which had to be dug nine inches lower than the floor level to give it adequate clearance, was the partly assembled radiological unit.

I had the movement motors working when suddenly our radiologist, Dr. Dso Li-Liang, entered. He was a brilliant Chinese, who had had postgraduate training in my own alma mater, McGill University, and at the Royal Victoria Hospital, both in Montreal. With a look of surprise, he shouted excitedly, "Where did you learn to assemble this kind of machinery?" He had only just heard I had been working for some days to put this much-needed apparatus in working order. "I did not know you were a mechanic or an electrician."

I pointed to the book of instructions lying on the table beside me for easy reference. "If you just follow what is said there, and you can put the nuts on a number of bolts, it's easy," I replied, gleefully watching the amazement on my friend's face.

For more than a year this radiological unit had sat idle in the hospital. It already had a history. Long before the Communists had taken Shanghai in May 1949, it had been ordered from Chicago. Subsequently it had been re-routed via Hong Kong and flown into Chungking just a month before liberation. After giving the new government time to settle in, we tried in vain for many months to get permission to bring Bob Edwards, our mission electrical engineer, to Chungking to assemble the unit. Bob was located in Chengtu, three hundred miles to the northwest. Early in May 1950 he made a personal visit to the Chengtu city authorities in the Foreign Affairs Bureau but failed to convince them of our need. Nor would their Chungking counterpart take any action. All personal persuasion failed to break down a wall of stony-faced, unsmiling officials who seemed able to say only one word—no. Reasons for their attitudes were never given. Argument was useless. One accepted their decisions with an external calm which belied other feelings held rigidly in check.

Perhaps, I thought, if one of the government organizations that desired to use Bob's services, or even the apparatus itself, might say a word in our favour, the barriers might be broken down. The 20th Arsenal had in fact requested Bob's services. So I sent our electrician, Tsui Tien-min, to get an invitation from them for Bob to come. Tsui brought back what seemed a suitable letter, but evidently it did not say the right words, for all further efforts, including those of both the radiologist and the hospital manager, failed to achieve any significant results. To the Foreign Affairs Bureau there seemed no good reason why it was necessary to bring a foreigner three hundred miles just to do this simple thing when some local Chinese might be found to do the task. Patience exhausted, I had decided to do the job myself, just to prove the authorities could not balk our plans.

I went home for lunch on this still ordinary-seeming day and then returned to my office to do the inevitable desk work that falls to the lot of a superintendent, trying to smooth out the innumerable and unusual questions that arise when living under a Communist regime. The nursing school principal, Tang Chuon-hwa, had a difficulty to discuss. She was followed by the hospital manager, who had his special problems. New to the position, he kept consulting with me to ensure he was doing things properly, lest he fall foul of the authorities or, worse, the several

Communist spotters known to be watching within our hospital ranks. His main fear was of possible government action against the hospital if there were any financial or legal complications involving the hospital and the authorities. He believed that I, as a foreigner, would not be troubled but he feared he himself might be imprisoned, as his predecessor had been.

Chang Chi, the secretary who handled my English correspondence and business, had difficulties of his own to discuss. I found him busy preparing a lengthy document. It seemed that a few days before, while passing by the registrar's office, he had overheard an altercation between the cashier and a patient leaving the hospital. The patient angrily claimed he was being charged for medicines he had not received. The cashier was relentless: "These are the accounts I was given. They must be paid before you leave." Trying to be helpful, Secretary Chang had intervened, questioned the patient and then checked his story, which proved correct. A nurse had failed to report and return the unused medicines to the dispensary. When the patient was told of the situation he left satisfied, after paying the corrected account. On the following day, a nursing student who was also a Communist Youth leader, met Chang Chi on his way home. With fire in her eye, she demanded sharply, "Why did you say this was a nurse's fault? Don't you realize you have made us lose face? You should know this is not done. You should apologize, or there may be trouble."

"But why is it necessary for you to make a long statement of this kind?" was my natural question. "What you said was quite correct, and the nurse was at fault. Why should you apologize? After all, as a Communist she should be prepared to accept criticism for what she has done. Doesn't the Party demand confession by its members and self-criticism of their faults in order to improve themselves?"

"Yes," replied Chang, "that's very true, but you must realize that what they say is good for other people is not necessarily what they are prepared to accept for themselves, at least not just yet. I would rather take a little trouble and apologize unnecessarily than win their enmity. That is why I am writing this lengthy letter. Better safe than sorry is my motto."

And there I let the matter drop.

At four o'clock there was a knock, the office door opened and a hospital messenger boy appeared.

"Here is a letter for you. Will you please sign for it?"

I received my letter, noting that two others had already signed their names to the chit book—Chang Chi and Shiung, the hospital business manager. A fourth letter had yet to be delivered to Constance Ward. She had gone across the Yangtze to Chungking city proper. She would soon be back. I signed for both of us and received Constance's letter.

Full of curiosity, for the envelope bore the stamp of the hospital labour union, I opened it and started to read the characters of the enclosed missive. It was an invitation to attend a meeting that evening at eight o'clock, but for what purpose I could not decipher. I went to ask Chang Chi in the next office.

For a moment he said nothing, but his ready smile had left his face when he replied. "You are invited to an anti-Austin[1] meeting. I wonder what they plan to do?"

"I see you got a letter, too, Chang. Was it for the same purpose?"

"Yes, apparently the four of us are all asked," he said in a worried voice. "I was afraid they might make it difficult for me, but I think all of us should go."

Manager Shiung replied in a similar vein when I went to him. "It is better to go than to stay away, even though you may not like listening to an anti-American meeting," was his opinion.

I decided to attend the meeting, much as I preferred to absent myself. At best it would be a turbulent, perhaps a nasty meeting. At supper time I gave Constance her letter.

Dinner conversation centred on the coming meeting. What was going to happen? Was this to be just another opportunity for the Communist enthusiasts to make their voluble, bellicose demonstrations of patriotism? Would they whip up the student body, hospital staff and workmen to vilify

---

1 Warren Austin, head of the American delegation to the United Nations, had angered the Chinese Communists when, in a speech before the Security Council on November 28, 1950, he had listed all the ways the United States had shown its friendship toward China over the years: treaties and agreements that supported China against Japanese or Russian imperialism; economic aid, especially the program of rural reconstruction begun in 1945 in co-operation with Chiang Kai-shek; medical missions to China; training for Chinese students in the U.S., and so on. Unfortunately, as much of this assistance had been given to the former government of China, headed by Chiang Kai-shek, a man they termed a "rotten bandit," the present Communist regime considered Austin's speech an open admission that the United States was guilty of imperialist aggression in China. Ironically, Austin, in a bitter debate with Andrei Vishinsky, the Soviet Union's delegate, had won the right to speak ahead of Wu Hsiu-chuan, the chief delegate of the Central People's Government of the People's Republic of China. Had he lost and spoken second, he might have been able to recast his prepared speech to respond to the blistering statements made by Wu. As it was, he merely gave Peking grist for its propaganda mill, enabling the Communists to fan the smouldering flames of hatred of the United States.

"American imperialism" and in particular Warren Austin, the American delegate to the United Nations, whose speech a month earlier had so enraged them? What active steps were they going to take to indicate their anger toward the United States for the "imperialist aggression" against China "openly admitted" by Austin when he listed ways the U.S. had helped previous Chinese governments?

We could not forget that already two anti-Austin meetings had been held in Chungking and reported in the local press within the past few days. One involved the Seventh Day Adventist Hospital. Its Chinese leadership was castigated for not having broken off its American association. Like a fireworks display, there was plenty of noise, and the affair passed over smoothly. In the other meeting, at the Catholic Hospital Nursing School, students denounced the sisters in charge, and demanded freedom from their control. Slightly more serious, it too had only minor reverberations. When I had read the reports of these meetings in the Chinese press, the thoughts When will my turn come? and Will our hospital be next on the list? had passed through my mind as only the faintest of probabilities.

Nor had we forgotten that on November 25 and 26 respectively, first Brother Pretat,[2] in charge of the Catholic Boys School, and then Rev. F. Olin Stockwell of the American Methodist Church, had been imprisoned. But the published charges against these men, alleged striking of students by one and spying by the other, had no worries for me. I certainly was not a spy, and I had never abused any of my staff. As recently as a month ago, the most ardent Communists among our employees had formally agreed with my policy that all internal contention between hospital groups must cease if hospital salaries and finances were to be maintained at the current level. Our salaries were then higher than in other hospitals in Chungking, all of which had been forced to decrease their salaries. Failure to end internal strife would cause the hospital to founder, leaving all at the complete mercy of the government, which would set its own salary levels. At least that was our argument.

---

2 Throughout his story, Dr. Allen refers to his Catholic fellow prisoner as Brother Pretat. Rev. Olin Stockwell, in his book *With God in Red China* (Harper and Brothers, New York), refers to the same man as "Father Petain, a French Catholic priest who had been helping in a high school." The editor has been unable to establish which name is accurate.

The one straw in the wind we should have recognized came from another quarter. Some days earlier, a former patient had let us know by a circuitous route that he had been approached by "certain individuals." They had enquired carefully if he had any complaints respecting a previous admission for treatment of a tuberculous anal fistula which, under streptomycin injections, had progressed exceptionally well. It did not matter against whom the complaint was laid; any name would do. This word was passed on to warn us. But even if we had recognized this warning, it would have been too late to save us; the Communist die had already been cast.

Although we did not know the real purpose of the evening's meeting, it seemed wise to prepare for the worst. The weather was cold, and sitting for hours in an unheated room at forty degrees Fahrenheit could be uncomfortable. "Better put on all the warm clothes you can, Connie," I suggested. "We may need them before the night is through."

"I think I'll go along and see what is happening," Ian said, a mischievous twinkle appearing in his eyes.

At first I laughingly agreed; on second thought, however, I suggested there might be ulterior motives in issuing the invitations, and since he had received none, it might be wise to just hold off. It could happen that he might be of greater use by remaining home. Constance and I had no choice in the matter. I knew the so-called "inscrutable Chinese" temperament could be volatile and easily swayed. Absence for Ian was the better part of discretion. How wise this decision was, events of the next few hours proved beyond question.

We had just finished making these decisions when I heard an urgent knock at the door. I opened it, expecting to greet the messenger who always came to inform us when meetings were about to start. On this occasion, however, one no less important than the heavily-built, five-foot-ten-inch Fung Cheo-wen, a dispensary coolie but also the chairman of the hospital labour union, stood outside, together with his diminutive assistant, a messenger boy named Tan Tse-gao. They greeted me with their most polished smiles.

"Would you please to come over to the nursing school? It is just time for the meeting to commence, and we would not wish to start without you."

Still we suspected nothing, though it was unusual for two people to bring the final courtesy invitation. Usually one sufficed and he would leave immediately, while we followed in due course. This time Fung remained while we put on our coats, waiting to escort us by lamplight to the nursing school auditorium, scene of the coming meeting.

Fung was a voluble talker. He had enough primary school education to read and write and had grandiose ideas of his own ability and some considerable leadership qualifications. A blustering bully at heart, he had earned among the missionary community the name of "The Big Wind," a title indicating both his actual name and his disposition. It was a useful covering appellation when he was being discussed in the presence of non-English-speaking Chinese.

He had secured his position in the hospital labour union by carefully using his friends and by creating fear not only among his fellow workmen but also among the staff, who hated him for his potential for setting others to work against them. He also had been singled out to keep the records of any known or suspected counter-revolutionary remarks or activities among hospital employees. These were kept by him for later use or reported to the authorities as he saw fit. Almost every meeting found him present as a participant. Always he had his little notebook at hand. Occasionally a few characters would be jotted down. If a committee was elected and he was not represented on it, he voiced his displeasure. But he did not always have his own way, as some made determined efforts to exclude him from hospital meetings whenever possible.

When Winnifred left for Canada in July, one of her last remarks was, "Look out for 'The Big Wind.' Don't let him catch you in any way. He can hamstring you if you aren't extremely careful." She is a shrewd judge of personalities. She had reason to fear him for she had crossed swords with him earlier in the year, in the period when the workmen, under his leadership, were beginning to feel the exhilaration of having an acknow-ledged and vocal place in the new Communist society. But I am anticipating this story.

Following Fung's light, Constance and I, like unsuspecting lambs, were being led straight to the slaughter. I did not know as we went with him that never again would I pass the threshold of my China home; that the door had closed on twenty-one years of missionary, medical, relief and other activities in China. A more than four-hour accusation proceeding faced both of us that evening, one of the most severe and mentally-dev-astating ordeals that the Communists have yet devised.

Chapter 3

Betrayal

W E REACHED the nursing school auditorium to find it filled almost to capacity. Two rows of seats had been reserved for special guests, some of whom had yet to arrive. Like us, the waiting crowd of two hundred people—nurses, staff, workmen, their friends and neighbours—had gathered to view or take part in what was about to happen. The windows opening to the verandah on our right were not yet crowded, as they were later in the evening, with the faces of people from the surrounding community who had heard about the "big doings" at the auditorium. With the exception of those especially briefed, everyone expected a meeting to denounce Warren Austin.

Hand-clapping and enthusiastic welcoming cheers greeted us as we took our seats in the guest section. All were thrilled that we, two foreigners, were also prepared to voice, or by our presence indicate, our displeasure at Austin's recent remarks. The noisy waiting audience sincerely felt we deserved the welcome they gave us.

Seated in our reserved places, we chatted amiably with those surrounding us. Secretary Chang Chi was a seat or two distant, a worried look occasionally clouding his usually smiling countenance during breaks in the merry conversation. There was no doubt he was upset. He handed me a letter which had just arrived from my daughter Margaret, who was to receive her degree in science the next term at McGill University. I read it, placed it in my pocket and continued chatting, waiting for the meeting to be called to order.

Comrade Fung appeared in the entrance and beckoned to Chang. I wondered if Chang was to be the scapegoat for the evening. Chang finally returned, his head hanging, his expression deeply troubled. As he seated himself without uttering a word, I thought: Poor lad, he is surely in for it tonight.

Behind this there was good reasoning. Immediately following the Communists' entry into Chungking, Chang had been strongly influenced by their propaganda. He accepted an invitation to act as secretary of the preparatory committee that was working to form a labour union at the hospital and in the early months he had made many personal difficulties for the hospital's administrators. Later, however, he became disillusioned with communism and finally decided to train for the Christian ministry. I felt grieved for him. Was Chang, who in the early days of the regime had helped force three other hospital leaders from their positions, himself to "eat bitterness" as they had done? There seemed good reason to think he would be the next to suffer. It also explained why I was there, since I had been invited to view the other employees' downfall, although it did not explain Constance's presence.

* * *

Through my mind flashed the memory of the ways those three men—the rigidly honest Tang Yuin-ho, the irascible Chang Tsen-hwa and the repentant Djang Gwei-han—had been disposed of by hospital Communists who considered them enemies. These episodes illustrated how the hospital Communists' skill at removing an enemy increased as time passed.

Tang Yuin-ho, our hospital manager, was the first to experience an attack. He was a staunch fundamentalist Christian whose great aim in life was to teach and preach Jesus Christ. Over sixty years old, he was an honest man who deplored the tendency among some members of the staff to add to their salaries in minor illegitimate ways.

Four weeks after the liberation he decided to leave his work, saying that skyrocketing inflation and the many months of difficult hospital financing it had caused were threatening his health. When clearing his hospital business affairs, Tang followed the new Communist practice of throwing open his financial dealings and business affairs to the hospital staff for questioning. He posted a notice stating he would be pleased to answer any legitimate questions from the staff, expecting this to be done in his own office.

The sudden announcement one afternoon that he would instead be called upon that evening to publicly answer questions from hospital staff, workmen and nursing students terrified Tang. He hurried to the local police, protesting what might happen, for he knew that in his financial strictness he had made enemies. The police reassured him, telling him if he answered questions fully he need have no fear for his safety.

As superintendent of the hospital, I should have attended that meeting. In the early days of communism, however, it seemed wiser for a foreigner to let the Chinese handle their own affairs, provided they did not exceed the bounds of normal decency. I also felt Tang could handle the situation without my help. Hence, the first "struggle" meeting was held without me. I repented my decision when I learned what happened that evening, and I vowed always to attend in future.

Next day, although Secretary Chang told me all had gone quietly, Tang had a different story. He was furious. The young, uneducated whipper-snappers had shown him no respect. They had made first one demand of him, then another, trying to confuse him in his statements. They had implied he had been dishonest.

"Last evening, among other falsehoods, they claimed I had personally cashed the 2.3-billion-yuan cheque given to me to purchase a hundred rolls of cotton cloth from the Yu Hwa Cotton Mill back in 1948. They said I had delayed payment, had invested the money at fifteen percent interest for a month, and thus had illegally made money out of the hospital. They stated you had given them this evidence. Did you do so, Dr. Allen?"

As often happened in struggle and accusation meetings, the facts in the matter had been deliberately twisted to make it seem I had criticized Tang. I assured him I never had made such a statement. To prove this to him and his accusers I found the cheque stubs and bank accounts showing the accusation was false: that the cheque had been made out in favour of the company concerned; that Tang, therefore, could not have cashed it; and that the bank book entry showed the cheque had been cashed the same day. Having made these points very clear to his accusers, and to Secretary Chang in particular, in plainer language than I had ever previously used to a staff member—for I was outraged at these lying tactics—I prepared a written and signed statement and posted a copy of it on each of the hospital notice boards. It quoted the evidence and stated there was no factual basis for the accusation. This declaration cleared Tang's name completely and finally.

Tang left Chungking in February 1950, after being assured by the now-repentant Chang Chi that he would not be interfered with further.

The hospital business manager, Chang Tsen-hwa, was next to suffer under the new regime. His removal came about in a different way, but also involved a form of the struggle meeting. Short-tempered Tsen-hwa had never been popular with the workmen whom he supervised. Just before liberation, in unwarranted annoyance he had struck a workman. This had mortally offended the remaining workers. He would have been dismissed immediately, except that other work was hard to find then and he was the sole support for a family of five small children. Instead, he was severely reprimanded and warned he might expect later repercussions from the workmen.

Late in February I was awakened just after daybreak by a Communist policeman waiting at my gate. He asked me to come with him to the home of Tsen-hwa, who was being arrested. I was needed to witness that everything was done according to rule.

We found Tsen-hwa in his courtyard, hands tied behind his back, standing between two military policemen. He was given scant opportunity to talk to me. Arriving immediately after me was Chao She-hwei, chairman of the preparatory committee of the hospital labour union. He followed the proceedings with obvious approval. Number Two on his slate of removals was already on the skids.

The police officer systematically searched the house, carefully selecting suspicious articles. He asked Tsen-hwa's wife to check them as he listed them and then to sign the list. All articles not needed would be returned, as was the usual procedure. Then he stated courteously, without amplification, that they had evidence Tsen-hwa was a criminal. Before they led him away, Tsen-hwa said to me: "I shall expect you to see that my family is cared for until my return. Please see that they do not lack. Sorry."

As Chang Tsen-hwa was led down the stairway, Chao She-hwei callously called out, "Do not forget, even though you will not be there, we will call a *deo dseng hwei* (a 'struggle' meeting) against you this evening."[1]

A struggle meeting is a terrifying Communist innovation. It has many features of the more serious accusation meeting. In the latter, too often

---

1 Chao She-hwei, in the brief three months under communism, was already earning the reputation for nastiness that eventually revolted even the other Communists on our staff. After failing to win election to the hospital labour union's representative committee (its executive body), he was discredited and was later forced to leave for a new position elsewhere, a sadder and wiser man.

the accused is given no chance to protest his innocence and is condemned out of hand. In the struggle meeting, as a rule, any one of the hundreds attending may use the opportunity to lay complaints, justified or otherwise, against the defendant, requiring him to respond to impossible questions whose answers can only condemn him. All do their utmost to so confuse the defendant that he will admit to uncommitted or actual faults which can be used for a later, and more serious, action against him. Sometimes the group wishes only to expose acts that would show the defendant was a menace to society, making him lose the face so important to the Oriental, thus shaming him and forcing him to leave the neighbourhood or destroy himself after his confession. It is a real struggle between the supposed or actual oppressor and the oppressed in every sense of the term, hence the name.

That evening I decided to witness the meeting and see who was taking part in it. With no defendant present, the meeting went smoothly, starting with the prepared statement by the police who had taken Tsen-hwa to prison that morning. They accused him of harbouring an enemy of the Communist regime at the time of liberation and of associating with members of secret societies. I knew Tsen-hwa was guilty of sheltering a friend, disobeying my order that only hospital residents and patients should be on hospital property at night during the uncertain period of liberation. On the second charge he was perfectly innocent of criminal intent. As the police statement continued, it became obvious that informers from the hospital had reported some of Tsen-hwa's previous faults and actions. Then came statements and accusations from the floor, each accuser vying to outdo the one before. Some charges were true, others false, all of them highly coloured. About 11 o'clock the meeting broke up.

The following morning Chang Tsen-hwa's wife sought me out, her face tear-stained. "Were you there? Did you hear all the things they said about my husband? Not a single person defended him."

"Yes, Mrs. Chang," I replied, "there was little one could do. You know he had many enemies who were eager to give their accusations, and most of them magnified the injustices they felt they had received at his hands. Nobody dared to defend him. He does not deserve to be imprisoned, true, but under the Communists, conditions are not as they were. There is no help one can give your husband. I am sorry for you, but all I can offer is to see that you and your children do not starve until he returns to you."

When all her husband's special hospital benefits had run out, she worked as a dresser in the hospital for two months. Finally, she resigned, knowing I had been told bluntly that I would receive no co-operation from the union, so long as she remained on the staff. In mid-September, with money I loaned her, she set up a street stall where she earned enough to feed herself and her children.

Late in March 1950, the third candidate on the list for expulsion, Djang Gwei-han, our chief accountant, was called upon to attend a struggle meeting with an important difference. His accusers had no factual evidence that could prove he was involved in shady financial or other deals. His accounts were always accurately kept and a thorough audit later failed to reveal any deficiencies or errors therein. But certain members of the preparatory committee were determined to force his resignation, no matter what the means. A number of minor deviations from his normal routine were recalled and seized upon as possible ways to incriminate him. Under expert Communist tuition, certain of our employees were learning that any irregular action or movement could be made grounds for suspicion or serve as material evidence for initiating accusations or investigations.

In Djang's case, for instance, they remembered that, while temporarily in charge of business affairs during the absence of hospital manager Tang, he had paid for fifty kilos of salt from a lot purchased cheaply by the hospital. Hospital families had the privilege of purchasing certain articles from the hospital at cost. Hospital salaries were not high, even though our staff received more than the average wage given in government hospitals. Fifty kilos, however, was considerably more than enough for personal use. Later he sold the salt at a profit to himself. Though not illegal, it was a small abuse of his privilege as a staff member.

Another time he had gone to our out-patient clinic in the city and collected a number of special vouchers issued in lieu of currency, which could not be printed rapidly enough to keep pace with inflationary changes. Sometimes it took a few days to negotiate the vouchers. Djang's enemies could reason that Djang might have been tempted, as many Chinese were at the time, to pocket the interest earned on the vouchers until they were cashed. A few hundred million or billion yuan placed on loan even for one or two days at one-half per cent daily interest could bring him at least enough to purchase a bushel of rice.

Having collected a few other similar suspicions of activities not necessarily fraudulent yet not wholly aboveboard the Communists were ready to confront Djang. At his meeting his accusers carried out one of the most adroitly planned manoeuvres I had ever witnessed. They implied here a suspicion and there a suspicion, waiting for him to admit anything, no matter how small, and give them the evidence they needed. Had he been as clever as they, he might have demanded the factual evidence on which they based their insinuations, or he could have stated he knew nothing of what was being implied. But he had a somewhat guilty conscience and the implied barbs struck deeply until he wondered just how much they knew of his actions. After two hours of severe public grilling, without his accusers having produced any bona fide evidence on which to base an accusation, Djang finally confessed to having made several minor manipulations of inflated currency vouchers back in 1948 along the lines suggested above. His transactions could have yielded very little personal profit, however, because hospital finances were closely controlled, the carriers of currency were known and the amount of the vouchers was too small.

The Communists had claimed all who confessed to their faults would be forgiven their previous errors, and their punishment ameliorated or dispensed with entirely, depending on the circumstances surrounding the case. Believing his accusers had actual evidence from unknown sources, rather than mere supposition, concerning his activities, he decided it was better to confess and retain his present or a lesser position, which he knew would be denied him if he failed to confess with known evidence held against him. Staking everything on government or hospital leniency, he volunteered to make restitution for his action, though, as he stated, the hospital had not actually suffered from any action of his.

But once he had made his confession, his case was hopelessly lost. His accusers had gained their end and nothing Djang could do would save him. The union was determined to force him out of the hospital. It agreed to his staying on condition that he pay five hundred times the three month's salary he had volunteered to give in restitution of his faults. He could not possibly do this and support his family, so he had to leave.

Early in 1950, I too had crossed swords with the union's preparatory committee. As explained in Chapter 1, the economy was so disrupted as the Communists set up their government in Chungking that businesses, banks, hospitals and other groups had to feed their employees in order to prevent starvation. Our hospital staff were more fortunate than most, but by mid-February payment of non-staff wages was one month in arrears. Employees at all other medical institutions in the city were much worse off. Nevertheless Communist class-consciousness was developing, and our hospital employees were aware they had a bargaining strength, hitherto unknown, against the capitalist managers and department heads.

Realizing this, I prepared a statement to discuss with all employees in full council. In theory, communism dictated that even the lowest category of employee had a right to be consulted. The draft of my statement was being translated into Chinese when a delegation from the preparatory committee waited upon me to consider the matter of unpaid salaries. Discussion was amicable. They wished to know my plans and I told them the assembly could take place that evening, but I did not want to go into details until then. Some seemed annoyed at that, but they said they would make the necessary arrangements.

Anticipating a long meeting to consider the issue of back pay, I waited that night to be introduced to present my statement. But the chairman of the preparatory committee, Chao She-hwei, called the meeting to order and immediately began to criticize my plan to talk with all employees. I believed my wish to speak with all employees was consistent with the Communist philosophy that all should have the right to be heard. Chao, however, persuaded the crowd to agree that I should have been willing to trust the preparatory committee and discuss the matter with them as the employees' chosen representatives. He gave no one the opportunity to disagree. In five minutes, his audience trooped out, leaving the committee to do its appointed job of meeting with me. There had been no chance for me to publicly explain my position or to receive their suggestions. Thus ended the shortest meeting in my twenty years of hospital administration.

We reassembled as a committee reinforced with five uniformed labour union leaders and cadres sent to observe my reactions and attitudes. I kept my temper, in spite of the hostile means used, as we decided how to resolve the problem. It had been almost a struggle meeting, but so soon after liberation the hospital Communists had not dared to take outright action against a foreigner. As for me, I now realized that the powerful forces I was dealing with would require delicate handling in future. It was my first real down-to-earth lesson in Communist techniques.

* * *

These four incidents flashed through my memory in the few minutes before the fateful December 20th meeting began. In each, Chang Chi had been one of the background planners. Had his turn now come? So it seemed.

But wait. There was a commotion at the door and uniformed government representatives entered, seating themselves in the first row so as to block the exit. The announcer, the planning committee and the meeting chairman followed.

"*Kai hwoi,*" shouted the announcer, restoring order. "The meeting is now open. Fan Sheo-yin is to act as chairman."

Miss Fan, as I called her, was the twenty-six-year-old dean of studies in the nursing school. This diminutive, black-haired, ninety-pound ball of fire stepped to the platform and raised her hand for order.

"We are met here this evening because of what our American oppressors and those who believe in imperialism have done to our country. We are now discovering their hidden purposes. Warren Austin has shown how the Americans have long planned to infiltrate our country and make our beloved China a colony of the United States. An American, Dr. Rappe, whom we used to love, always said 'we Chinese' when addressing a group of us. We thought he was one of us and were honoured when he so spoke. Now we understand what he meant. Warren Austin has opened our eyes. Now we know Rappe meant that one day he expected America would swallow us, through her cultural and religious aggression policies."

She was interrupted by a series of shouts from each of three appointed cheerleaders who led small groups in the audience: "Down with the American imperialist, Warren Austin. Death to the American aggressors!"

Miss Fan continued, "We should have seen the threats around us, but we were blind. Even here in this hospital there are imperialists who pretend to be our friends. Superintendent Allen has been following the same cultural aggression policies as his American friends. He is a friend of the American spy Olin Stockwell, who has already been arrested. Tonight, therefore, we are met especially to denounce Superintendent Allen. This is his official accusation meeting. Now you will hear the kind of person he has been, all the while posing as our friend."

A surprised hush spread through the room, but Miss Fan's words were all I heard.

"We have been watching Superintendent Allen for some time and now we are going to tell you how, during these years among us, he has been oppressing us in many ways. It is thanks to our liberators that we are able to accuse him. Representatives from the People's Liberation Army—from the Public Safety Department, the local police station and the department of education—are here with us. Also with us are representatives of various hospitals and schools that other missionaries have used for their nefarious purposes. All of us wish to share in these accusations together. For all this we thank Mao Tse-tung, our glorious leader."

Triple shouts of "May Mao Tse-tung live forever" and "Long live Mao Tse-tung" concluded the introduction.

Unwilling to believe what I had only too acutely and painfully heard, I still could not conceive that this outburst was more than a passing response designed to satisfy the authorities that the Chinese employees of our mission hospital were as patriotic as the community at large. Before the night ended, however, I was to be taught another lesson in how easily a small group of Communists armed with well-prepared propaganda could sway a once sympathetic crowd to unjustly condemn two of its staunchest friends.

The stage was set for the destruction of the innocents, as Miss Fan announced the first of the accusers.

Chapter 4

Accusation

THOSE WHO BECOME Communists are either idealists or opportunists. The idealists at first know nothing about communism's methods and techniques, but they listen earnestly to its philosophy and propaganda. They believe a utopia will emerge when the capitalistic system with its acknowledged injustices and inequalities gives way to a classless society. Everyone will have part ownership in this new society and all will share in its benefits. Idealists who believe the expected end justifies unpleasant means remain committed; those who come to abhor the means fall away from communism.

Opportunists, on the other hand, use communism as a way to settle the score for some real or imagined wrong. They are the most difficult to deal with, at least while the Communist system is being inaugurated. Initially, Communist organizers seek out these aggrieved individuals and give them the strongest encouragement to voice their complaints. The result is two-fold. First, the aggrieved feel gratitude and loyalty toward the new government for freeing them from fear of their so-called "oppressors," and second, the government gains vast records of grievances it can refer to in future actions against those it sees as enemies of the people. The whole process is calculated to bring everyone under centralized state control.

Miss Fan was an opportunist. Besides being dean of studies of the nursing school, she had been acting school principal for a few months during the 1948-49 session. During that time she had played favourites with some of the students, relieving them from certain night duties and tuberculosis ward duties, and accepting bribes. These matters were discovered when the permanent principal, Tang Chuon-hwa, took charge later. Tang quietly removed Miss Fan's authority for arranging the practical training periods. Naturally Miss Fan lost much prestige and hated the principal.

I knew nothing of this situation until a graduate nurse circulated a petition signed by almost all our locally-employed graduates. They denounced Miss Fan, accusing her of accepting bribes and undermining the principal's authority. Other minor complaints could not all be proved. I had good reason to suspect the graduate nurse initiated the accusations for personal reasons. Although the charges against Miss Fan were serious and she should have been fired, I let her off with a warning heart-to-heart talk. At the time, liberation was only weeks away and I thought it wiser to smooth over the affair so it would not be used to make enemies. I might have saved myself the trouble. With the arrival of the Communists, Miss Fan adroitly manipulated her position to ingratiate herself with the several Communist-planted leaders in the student body. Often in 1950, she deliberately avoided me in the hospital corridors or failed to greet me. Had I been naturally suspicious, I might have taken these changes seriously. However, other affairs, seemingly more important, occupied my time, and meanwhile Miss Fan laid her careful plans. She was now to enjoy her revenge.

She called upon Huang Tse-min, a friendly, illiterate hospital messenger boy, to be the first speaker. Going to the platform he denounced me as a "bloated capitalist" and an "oppressor" of the hospital employees. He said I had a herd of cows that gave me milk, while the coolies had nothing but water from a reservoir polluted by manure from a stable I had built.

A U-shaped valley separated the hill on which our three missionary homes were built from the opposite hill where the hospital, staff residences and nursing school were located. To supply the water needs of this small community of five hundred, including patients, staff and missionaries, two water reservoirs had been built in the valley. The upper pond, used by the missionary community, was separated from the stable by two hundred yards of vegetable garden. The lower, much larger pond was separated from the first by another vegetable garden. Usually, drainage was not a problem, but during my furlough in 1945-47, hospital gardeners neglected to remove barnyard manure and this caused some pollution. On returning, I ordered the manure removed and the water was again sanitary. My accuser did not point out that the missionaries' reservoir was the first to be contaminated, an omission that did not matter to those seeking only convenient accusations for destroying an enemy.

Huang concluded, "This Allen has everything to eat, but he gives us cow dung for our nourishment. What is that but oppression of our people? Now we all have equal rights and such conditions should no longer be permitted. This is clearly a case of oppression of the common people."

While the implications of his accusations were nasty, Huang obviously had said no more than had been put into his mouth by others. He had always been a friendly, courteous lad. Fear of the consquences had forced this weak accusation from him. Nevertheless, his statement was enough to stimulate the crowd. One of the accusation committee members in the crowd shouted, "Get Allen[1] on the platform. We want him on the platform." Sensing the developing mass hysteria, Constance leaned toward me, remarking, "It looks as if our work is finished here. There will not be much we can do after a meeting of this kind."

The shouts were growing more vigorous, so to humour the crowd I rose and went to the platform, where I stood hesitatingly. "Make him kneel. Make him kneel. Make him bow his head to Mao Tse-tung." (Mao's picture, draped with the five-starred flag of China, decorated the wall behind the chairman.) Better, I thought, to yield gracefully than risk having the crowd stirred to violence. I knelt before the now cheering, hand-clapping, foot-stamping crowd. Keeping my feet over the edge of the wooden platform, I made myself as comfortable as possible, tucking my overcoat tails under my knees to soften, even a little, the bare wooden floor.

Immediate quiet followed the raised hand of the chairman as she announced the next accuser, a young workman named Wang Yin-chieh. Quietly and obviously under pressure, he gave his short story. Early in the year, when he asked for an advance on his salary, as he had done in other years, the hospital refused. (Wang did not mention, of course, that after liberation the hospital suffered from a chronic lack of money and that a loan to one would have led to demands from all.) Instead I had made him a personal loan of thirty thousand people's currency notes. "Allen knows that our salaries are paid according to the value of the quantity of rice we should receive. But when I repaid my loan, I gave him fifty thousand yuan. He never even offered to accept payment in terms of rice. Rice prices had dropped between the time of loan and repayment.

---

1 From this time onward I was officially stripped of all titles. Throughout 1951, no one ever again addressed me as Superintendent or Doctor.

That difference did not matter to him, since he is a capitalist. But I am a poor lad on the very lowest wage. He should have remembered my plight. So, not only is he a capitalist, but by his inconsiderate action, he oppressed me. He thus oppressed the poor people of our country. That is my accusation."

The next day, Wang was one of my temporary guards, and when nobody was near he did everything short of apologizing to gain face with me. We both understood perfectly. I am certain he knew I forgave him for what he had been forced to do.

He closed his evidence and the cheerleaders led the shouting of slogans. As the evening wore on, they voiced their contempt of me, cursed "foreign imperialism" and made a hundred other comments, such as "Down with the running dogs of Chiang Kai-shek," "Away with Truman," "Follow our glorious leader," "Long live Mao Tse-tung."

A nursing student took the floor. Shouting at the top of her voice, she began passionately to vent her anger on my absent wife, Winnifred, and Constance Ward. She objected to Winnifred's coming to a graduation ceremony, "strutting like a queen in her fine clothes and taking one of the best seats in the gallery to avoid sitting with us on the benches outside." (The student conveniently forgot to mention that Winnifred had been invited to take this seat, since she had been ill and her presence was especially desired.) Next the student complained of being sent dirty undergarments that had belonged to Winnifred. Screaming her accusation, she held up samples and then threw them at Constance and me. "This is the kind of woman who was our superintendent's wife, and he is no better," she shouted in a rage so great her words literally sputtered from her lips.

She had put on a marvellous show during which I had temporarily forgotten my beginning-to-ache knees. I relaxed and sank back, sitting on the calves of my legs to relieve my tense thigh muscles while I made mental note that at least the evening was not going to be dull. Once they have demonstrated their loyalty, I thought, their accusations will surely ease off. Official Communist visitors were present and a realistic show of humiliating a foreigner must be given for their benefit.

What had happened to give this student the ammunition to make so bitter and completely unjustified an attack upon my wife? Winnifred and our two children, Phyllis and Marion, fourteen and seven years old respectively, had left Chungking in haste on July 9, 1950, to make suddenly altered connections for their return to Canada. Some clothing Winnifred

wanted thrown away was instead given by Constance to a group of
Chinese Christians who turned cast-off clothing into shoe soles.

The more serious result of this student's accusation was to introduce
Constance Ward as a principal figure in the evening's proceedings. She
took her place, also on her knees, on the right side of the platform.
Meanwhile I adjusted my position, planning to rest each knee alternately
for a time. I had been gazing about while Constance was mounting the
platform. A nearby student noted my actions and drew them to Miss Fan's
and the audience's attention. Taking her position and authority seriously,
Miss Fan strode over.

"Get kneeling properly, and bow your head in penitence, as you
should. You have no right to be looking about the room," she ordered,
pushing down my head viciously. I held myself in check, knowing it best
to accept any such minor indignities, but my mind was in hot rebellion
at her action, which in Chinese tradition constituted violation of one's
person, doubly serious and demeaning when two of the opposite sex
were concerned, and the male in the inferior situation. But as the meeting
continued, I not only ceased to bow but instead kept a very close watch
on as much as I could of the proceedings.

For a while no accusations were made against Constance, the most
innocent and gentle of persons, beloved by both her Chinese friends and
associates, and her fellow missionaries. That she should even be considered a menace to society was a monstrosity of thought. I deduced she
was there merely because we were foreigners together. The temper of the
meeting was growing more nasty, no question of that. But beyond an
intensification of the slogan shouting, increasingly bitter in content as the
meeting progressed, no further attempt was made to lay a finger on either
of us.

Now Fung Cheo-wen came to the platform. By the close of the year
he had assumed a position of considerable importance as head of the
hospital labour union and ruled with a rod of iron. Almost without
exception he remained civil to me, but he had already made trouble for
me during the year. He now began a long, vindictive and insolent account
of an incident that had angered and humiliated him in February 1950. He
claimed that I put patients' needs ahead of hospital workers' needs, and
that was wrong in the new China.

What had happened was that Fung and several workers had come
one Saturday afternoon to collect partial payment of their salaries. It was
a week after that unexpected meeting I had had with the union to decide

how to handle the delayed salary payments and I had said the earliest that money could arrive from Chengtu would be Saturday, a day when the hospital offices were closed. I was visiting a patient at another hospital on my afternoon off. Fung came to the hospital accountant and demanded payment. The money had not arrived and Djang did not know what to do, so he came to my house to get me and then dared not leave until he had seen me. Winnifred invited him in to await my return. Soon Fung and his men knocked on the door and demanded to know why Winnifred was "hiding" Djang. She invited them in, but Fung said he would not enter the home of a foreigner. He said I should be there to take care of the workers' needs before any patients'. Quite a crowd was gathering outside the door, including J. B. MacHattie, the assistant superintendent, who tried to calm Fung. Enraged, Fung turned to leave, calling his men to follow. But some accepted Winnifred's invitation, went in and reassured Djang that they meant him no harm. Then they left. Meanwhile, Fung waited at the gate, burning with humiliation and incensed at having lost face.

He was not one to forget. Now, for the benefit of his audience, he described the incident with full Chinese embellishments.

Other people in the audience rose to denounce other foreigners besides Constance and me. Before the evening was over, MacHattie, the most mild-mannered, quiet and kind-hearted of men, now for months safely at home in Canada, was accused of having threatened the nursing students with starvation. He had only said, "You won't starve if you have to wait a few moments," when the impatient students came at an inopportune time and complained because they had to wait for him to get some rice for their kitchen. Slighting remarks were also made toward two other former missionary workers, but it was obvious to me that the speakers attacked missionaries who had left the country in order to avoid having to accuse me.

Next came "testimony" from two nursing students who had been patients in the hospital. From the beginning of the Communist regime, the Communist student nurses had been our most difficult problem. One, Miss Li, supposedly recovering from an operation, left the hospital several times without permission. Finally, I suggested she should be discharged, since she was well enough, and she agreed, asking when she might return to work. I said she could return any time, and she came back without delay. Now, she accused me of having "forced her to return to work on the day following discharge," which in her opinion constituted oppression of the workers.

A probationary student, Miss Tao, had to be treated for tuberculosis of the kidney. She was told she was not strong enough to continue her studies and should rest and cure her disease. Hospital policy, agreed to by the hospital labour union, required students and staff to pay half the cost of their medications. She could no longer be considered a student under the circumstances, but under pressure from her father and a Communist official, we agreed to treat her as an indigent patient and pay for half the treatment, if the father would pay the other. Treatment with streptomycin ran from April to the fall, except for ten days when supplies ran short, and the disease was arrested. However, her father made only one payment and defaulted on the rest, and in the fall he insisted she return to school because he could not afford to have her at home. Although her doctors felt she risked a breakdown, they agreed to let her try returning to work. In every respect I had done my utmost to co-operate in her treatment, but even the many concessions I had made to her provided no immunity for me on this occasion.

Now, two months later, Miss Tao stood as an accuser and twisted every fact. I had "oppressed" her by forcing her from the nursing school (but only the school principal could do this); I had not maintained her treatment properly (but the shortage had been beyond my control); and I had given her cheaper streptomycin rather than the newer, more expensive dihy-drostreptomycin (but she assumed, wrongly, that newer must be better).

While Li's and Tao's accusations seem trivial and did not even earn a place in later interrogation, this is the type of material that provides the needed basis for action against those whom the Communists wish to expose or condemn. They illustrate extremely well how good intentions and the simplest of facts may be distorted by Communists to further their ends. If the Communists have slated one for elimination from their society, there is no way to escape from their all-entangling net. The only options are conformity or annihilation—or deportation, for foreigners.

For about two hours such accusations as these continued. Even in this Communist society, no accusation yet made had been serious enough to cause me undue worry. It seemed clear that all but Fung were acting under pressure from above. Physically I was becoming more and more uncomfortable. My back and thigh muscles were not only aching but weakening and twitching. Constance, however, seemed to be bearing up extraordinarily well under the severe physical strain.

No accusation meeting involving me could have been complete without a reference to Chang Tsen-hwa, the hospital business manager whose family I had helped after he was arrested. According to my accusers, Chang Tsen-hwa had confessed and been convicted of "counter-revolutionary activities." By helping his wife and children I had been "protecting a counter-revolutionary, a most serious crime against the government." The government had clearly stated that those who helped counter-revolutionaries would be punished. To them it was irrelevant that no one had ever officially informed us Chang Tsen-hwa was a counter-revolutionary.

Now came the biggest surprise of the evening. With this next accusation, by Whang Dung-min, chief laboratory technician, the crowd's attention turned to Constance. He told of a conversation he had had with her. He spoke of this and nothing more. There was no bitterness, no shouting, merely a statement of fact, but it was enough to condemn her in the audience's eyes.

Whang was one of the best-liked and most reliable Chinese members of the hospital staff and had been active in church affairs. We had been the closest of friends. But shortly after liberation, he began to be persuaded by Communist philosophy, newspaper stories and the urgings of Chao She-hwei that the new government's policies were good, as many of them were up to that time. The more disagreeable aspects of communism had yet to become manifest.

One night, after an English class taught by Constance, Whang and she had a discussion about communism. She tried to explain to him that his government was presenting inaccurate information about events in Korea and about the relationship of other countries to China and the living conditions of citizens in those countries. He argued that while Chiang Kai-shek's government had lied to the people, everything published by the Communist government was thoroughly documented and illustrated, so it had to be the truth.

When Constance told Ian Robb and me the story on her return home that evening, we were shocked at what she had done, and said, "Do not ever get into that kind of a conversation with a Chinese again. They could very easily make plenty of trouble for you if they wished." In complete innocence she had left herself wide open to the accusation Whang was now making.

Had our minds acted quickly enough on that occasion, we might have advised her to apologize to Whang for prolonging the argument. He had probably mentioned the conversation casually to one of the Communists, perhaps Chao. Now he, too, was under pressure to make his accusation.

He would have been told he must speak or take the consequences, and for the Chinese, consequences could be serious indeed.

Whang concluded his testimony: "I talked with her for more than two hours trying to convince her that what our government said was not propaganda but the truth. She would not believe me." Those words were Constance's doom. After his accusation she too could no longer work with and among her beloved Chinese friends. How her heart must have ached for Whang that evening as he publicly committed himself body and soul to the Communist cause. To have him so calmly, and in so considered a fashion, denounce Constance, who had befriended him so freely, seemed incredible. If such as Whang were against us, then surely our work had gone for naught.

After this accusation, pandemonium broke out. It became increasingly difficult to follow all that was happening. Accusations continued to rain on my head. The clamour of the bystanders outside; the triple shouting of slogans by the crowd; the continual watching to be sure the frail, greying woman kneeling beside me with her head bowed would not crumple under the strain; the attempt to listen to and remember evidence regarding which I would ultimately have to make my own statements—all were part of a terrible nightmare which, even as I pen these words [in late 1953] almost three years after the event, is still vivid and almost overpowering in its mental clarity.

But on and on the accusations went. Three hours passed, then four. A nursing student, Miss Mung, who like Fung had been observing my alleged mismanagement of patients, oppression of the nursing students and other misdemeanors, read from pages of notes. Then a uniformed outsider I had never seen before rose and accused me of allowing Christianity to be taught in the nursing school, violating the government's law forbidding religious services in teaching institutions. It was true I had never made any attempt to stop the church from holding its services in the auditorium of the nursing school, where I was then being accused. But the school was not under my control but that of a board who alone had the authority to refuse to allow services there. In no sense could I be held responsible for the situation. But when a Communist speaks officially, his word is believed. I was judged to be at fault and later had to confess my guilt.

Other denouncers followed and accused me of alleged personal statements that showed my lack of sympathy with the government and attempts to undermine its influence. I was even accused of engaging in spying activities in connection with Rev. Olin Stockwell, who had already been imprisoned for spying.

In all this long evening, Constance and I were given no opportunity to defend ourselves or even confess our guilt. Any statement we might have made would not have helped us and might have incited the audience to violence against us. Properly for that occasion, our tongues were as silent as if they had been removed. But we did have our defenders. It might have been wiser for them had they, too, remained silent, as did other friends.

About midnight, one of the student nurses, a nineteen-year-old orphan with strong Christian convictions, was called upon for her accusation. In the year since liberation she was one of the few students who had remained faithful to her beliefs in the face of possible persecution by students inclined toward communism. As she rose and walked to the platform a great sadness came over me. Had the plausible-sounding accusations made against me that evening caused her to lose her profound belief in God and her accepted Saviour, Jesus Christ? Had she also lost faith in me, as others seemed to have done? Who could expect her to disbelieve her own people and her own ears in favour of a foreigner, even if he had helped her in many ways? I had expected most of the others to say what they did, even though I knew these accusations were forced upon them and they had no recourse. And I knew it was dangerous for my undoubted friends to speak on my behalf. As she spoke I prayed silently for her, the only time I did so during that bitter, unhappy evening.

She spoke with quiet dignity: "I have always been a Christian. I was brought up that way by my grandmother. My parents are both dead. I have only a brother remaining. I have always been true to my God. Tonight I have heard many disturbing things. I have heard many accusations against one who calls himself a Christian. I do not believe that anyone who is a real Christian could do the things with which he is charged. I did not realize that there was a devil among us tonight, until I saw what I have seen and heard what I have heard. I know that devil will receive justice for what has happened tonight."

She said no more and my heart sank completely. She, too, had betrayed me, I thought. A loud roar of cheering and hand-clapping arose, led by the Communist members of the audience who were thrilled to have gained her, their "most stubborn opponent," as a convert. But both they and I had completely misunderstood her. She had carefully chosen her words to convey condemnation, but the next day it became clear to the organizing committee that she had condemned not me but those who had accused me, including themselves. It was not long after my release that I learned how heavy a price she paid for her courageous action. She was condemned to nearly six months' imprisonment to atone for what she had said. With her went another student who had refused the committee's demand to accuse me. The third member of this Christian trio was ill in hospital that evening. When she learned her friends had been imprisoned, she unsuccessfully attempted suicide.

At something short of one o'clock in the morning the accusations finally ceased and Miss Fan completed her indictment. "You have all heard what has been quoted in evidence this evening against this man, Allen. This is the devil, who has been in our midst trying to enslave us. Tonight we have uncovered his nefarious activities. We have liberated the hospital from his power. Likewise, the nursing school has found a new freedom. What is right that we should do to him? Nothing is too severe for a man like him and his accomplice, Constance Ward."

The excited throng, wrought to the highest pitch of psychological tension and hoarse by this time, shouted as one voice, "Let the government investigate this evidence. Let them be sent to prison."

To one other I wish to pay my tribute and gratitude. She was an unlettered Christian Chinese woman, who rolled bandages, assisted Winnifred in her work as keeper of the linen stores and helped in other ways in the hospital. By dint of much work and with covert assistance from the hospital, she had placed her son in training as a laboratory technician and her daughter in training in a midwifery school, while a third child still attended primary school. As the shout went up to "Send them to prison," she rose and courageously cried out, "You can't do that. You can't do that." Only that once did I turn my head to make certain who had spoken on our behalf. Memory of that scene still remains as vivid and clear as I saw it that night. From every direction hands were stretched out to pull her down to her seat, much as a pack of hounds would pull down a doe at bay. I thank God for the memory of that mother and the young orphan girl and the many who wisely remained silent, perhaps thus saving me from more serious consequences than what resulted from that meeting. They and their families have perforce to live their lives under the conditions that will develop in the future, conditions under which few of us would care to exist.

The government investigator, sent to ensure that such meetings are "properly" conducted and ostensibly to hold the crowd in control should it attempt excessive violence, then rose to his feet. "If that is your wish, then I must tell you that none of us can take action against these two. They are foreigners and according to the law they have to be dealt with through the Foreign Affairs Bureau of the Public Safety Department. Those arrangements must first be made. In the meantime you must not harm them in any way. You must see that they are properly and suitably cared for in the interval."

The crowd started to disperse. Constance and I rose from our knees, grateful to relieve our aching backs and other muscles. We were conducted to a small lecture room in which benches and other furniture had been temporarily piled to clear the auditorium. At last we could relax our overwrought bodies. We were told to remain there while the organizing committee met to discuss suitable action condemning Warren Austin, whom everyone except the accusation committee had long since forgotten. During the next half-hour, Constance and I had our last opportunity to speak together before we were finally separated, yet we said little. The events of the evening had concluded on much too serious a note for talking and each of us was deep in thought.

It was obvious that months of investigation must pass before I could possibly free myself from the web of false statements that had been tightly woven about me by that small core of Communists. They were bent on removing, once and forever, any trace of foreign involvement in the United Church of Canada's mission hospital in Chungking.

Of the more than fifty charges laid against me that evening, those made during its later hours became a mental confusion in the general pandemonium that reigned. It was only afterward in prison, when the more important items were brought up individually for investigation, that it was possible to develop a clear picture of the devious methods used in the preparation of this alleged or implied evidence of so voluminous and accusing a character. The government itself could not have issued a warrant of arrest on the basis of any evidence given had the hospital personnel and nursing students not been previously stimulated to take initial action.

The meeting at an end, we were escorted along the dark, winding pathway from the nursing school to the women's wing of the hospital. We said our goodbyes, wishing each other well in the unknown trials that were to come to us. Constance went to her room, I to mine, a room pregnant with memories of scores of patients whom I had helped back to health. It was hard to accept the fact that our more than fifty combined years of work in China had ended with betrayal by our erstwhile friends under the overwhelming influence of communism.[2]

---

2 Constance Ward fared inordinately well. After ten days of detention in the hospital she was questioned and confessed to the accusation made against her. She was warned not to repeat a similar offense, and to report at regular intervals in writing to the Foreign Affairs Bureau. Both she and Ian Robb were permitted to leave later on without further gross inconveniences. Constance left Chungking en route home on August 6, 1951. Ian was advised by certain Chinese friends to take no further responsibilities at the hospital from the time I was arrested until his departure. He continued to attend his patients for a short period thereafter but, noting the general trend of political activities, finally decided to cease his medical work. A previously requested exit permit was granted and he left China in March 1951.

Chapter 5

Facing the Political Court

U TTERLY EXHAUSTED, I woke late the following morning, December 21st. One of the hospital workmen was stationed on guard duty outside my room. Lao Hsu, our house servant, brought my breakfast and various necessities from home, but I was not allowed a razor, for fear I would attempt suicide. Ian Robb sent reading matter and writing paper. I immediately started preparing urgent statements and instructions as I sat huddled in bed, clothes well tucked in to keep warm in the near-freezing room. As the guards came on duty, they chatted amiably with me, avoiding any reference to the previous evening. Two department heads visited me during the day and from things they let drop in the course of conversation, I gathered a meeting of hospital, church, government and other representatives was to be held to discuss my future.

News of the accusation meeting had spread widely and swiftly. Toward mid-morning a noisy crowd gathered to see or at least shout slogans at the foreigner who was locked up under the control of his own hospital employees. Above the noise I could hear my secretary exhorting them to be quiet for the sake of their countrymen who were ill in the hospital. That worked wonders and the crowd dispersed. In the afternoon, however, students from the nearby Chungking Girls High School asked the nursing students to let them see the "imperialist" foreigner. My door was thrown wide and group after group came to peer in. I turned my back toward them as I lay on the bed. Some commented sarcastically that I had been given too comfortable a bed. Others taunted me to pray, since that is what they had heard Christians did when in trouble. Although distinctly embarrassed, I managed to keep my temper under control.

During the evening, labour union chairman Fung, now in complete control of operations, came up to see that I was being well looked after. I thanked him for seeing that my normal requirements were being met but said it surely could not be his wish that I should be exposed as a public spectacle for the crowd's pleasure or abuse. He agreed, saying I would have no further cause for complaint.

His instructions to the nursing students to cease taunting me angered the ringleader, Ho Yo-lan, chairman of the student body. The next morning, she appeared at my door, blocking the exit as I was about to go across the corridor to the washroom. She was short, plump and red-faced and many people feared her nasty temper. I tried to pass her. Immediately she flung her arms out to stop my progress. I drew back and asked what right she had to stop me, since my guards were members of the hospital labour union, not the student body. I courteously asked her to move aside, but she made no move at all. Thoughts of yesterday's taunts from the students she had escorted past my room, together with the memory of her obstructive activities all year, made me cast all discretion aside. With no further warning, I walked through the doorway, as if she were not there at all. Her face flushed deep scarlet with anger as others in the hall witnessed her discomfiture. I knew there would be a reaction. What I had done was neither gentlemanly nor becoming of a Christian missionary, but the sudden temptation to even up our score just a little was too strong to resist.

She lost no time in getting her revenge. An hour later she had a crowd of off-duty students on the march. My guard at the time was Fung's lieutenant, Tan Tse-gao. Hearing the demonstrators and discovering this exhibition was for my benefit, he opened the verandah door and pushed up the window, the better that I might hear the noise, which by this time would have penetrated any but a concrete or brick wall. Tan did not know I was partially deaf. I rolled over in bed and put my one good ear in the pillow, turning my deaf ear upward. After half an hour the students left.

Meanwhile I began to wonder just why I was being held so long without official action. A short note from Ian that morning had indicated what Fung's action was likely to be, but nothing official had been said to me. When Fung made his daily visit, I asked him about the inaction, saying I should be permitted to put my case before the Foreign Affairs Bureau. For the first time since the accusation meeting, Fung referred to my situation and informed me that I had many charges laid against me, that I had been found to have many faults. Without further comment he left.

Several of the workmen guarding me had tried to reassure me there was no need to worry. I appreciated their obvious concern for me, which conveyed the sympathy they dared not express openly. In spite of what had happened, they were still my friends. They told me the whole matter would soon be cleared. In their inexperience, not fully comprehending the destructive capabilities and designs of the Communists, they did not then realize how far their own actions were to lead. But I knew that since I had been charged with spying, much explaining would be required before I would again be a free man.

The cheering note from Ian had come with some medical journals and a Bible. My guards later took the Bible from me, however.

After lunch, two representatives of the Foreign Affairs Bureau, Comrades Tai and Kao, whom I knew well, came to my room with Chairman Fung and a few hospital representatives. Without preamble Comrade Tai handed me a warrant, enquired if I understood its meaning, then ordered me to collect my belongings and accompany him. I gave the terrified Lao Hsu a list of my bedding and clothing needs for what I presumed would be incarceration in a common, ill-kept prison. I stuffed my towel, soap and a few other personal articles in my pockets. My hands were not bound, thanks to Comrade Tai's considerateness, so I knew I was merely under investigation and not yet deemed an actual criminal.

On leaving the building I was surprised to see a crowd had gathered to witness my departure. There were few members of my staff present, but students of the nursing school and girls high school, together with their teachers and many neighbours, were gathered in force to view the arrest. I faced them as calmly as possible, walking down the long flight of stone steps to the gatehouse while the crowd, momentarily quiet, watched. Once my two escorts and I had passed through the gate, the mob suddenly closed in behind, bursting forth in a torrent of name-calling and following us most of the way to the river. When we reached the street that wound through the village of Shuan Tan Miao, about a hundred feet above the Yangtze, Comrade Tai decided the demonstrations had been adequate. Turning, he ordered quiet and commanded the crowd to go home. Free from the howling escort, we three continued to the ferry dock and crossed the river.

An automobile and armed guards awaited us at the top of the broad stone steps that led from the river to the entrance to Chungking nearly two hundred feet above. Passersby here were unaware anything unusual was happening. Seated in the car with the armed but courteous guards, I was quickly driven through the city, up Iron Workers Street, to a point opposite one of the city's famous Buddhist temples, newly rebuilt after its destruction by the Japanese. Here the car turned right down a muddy road leading to the Political Section of the Public Safety Department.

A group of officials met me there, brought me into their headquarters and took me to my cell. The building had been the five-storey residence of a wealthy Kuomintang official before the Communists arrived and had housed not only his own immediate family but many close relatives as well, together with their numerous servants. My cell was a room just over eleven feet square. It was almost dark, for the windows on the east and north sides had been boarded up, leaving but a few chinks where daylight entered. A guard switched the electricity on, revealing a sparsely furnished, cement-floored room that had been plastered many years ago. It was dirty, unattractive and unheated. The temperature in the room was about forty degrees Fahrenheit.

I was immediately stripped, and my clothing and person searched. While I was giving my name, age, residence and other details for the official records, a man later identified only as Wu, an investigator with the Political Section, entered. Like others in his department, he proved to be highly intelligent. He wore dark, heavy, horn-rimmed glasses and his face was expressionless and without humour. In a very businesslike manner he asked his comrades for the contents of my wallet and pockets, which had already been listed. Some of my clothing was examined and returned to me and I began to dress. In fifteen minutes the formalities were over. My examiners left, taking my belongings and giving no receipt for them. They locked the door securely outside. I sat on the bamboo bed in one corner, awaiting my remaining clothes and bedding and wondering how long I would be kept there.

My first supper under detention was a surprisingly large and tasty dish of steaming noodles and meat balls, so good that at the time I thought it had been purchased at an outside restaurant. I made myself as comfortable as possible for the night. My bleak, comfortless room was furnished with a square four-legged stool, a desk-table and a bed with inch-wide strips of interlaced bamboo for springs. On this I arranged my sleeping bag, two blankets and a quilt.

I took stock of the situation. How was I to get out of this mess? Was I to be forced to confess to things I had never done or said? Only a few days earlier, Ian, Constance and I had discussed the arrest of Rev. Olin Stockwell, a missionary of the American Methodist Church, who as appointed treasurer for the American Methodist Hospital, had helped me see that certain medical supplies were distributed earlier in the year. Olin and his wife, Esther, had been in Chungking since 1949. At the time of his arrest, I had made the mental decision that if ever I found myself entrapped as Olin was, I would say no more than necessary until I knew I was on safe ground.

Suddenly the door opened and a guard escorted me up two flights of stairs and along several corridors. We arrived at an outer room where I was given a chair. A few moments later I was called into the main room, where I found myself standing at one end of a long table. At the other end sat Chairman Lan, head of the Political Section. At the sides of the table sat eight others with paper and pencils in front of them. I had met Lan before under friendlier circumstances.[1] He motioned me to sit down some distance from the table, opposite him.

"Do you know where you are and what august body you now face?"

I knew where I was but I was sorry, I did not know the official position of the group before me.

"This is the Political Court and we are here to question you on matters of which you have been accused. We want you to tell us everything you know, freely."

I had difficulty following his Shantung accent, and he asked if I wanted an interpreter, to which I said yes, one might be helpful. A grey-haired man named Liu, who looked like a Shanghai stevedore, interpreted for the remainder of the interview.

"From the evidence at hand, we believe you are a spy. Are you prepared to admit that this is so?"

I replied bluntly that I was engaged in no such activities. There was absolutely no evidence to support this supposition.

"If this accusation is not the truth, then please tell us who was the woman in your home on November 28th. What was she doing there?"

For a moment I simply could not think. How could I remember what had happened on that specific evening? I could not reply.

"Just think a little harder. You must tell. Just to help your memory a little we will tell you she was a China Inland Mission Language School

---

1 Dr. Allen is probably referring to the hearing he attended in November 1950, regarding the hospital's failure to pay tax on two sales of medicine. See Appendix A.

student admitted to your hospital. Now do you remember? Who is she? What does she do? What was she doing in your home? What did you talk about?"

With these hints, I recalled the visit of Lizzie Toft, a Swedish missionary nurse who had been in hospital for an operation and who, a couple of days later came to my home to recuperate, as foreign patients occasionally did. We had had no serious conversations.

"You have not answered my question," the judge said sharply. "What was she doing on the night of November 28th in your home?"

I could not answer and said so. How could I be expected to remember exactly what had happened on a night four weeks ago? This annoyed the judge, who decided I was being perverse. He went on to another subject.

"If you will not answer that question, then tell us why you were found in the Juan Ren (City People's) Hospital late one evening last summer? Why were you not at home at that time? How many nights have you spent in the city and where did you stay?"

Being out overnight without registration was not permitted, either for foreigners or Chinese, but I had had good reason. I explained I had spent the night in the city only twice in the past six months, both times because the ferries had been taken out of service and I could not get back across the river. The first time, I had accompanied my wife and two children across the flooded river so they could catch a steamer on their homeward journey, but it had been the last ferry of the evening because the flooded river was too dangerous to cross in the dark. I had planned to stay at the Canadian Mission Business Agency in Chungking but decided to take a walk before checking in there. Along the way I happened to be accosted by several persistent prostitutes in the former British consular area. I decided the only way to rid myself of them was to stop at the American Episcopal Mission Hospital, which was also in the neighbourhood. The second time I stayed overnight in the city, I had been called across to Chungking late at night to attend a patient there and had to remain in that hospital until morning when the ferry service began again.

"Liang Tseng-luen, do you expect us to believe that nonsense? It is obvious that this is just a made-up story to cover your illegal and ulterior motives. You definitely went to the hospital to spy on something. What was it?"

"I have told you what happened," I said decisively. "I have nothing further to add."

Finding I could not be induced to speak further, Lan moved on. "You say you are not a spy. When have you helped our government? What assistance have you ever given to us? You have never shown any co-operation with us at all."

I thought I was getting a break here, for of course I had helped. "While I was in charge of relief work," I began, "I helped secure medical supplies for your International Peace Hospitals in Yenan. When your soldiers of the People's Liberation Army came to Chungking I gave them every assistance. I treated one of your police station officials and operated on him free of charge. These are only some of the ways I have helped your government."

"We have heard and know all about that," said Lan, not even letting the interpreter finish. "It is no more than should be expected of you. What else have you done? Nothing!"

Although I was doing my best to co-operate and answer their questions, I was getting nowhere rapidly. They did not believe me and clearly thought I was withholding information. Lan's bludgeoning attacks did not help extract the desired information. If the official attitude was to be one of disbelief, then the sooner I ceased giving information that might lead to later entanglement, the better. Why should I take chances when I was unsure what answers they wanted or why they asked? I would not play into their hands or be caught by their tactics.

"You are charged with attempting to kill, or at least to maim or injure, some of our Communist officials. You have operated upon them. They have had complications that were deliberately caused by you. We know you have operated successfully upon high officials of the false enemy government of the traitor, Chiang Kai-shek. They had no complications. But these three men"—and he named them—"each have suffered at your hands. What have you to say for yourself? *T'an beh, t'an beh.*" (Tell everything you know, both good and bad.)

I explained. In the first operation, chest surgery for tuberculosis, an alarming hemorrhage occurred when the first rib was removed. A gauze pack left in to control the hemorrhage was removed the next day and the incision was closed. Miss Mung, an accuser at the December 20 meeting, had stated this was an improper technique and had caused the resulting infection. As the surgeon, I had the choice either of not using a gauze pack and risking a later fatal hemorrhage or of using the pack and risking a temporary minor infection. The latter course was the safest.

In the second operation, also chest surgery, a secondary hemorrhage followed some days after the second stage operation. This was a normal complication which occasionally occurs even in the best of surgery. In this particular case the patient's life was never in serious danger.

In the third case, a wound became infected following kidney surgery done in the heat of summer, when perspiration from surgeon and patient could cause self-infection. Though the surgery could have waited until fall, the patient had insisted the operation be performed without delay, since it would be difficult for him to arrange a further sick leave. Against my better judgment, I yielded to his pleading. A minor superficial infection resulted, delaying his discharge for some weeks.

I was willing to admit to any reasonable fault, but I contended these were unavoidable complications. On one point I was firm: I was entirely innocent of deliberately seeking to injure or maim these patients.

Again my evidence was not accepted. "That is your story, Liang Tseng-luen. We have proof that you did these acts deliberately, and we will investigate further. Now, tell us of your relationship with Chang Tsen-hwa."

Chang Tsen-hwa, if you recall, was the unpopular hospital accountant whose arrest I had witnessed and whose family I had helped after his imprisonment. The Police Bureau had already learned everything about him at the accusation meeting held against him. I told Lan I had nothing to add since I knew nothing of his activities outside the hospital. In fact, I had made a point of not investigating the personal affairs of staff members, in order to avoid possible charges of favouritism through too-close personal relationships with them, even though some, by virtue of their position, had more intimate contact with me than others.

"But you have been helping his family. Liang Tseng-luen, you say you are not a spy. If you are not, then you must be a counter-revolutionary. Otherwise you would not have been helping them. You know he is in prison for counter-revolutionary activities."

I refused to admit to being either a spy or a counter-revolutionist. I said I had never been specifically told Chang Tsen-hwa was a counter-revolutionary, though there had been gossip to that effect.

"Liang Tseng-luen," he said, "you are not being helpful this evening. You have not been frank with us. You have not confessed to any of the accusations against you. Let me warn you, if you continue to be so unco-operative, you will have trouble when you appear before the next court. Things there will go badly for you."

"I'm sorry," I replied. "I am doing my best to be co-operative. I wish to clear these charges as quickly as possible. If you would permit me to have a personal conversation with your interpreter, I may be able clear up many points which, as yet, I do not understand."

"That should not be necessary. You are a very intelligent man and the questions we ask are simple enough, but you will not be frank. Go back to your room and think over your problems. When you next appear, you must be more co-operative."

I was led back to my cell. None of the evening's events at this court seemed to make any sense. We were poles apart in our thinking. As I paced my cell I wondered why they persisted in these ridiculous charges of spying and counter-revolutionary activities, especially on such trivial evidence.[2] There were many accusations which would demand detailed explanation. Well, I told myself, keep your head cool and take your time. You have committed no serious fault, even under their laws. There will be plenty of time tomorrow to think over your problems. Let each day take care of itself. Now is the time for sleep.

Preparation for bed took only a few minutes. I went and switched off the electric light, but even before I could reach my bed, only six feet away, I heard the guard shout: "Turn on that light. It must remain on all the time. You are not to sleep in darkness." He did not add that he would be using the peephole in my cell door to watch my activities at intervals during the night. Until the following May, for me the welcome dark of night was always dispelled by the dim light of a single electric bulb.

---

2 After my release I learned that almost every foreigner brought to these courts was accused of one or other of these charges, all on most unreasonable evidence.

Chapter 6

Interrogations Begin

ON THE MORNING of my first full day of solitary confinement in the Public Safety Department I was surprised to be given a breakfast of milk and toast, evidently a move to make me feel I was being treated well.

Following the reprimand from the Political Court I was left alone for several days to think over my plight. I had answered all their questions truthfully, but they had not believed me. I had tried to co-operate, but they told me I was unco-operative. I tried to read the one book I had been allowed to keep, a text on practical anatomy, by J. B. Jamieson, but I absorbed none of it. Unable to read, I paced the floor, thinking how I could convince these suspicious investigators that I spoke the truth. The senseless accusations against me had been twisted to put me in an impossible and highly embarrassing predicament. For now, I decided to hold back no relevant information, tell all the truth as I had been doing and scrupulously avoid any statement that might implicate others. It seemed incredible that any group of fair-minded individuals could fail to see my point of view.

All this thinking at least shed sudden light on the Political Court's question respecting my relations with Miss Lizzie Toft. A Swedish mission-ary nurse studying Chinese, she had been admitted to our hospital for an operation. During part of her recuperation she had had to stay in the hospital, rather than with a missionary couple only blocks away, because of a ruling in October 1950 by the Foreign Affairs Bureau of Chungking. It prohibited members of the China Inland Mission Language School from staying away from home for longer than ten days. The ruling was designed to prevent them from preaching Christianity among the Chinese. The missionaries got around this and still continued their practice postings by returning to the school before the ten-day period ended, staying at school a few days and then returning to their post. All would have been well if I had not rocked the boat by asking for special permission to have a missionary serve an extended period as nurse for a fellow missionary who had been hospitalized with us. I was told to use Chinese nurses for the job, but the request got the government suspicious and it questioned all the language school students and then ruled they must have permission for any night's stay away from home.

On the night in question, Miss Toft had been invited along with Rev. and Mrs. Ralph Toliver, another missionary couple who were also friends of hers, to a belated birthday dinner for me in our home. Her return to the hospital was delayed when Ian Robb, who was to escort her back, asked her to wait until a Voice of America radio news broadcast ended. Her late arrival at the hospital annoyed the night nurse, and the fact that the day nurse had forgotten to make up a bed for Miss Toft made matters worse. Furthermore, my friends Rev. Olin Stockwell and Brother Pretat had been arrested as spies just two or three days earlier. I believe the nurse grew suspicious that Miss Toft and I were collaborating as spies, since otherwise she could not understand why a non-emergency patient should enter the hospital so late.

The more I thought about the incident, the more ridiculous the evidence seemed. It would be easy to clear the matter at my next examination. I made a complete written report a day or so later and was never questioned on the matter again.

On Christmas morning I awoke rather upset. The contrast between the way I had expected to spend the day and the reality was distressing. We had planned to have Christmas dinner at our home for the United Church community present in Chungking at that time, and here I was in a prison cell, alone. My depression was lifted somewhat when one of the guards came in with a package of oranges, a gift from Ian Robb, I assumed. Still I was downcast and wondered how I was going to face the problems ahead of me.

Then, as if the thought of Christmas became transcendent, I started to hum some Christmas carols. One carol led to another and to hymns that were being sung in all Christian churches that day. My mood improved with each carol, and finally I came to a solo I knew well, one I used to sing at home in Naramata, B.C., with my sister Margaret accompanying me on the piano. It was called "The Star of Bethlehem." After humming

over the first part of it and starting the words of that delightful sacred solo,
I came to the final lines:

> And onward, upward shone the star, until it seemed to me
> It flashed upon the golden gate, and o'er the crystal sea,
> Then the gates rolled backward, I stood where angels trod.
> It was the star of Bethlehem that led me up to God.

In the midst of the magnificently increasing tempo at the close of the
solo I stopped and began to think. Why should you be worried, I told
myself. You are a Christian. This situation should not upset you unduly.
You will come through it with no harm, because you know the Communists do not want to create a bad impression abroad about their treatment
of foreigners. So there is no need to fear injury or serious maltreatment.

Then and there I decided only one way was open to me. Few people
in the recent past had experienced the situation I was in. I had a unique
opportunity to observe at first hand how the Communists altered the
political, social and cultural fabric of the Chinese nation. I would use my
favoured position to describe intimately what happened to those who
appeared to be opponents of the Communist regime. I would note what
was happening, so that I could tell my story later on. I would deal with
the situation from day to day.

On December 26th, Investigator Wu unlocked my door and entered.
I rose, offering him the only stool available, seating myself on the bamboo
bed. It was Wu who had directed my admitting examination, checked the
contents of my pockets, taken what he desired for examination and
returned the remainder. With his horn-rimmed glasses, he looked like an
overly-studious university student. Although at first he was quite affable,
during later periods of interrogation I discovered him to be taciturn,
unsmiling and severe to the point of rudeness, not at all characteristic of
the usual Chinese temperament. I learned to dread his investigations much
more than those conducted by the other two interrogators who worked
on my case for the next eight months. His sledgehammer methods of
questioning were designed to overpower the prisoner, not put him at ease.

Wu spoke excellent, though stilted, English during this first interrogation. It was the only occasion any of the investigators carried on a complete
conversation in my native tongue, though nearly all were able to do so.
To use the English language in an official capacity was strictly forbidden

under the People's Government—all conversation and questioning must be in Chinese.

He began pleasantly enough. "You did not make a very good impression the other evening, Allen. What is your attitude toward this whole investigation going to be? Will you be co-operative and work with us to clear your problems, or do you intend to be stubborn and make difficulties for yourself and everyone else?"

"I intend to get this business straightened out as quickly as possible," I replied. "As far as I am concerned I have nothing to hide, and I wish to be co-operative, but frankly, I am not clear about many things of which I am being accused. I am prepared to clear all obscure points if you will state what they are. I do not intend in the least to be stubborn and I will tell you all you wish to know if it affects accusations that have been made against me."

It appeared to me we could talk each other's language. Our conversation seemed to be off to a good start.

"Do you know you are not alone here? Do you know that Rev. Olin Stockwell is here? And the Frenchman, Brother Pretat, too. I think you know them both. Perhaps you have some relationship with them."

I said I knew them both slightly (for this was no time to know others too well, especially when spying charges were being levelled against at least one of these men). In answer to all the questions Wu asked concerning them I gave only the minimum of information sufficient to satisfy him.

Casually, he remarked at last, "The charges against you are the same as those against Stockwell. Do you know what they are?"

"Just what I have seen in the local papers. I know nothing official."

Suddenly he faced me, the first hard glint appearing in his eyes. Stony-faced, his voice now harsh, he said, "Allen, we have evidence you have been working with Stockwell. You have been going to his home weekly and there, together, you have engaged in espionage activity. We have people who are prepared to swear to this if brought to the witness stand. What have you to answer to this charge?"

The abrupt change in his attitude and the un-Chinese directness of his charge that I was guilty instantly set my adrenalin flowing. I was mentally furious, but keeping my voice under control, I replied bluntly, "No person in this city would dare make such a charge, unless he lies. No one can state I have been in the Stockwell home weekly, for I have been there only once since he came to Chungking just over a year ago. I have met him weekly at Rotary Club meetings as long as they were permitted. They ceased two months ago upon your government's order. In any case, we parted company when the meetings ended."

Without further comment he asked how I used my Thursdays when in town. I said my mornings were spent in our city out-patient clinic and noon time had been reserved for Rotary Club as long as it lasted. The afternoons were spent on hospital business matters and attending special meetings dealing largely with hospital problems, visiting patients at home, giving special consultations and handling any personal business matters that might arise. I returned to my home and the hospital on the south bank of the river at any time between five and eight o'clock in the evening. If he implied my Thursdays in the city were used for ulterior purposes, his information was grossly at fault. I was not involved in any but conventional matters, certainly not espionage.

Wu paced the floor and suddenly turned on his heel to face me. I stood opposite, prepared for a second direct attack. This man had to be watched. I must not be caught off guard. The attack came, as unequivocal as the first false accusation. He could not easily be turned aside.

"You are going to be charged with concealing medical supplies which did not belong to you, the drugs you took from the Joint Committee for Rural Reconstruction (J.C.R.R.). This you already have confessed to."

I had done nothing of the kind, and this I tried to show him as I reviewed the case.[1] The medical supplies in question had been donated by Western nations to China for post-war recovery. In mid-November 1949, just before the Communists entered Chungking, I, as chairman of the West China Medical Committee of the International Relief Committee of China, was asked to take charge of their distribution. Half the supplies had been designated for the Chinese government's use, the other half for private organizations, such as mission hospitals and the Red Cross. I made documented efforts to inform the new government of the location of the supplies, but I was not permitted to handle the actual transactions because I was a foreigner. The vice-chairman of the committee, a Chinese doctor, therefore made the final arrangements with the Military Commission in Chungking. In December the Military Commission collected the government's share for government use. Between April and August the following

---

1 See Appendix B for a more detailed account of this issue.

year, I authorized the actual distribution of the remaining supplies previously designated for private organizations. Brother Pretat, Rev. Olin Stockwell and Dr. Yu Enmei all helped with the distribution.[2] Only after this was completed did representatives of the Foreign Affairs Bureau of the Public Safety Department come to me wanting me to retrieve the supplies I had just distributed and return them to the government, claiming these were the ones designated for its use. They apparently never received the documentation I had so carefully prepared to prevent just this kind of confusion. The representatives insisted the agreement made with the old government held for the new one as well, and since they claimed they had no record any medical supplies had been received in December 1949, then clearly I had misappropriated the government's share and distributed it in 1950.

I explained all this to Wu, pointing out that his government had repeatedly stated that it had no jurisdiction over any actions taken under the previous Nationalist government. But no argument could penetrate Wu's armour.

"You are to be charged with concealing supplies belonging to the People's Government," he repeated, as if he had heard nothing I had said. "On all the subjects I have questioned you about, I request a full written report. Paper will be sent to you for that purpose. I shall send you our interpreter in case you need his help. Give us your co-operation and we will gradually get this case cleared."

In due time, paper appeared and I made one of my first reports. It irked me that in the Political Department's investigation of this charge regarding the distribution of medical supplies I was expected to report from memory when detailed documents were on file at the Foreign Affairs Bureau. I had played a minor role in a distribution that I had not wanted to handle in the first place. We had tried to protect ourselves against the very complications that occurred, but we had not counted on dealing with a government that acted contrary to its own previous statements. It may never be known how many Chinese people have had to pay the severest penalties for non-criminal actions committed under the old regime that were judged criminal retroactively by the new Chinese People's Govern-

---

2 All three were imprisoned, although not officially for their connection with this medical supplies issue. Dr. Yu Enmei's story is told in a note in Appendix B.

ment in its eagerness to get rid of undesirable persons. Many others, both Chinese and foreigners, were involved equally with me in this distribution of medical supplies, and some were imprisoned, but I know of none but myself who was officially condemned for this or a similar reason.

A day or two before the new year, I received the translator's promised visit. I had been in solitary confinement for over a week. I was calm now and eager to talk with this amiable old man, Liu, about points that needed clarification. He wanted information and I was eager to explain my position and to clear myself. We got along famously for perhaps half an hour.

He urged me to tell all I knew (*t'an beh*) about my faults and actions, advice I was to hear often during the months of interrogation. I told him how frustrating the investigation of my case was for me, since when I gave information, I was not always believed. I also explained that I appeared to have been condemned for trying to do what seemed right for my staff and for the good of all. Was that not what communism stood for?

As an example, I told him about the time in June 1950 when our short-lived hospital services committee decided the cost of streptomycin to treat tuberculosis among hospital staff and labourers would be paid half by the hospital and half by the employees. The Communist representatives of the hospital labourers argued for an option which would actually have been even less to their advantage but was the one they had settled on among themselves beforehand as the best. After a long and bitter discussion, the vote was taken and the majority chose the fifty-fifty option. The next day the Communist members of the committee resigned, saying I had not been democratic in my handling of the matter. The committee never met again. (Its duties were taken on by the hospital labour union's representative committee.)

Truly, I had not been democratic in the Communists' sense of the term. To them "democratic" meant that everyone must talk a problem through until all are in unanimous agreement—and these three representatives would only have been satisfied if their option was the one imposed on the whole hospital body. I was "undemocratic" because I adopted a majority decision that showed the two groups were divided on the issue. Under Communist democracy, all persons must think and act as one.

The interpreter could not see why the labourers wanted an option that was less beneficial for them, and he began to favour my position, something no well-taught Communist would allow himself to do. Indeed, the interview came to a sudden end when Wu, who all along had been in the corridor listening to our exchange, appeared in the doorway.

"You are not asked to discuss problems with Allen," he said. "Your duty is to ask him questions. You need not continue further. Be gone."

The interpreter left and I was escorted back to my lighted and stuffy room to await my next questioning.

Never again did I face the Political Court.

On New Year's Day I was allowed to exercise with Olin and Brother Pretat under the supervision of an armed guard. All three of us felt our spirits rise, although we could not talk to one another.

A day or two later, shortly after our morning exercise, a guard led me up two flights of winding, wooden stairs and along a corridor to the open doorway of an interrogation room. Within, seated on narrow benches behind two long tables were Wu, a second man and a woman with fountain pen in hand and a quantity of paper lying on the table before her. All three were dressed in the same drab, ill-fitting, padded uniform of the People's Liberation Army. The guard took his seat in the corner of the room and Wu ordered me to sit on a narrow bench facing the tables. Pleading hardness of hearing, I drew my seat closer.

The interrogation lasted the greater part of the morning, during which Wu continued to pursue the subject of my espionage activity and claimed I had committed a number of offences against the government.

He asked me why I had asked my secretary to translate the regulations of the hospital labour union and I replied I had wanted to be prepared to deal properly with labour union issues. He said it was illegal to translate an official document into another language and charged that I had wanted to sell the translation to spies. I denied this vigorously. When I finally pointed out that the translation had never actually been made, Wu's face betrayed no emotion. He merely glanced at the papers before him and without a pause brought up the next topic.

Once more I had to defend my support for the family of Chang Tsen-hwa. Saying his young family could not be considered his accomplices, I argued that Christian charity would not let me watch them starve. On this point I felt I had done nothing wrong. Wu asked what the Canadian government would do if I had assisted the family of a political prisoner. I dared not offend him and China by saying there was no such person in my country, so I settled for telling him that only the criminal in Canada was forced to pay a penalty. If his family was in need, they could receive help and none would question the aid.

Wu was becoming distinctly annoyed. "Why do you not admit to your faults, Allen? Every time we ask you a question, instead of admitting your faults you defend your action. This attitude will slow down completion of your case. You must admit to your faults. You must have faults. If you did not, you would not be here."

"I admit I have faults, Comrade, and when they are brought against me I am prepared to admit them. But you have asked me to tell the truth. If I falsely admit faults when I should tell the truth, I would not be doing what you asked of me."

Wu now turned to the offences they claimed I had committed against their government: holding it up to ridicule, criticizing it and in general not giving it the support I ought as a guest of China.

To his charge that I was guilty of belittling the People's Liberation Army, I replied that on the contrary I had always tried to assist the P.L.A., both its soldiers and its civil servants. I tried to tell him some of the instances: the wounded soldiers of both governments who received treatment free of charge during the liberation period; the delivery of the baby of the Shuan Tan Miao police chief's wife in return for a token payment of her food and fuel allowance during her hospitalization; and an operation on the leg of a police subdivision head, for which he never paid, and the loan to him of my Willys Jeep station wagon to cut a bit of a dash at a wedding ceremony (it was returned damaged). Of course, I did not get the opportunity to relate all these helpful incidents before Wu tried again.

"Think a bit and perhaps you will remember what you said to your accountant."

My thinking apparatus was deliberately not working well that morning and I volunteered no comment. I was determined not to be caught by these "bogging down" tactics. Already I had learned never to speak until my interrogator gave some leading remark to indicate the answer he wanted from me. I had not long to wait.

"Don't you remember the time you told your accountant the P.L.A. had no accountants of its own? You should not have made that remark, for our government has very qualified accountants and other personnel for all branches of the work it must do. Your remarks were an insult to us. Are you going to deny this? Think hard, Allen, and tell us. Did you not make such a statement?"

Now I could be obliging as I replied, "Yes, I remember well that very occasion." Leaning forward and showing interest for the first time, Comrade Wu waited for me to give what he believed would be a full confession.

In the early part of April 1950, two men came to examine the hospital accounts, one of them in the uniform of the P.L.A., the other in ordinary clothes, obviously one of the people. They spent several hours examining the previous quarter's accounts and determining the amount of taxes due on them. Later in the day our accountant discussed their visit with me, reporting in detail the new taxation laws and our responsibilities to government. He, not I, then casually remarked that it seemed the P.L.A. did not have trained accountants in its organization. I made no such statement.

"And what was your attitude? Did you agree with him?"

"I am sorry. I cannot recall that I made any statement to that effect, although I expect I acknowledged the comment in an offhand way."

"Then, in effect, you agreed with him."

"If you wish to put it that way, then I must answer, 'Yes, I agreed with him,' although agreement certainly did not imply criticism. It just seemed an obvious fact that the individual in street clothing did not belong to the P.L.A. But if you feel this was disrespectful to your government, then I am prepared to apologize."

Fault number two was a similarly inconsequential remark, made out of frustration with the student nurses and their frequent absences from duty after liberation to attend propaganda activities. At the Department of Education's order, mission nursing students—including those at our hospital—eagerly learned new songs and dances, such as the *yang go* or harvest dance, joined processions and distributed propaganda for the new government's authorities. Their responsibilities to their patients mattered not a bit. Authorities could reproach any foreigner who objected that because of these propaganda activities patients were suffering from lack of nursing attention. The burden of care for as many as 150 patients at our hospital often fell on the shoulders of only twenty graduate nurses.

On the day of my ill-fated remark, I and a number of doctors and nurses watched from a fourth-floor window as the nursing students threw all their energies into learning a dance in the playground below. Thinking of their many recent absences, I remarked casually, "I wish they could put that much energy into meeting the needs of the patients." In the main the students worked hard on the wards to learn the practical side of nursing and malice was far from my thoughts, but like many others, I was irked at the Department of Education for having caused these nursing inconveniences.

Now, faced with the statement, as reported by Wu, I had no reason to deny it.

"You were interfering with their liberties. You also expressed yourself against their display of happiness which indicated their pleasure at being liberated from the bandit Chiang Kai-shek's government. You wished to put a damper on their pleasure. In thus expressing your dissatisfaction at the students' dancing, you have implied dissatisfaction with our government. This you should not have done."

Rather than argue the point, I parried, "If that is the way you feel, it is you who must make the decision. If you feel I am guilty, then I accept your interpretation. I am sorry I made the remark, but be assured I had no thought of embarrassing either the students or your government."

Two confessions in one morning! Both Wu and his associates were satisfied they were making progress at last. Personally, I thought it very weak stuff. Why argue for hours about such trivialities? If such apologies and confessions were all they wished, this ordeal would soon end. Wu called upon the secretary to read her version of the morning's proceedings. She read questions and answers in Chinese and I listened, making a comment or two where the meaning did not seem to convey what I had said. As I put my thumb-print to the evidence, indicating my acceptance of it as a correct version of the morning's proceedings, the gong sounded for dinner. I was led back to my cell.

There I pondered the events of the morning. If the charges against me could be cleared simply by orienting my thinking to fit their distorted interpretations without seriously compromising the truth and my own ideals, then my problem was not a very serious one. This questioning had not been as severe as I expected. However, the more serious charges had yet to be introduced. What other questions they might have tucked away, I did not know. That inch-and-a-half-thick dossier still lying before the interrogator, as on the night of my questioning by the Political Court, must contain much still to be investigated.

The procedure for dispensing justice in the Political Court, to which I was now subject, was different from that of the Communist civil court of Chungking, of which I had also had some experience in 1950. I had been co-defendant in a trial to determine responsibility for a death following a tracheotomy where I had been a consultant. The trial, though far different from those in Western countries, was eminently fair and the decision just. No lawyers were present, since lawyers in a communist society are considered an outcast class, the product of a "decadent" civilization. Behind the bench sat only two people, the judge and the court stenographer. The plaintiff first laid the charge and the judge investigated any point that needed clarification. From this part of the trial the defendants were excluded. The plaintiff's evidence complete, he was asked to withdraw and the defendants followed the same procedure. As a foreigner, I was permitted the services of an interpreter of my own choosing. Our evidence having been heard, the plaintiff was called in. With both parties present, all the recorded evidence was read and each had the opportunity to correct inaccurate interpretations before placing his thumb-print, thus approving the recorded evidence. The court then adjourned to examine the evidence presented.

Although I did not appear again, the main defendant was later called before a specially-convened investigating body of leading representatives of the medical profession, including specialists in ear, nose and throat work. He was given a thorough, detailed examination and questioned on all aspects of the case by this very competent body, many of whom were well known to him. That made no difference, however, since everyone knew that friendship, which formerly had meant so much in the way of protection and assistance in a case such as this, was now apt to have the opposite effect if used for ulterior motives. A few weeks later both of us were fully cleared of the charges laid against us.

In my present situation, however, I was not in a civil court where the issues were clear-cut and undistorted. This was an investigation by the Political Section of the Public Safety Department of Chungking. I had to use my own best judgment, tact and extreme care to avoid being trapped into a confession of fault. No lawyer was available to assist me in my defence. I had no access to the law of the land. In fact, the law was largely uncodified at that time. Decisions in political cases were based on the general interpretations of "reasonableness" by the committee that would ultimately render the verdict. Whether this would be made in accord with facts, or facts distorted to bring about a desired decision, remained to be seen. The situation was further complicated by another procedure completely absent from Western courts. Before trial the case must be fully investigated and clarified, the defendant must have confessed to his faults—real or implied—and, to ensure there was no possibility to retract, these confessions had to be sealed by his thumb-print. The court itself was a mere formality, including abject confession and sentencing of the prisoner.

Thus far the interrogations had not been difficult, and these few minor confessions pleased the committee. They indicated a "good attitude," a willingness to recognize and admit alleged faults. Such an attitude was essential before release could be considered. It also indicated how much "brainwashing" might be required to correct one's attitude toward communism.

THE ALLEN FAMILY IN NARAMATA, B.C. This photo, taken about 1916, shows Stewart Allen (at far right, in Scout uniform) on the steps of the family home in Naramata. From left, his mother, Mary Margaret Allen; brother Harold (also in Scout uniform); brother Stanley; sister Margaret (holding doll). (The girl in the gingham dress was a family friend.)

CITY OF CHUNGKING. This view of Chungking (Chongqing) was probably taken in the 1940s, from the south bank of the Yangtze River, where the Canadian Mission Hospital stood. The Kialing River flows into the Yangtze at the right.

MODERN LESHAN. In this 1994 view of Leshan (formerly Kiating), Sichuan province, a large new hospital rises in the centre background. Dr. Allen's first mission posting in China was to the Canadian Mission Hospital (a different hospital and the only one at the time) in Kiating, where he was superintendent until his return to Canada on furlough in 1936.

CANADIAN MISSION HOSPITAL, LESHAN. This view of the hospital shows a colonnade along one wall. In this hospital, in 1932, Dr. Allen came face to face with death when a mob instigated by an angry officer-patient tried to attack him (see Chapter 11). After that incident, he realized he might have to forfeit his life if he continued in missionary work, and he accepted the fact. It was the staff at this hospital who wrote the tribute to him (quoted in the Introduction) when he left China in 1936. (Photo taken in 1994)

FORMER ALLEN RESIDENCE IN KIATING. This 1994 view of the former Allen family residence in Kiating (now Leshan) shows the back entrance to the large house. In the early 1930s it was more secluded, but now many buildings encroach upon it.

ALLEN FAMILY RESIDENCE (FRONT). Modern Leshan surrounds the former Allen family residence in its oasis of trees. Here Margaret and Gwyneth played while their father tended to patients and hospital administration and their mother, Winnifred, entertained countless missionary and other visitors.

STAFF OF THE CANADIAN MISSION HOSPITAL.   Dr. Allen sits surrounded by his staff and family at a 1944 gathering in the residence compound of the hospital. At centre, he holds his daughter Phyllis, while his wife, Winnifred, holds their baby, Marion; to their left are daughters Gwyneth and Margaret. Seated at Dr. Allen's right is Dr. Marian Chang (in dark, striped top) and to her right is her husband, Dr. Dso Li-liang. Dr. Dso was the hospital radiologist and also Dr. Allen's good friend. The roof at the upper right belongs to the house the Allens lived in from 1938 to 1945.

ALLEN FAMILY RESIDENCE, 1948-50.   This spacious house, formerly the home of foreign nurses, was the Allens' home during their second posting to the Canadian Mission Hospital. The family often entertained foreign guests here for short visits or extended stays. The house had been the residence of Irene Harris before the Allens moved in. This picture was taken in 1981.

```
                                              3 Hsin Tsun
                                              Liang Lu Kou
                                              Chungking, June 2, 1945.



Dr. A. Stewart Allen
Canadian Mission Hospital
South Bank
Chungking.



Dear Dr. Allen:
              Hearing that you are planning to leave shortly on furlough,
I would like to send you a word of appreciation for your efforts in our behalf
as chairman of the Canadian Red Cross Committee  and as coordinator of relief
in Chungking. It has been a great encouragement to know that there are so many
friends sympathetic to the needs of our work, and I am hoping that you will
lend your abiding support to our projects. In particular, I trust that you
will endeavor to get the grant of 20,000 doses of typhus vaccine for us upon
your arrival in Canada, and have these shipped to us by air soon. We are able
to find transportation from Chungking by air promptly.

              Here is wishing you bon voyage and a happy home-coming, as
well as your return to us in China whenever facilities allow it.

                                   Very sincerely yours,


                                   Soong Ching Ling
                                   (Mme. Sun Yat-sen).
```

MADAME SUN YAT-SEN'S LETTER.   While under house arrest in Chungking, Dr. Allen was taken across the Yangtze River to his hospital on the south bank. There he was allowed to go through his desk and take anything he wished to keep. This letter from Soong Ching-ling, widow of Sun Yat-sen, founder of the Kuomintang, was among the papers he chose.

THE NURSES' RESIDENCE. This building, the nurses' residence, was part of the hospital compound. The photograph was taken in 1981. A large hall on the ground floor at the left side of the picture was used for church, staff feasts and meetings, including Dr. Allen's accusation meeting on December 20, 1950.

CANADIAN MISSION HOSPITAL, CHUNGKING. Dr. Allen visited his former hospital in 1981, now called the 5th People's Hospital of Chongqing. This shows the front entrance of the hospital building.

FORMER CANADIAN MISSION HOSPITAL, CHUNGKING. An unobstructed view of the hospital is hard to find in 1994. A wall and a building have been erected in front of the hospital, now called the 5th People's Hospital of Chongqing. At left is the original hospital and at right is the wing for tuberculosis patients, added by Dr. Allen during his tenure as superintendent.

FORMER TUBERCULOSIS WING. A close-up of the tuberculosis wing Dr. Allen ordered built to treat the many patients then suffering from this disease, which has since been eradicated in China. The hospital, now called the 5th People's Hospital of Chongqing, will celebrate its centennial in 1996. (Both pictures were taken by Margaret Williamson, 1994.)

THE ALLEN FAMILY IN MONTREAL, 1947. The entire family was together for this photo, taken the year before all but university-bound Margaret returned to Chungking. At back, from left, Gwyneth, Stewart Allen (seated), Phyllis; front, from left, Winnifred, Marion and Margaret.

FAREWELL DINNER PARTY FOR THE ALLENS, 1947.   Before Stewart and Winnifred returned to
China, they attended a cheerful dinner party in their honour, in the Westmount, Quebec,
home of Mr. and Mrs. Douglas Jackson. A number of friends from the Dominion-Douglas
Church were present. In the bottom row, from left, are Dr. Reg Sellers; his wife, Peggy;
and Jean Jackson. In the middle row, from left, are Mrs. Goodwin (the mother of Jean
Jackson); Winnifred and Stewart Allen; Mary Margaret Allen (Stewart's mother); and Evelyn
Smith, wife of the minister. In the top row, from left, are Mr. Goodwin; an unknown man
and woman; Dr. A. Lloyd Smith, minister; Connie Everson; unknown woman; and Ewart
Everson. (Mr. Jackson, the host, took the picture.)

REV. F. OLIN STOCKWELL AND HIS WIFE, ESTHER. An American Methodist Church missionary couple, the Stockwells had come to Chungking in 1949 to take the place of a longtime missionary of their church there, Dr. Rappe. Olin worked often in rural communities, but he also carried on some of Dr. Rappe's committee work with a nearby girls' school and the American Methodist Hospital. Thus he became involved in the medical supplies issue along with Dr. Allen and eventually found himself in the same prison as Dr. Allen. Two years later, he was released and deported as a "cultural imperialist." He and Esther continued their missionary life: by about 1955, when the above photo was taken, they were on their way to work in Borneo.

CONSTANCE WARD, LATE 1940s. Miss Ward was a Women's Missionary Society missionary, who kindly agreed to keep house for Dr. Allen after his wife and two daughters left Chungking for Canada in July 1950. She, too, was invited to the December 20th, 1950, accusation meeting, where she was made to kneel alongside Dr. Allen and bear in silence many unjust accusations. After several days of questioning she was released. She left China in August 1951.

OFFICIAL COURT JUDGMENT. On October 15, 1951, this official judgment was handed to Dr. Allen by the Chungking City People's Court. A translation appears in Appendix A. He is here sentenced to pay a fine for tax evasion and to be deported for concealing government medical supplies.

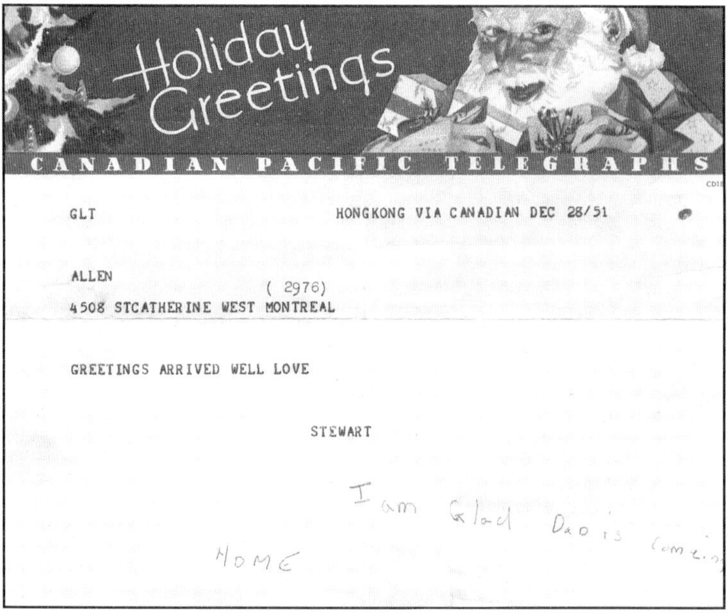
Holiday Greetings

CANADIAN PACIFIC TELEGRAPHS

GLT HONGKONG VIA CANADIAN DEC 28/51

ALLEN
(2976)
4508 STCATHERINE WEST MONTREAL

GREETINGS ARRIVED WELL LOVE

STEWART

I am Glad Dad is

HOME

THE LONG-AWAITED TELEGRAM. Almost the first thing Stewart Allen did on arrival at the Church Guest House in Hong Kong, December 28, 1951, was to cable his family that he was out of China at last. With typical understatement, he says merely, "Greetings. Arrived well. Love, Stewart." However succinct the message, it was received with joy at home, where his eight-year-old daughter, Marion, pencilled on it, "I am glad Dad is comeing home."

THE ALLEN FAMILY REUNITED. This happy family portrait was taken in 1952 by a *Maclean's* magazine photographer in the Allens' Westmount, Quebec, apartment. The April 15 article described Dr. Allen's experience as a prisoner of the Chinese Communists. The photograph shows, from left, Gwyneth, Marion, Stewart, Winnifred and Phyllis. (Margaret was married by this time.)

RETURN TO CHINA IN 1981. Members of the West China Club of Toronto posed for a group picture at the Nine Dragon Wall in the Forbidden City, Beijing. From left: Jack Mullett, Fred Taylor, Mary Agnew, Jean Stewart, unknown woman, Stewart Allen, three unknown women (the four unknown woman are possibly "the Sparling girls," Dorothy Small and the wife of Orlando Jolliffe), Ross and Ken Armstrong, Gwen Kitchen Armstrong (their mother), Mr. Armstrong, Muriel Kitchen Tonge, Walter Tonge, Orlando Jolliffe and Joy Willmott. All were former West China missionaries or their children or grandchildren.

RETURN TO CHINA IN 1994. The four daughters of Dr. Allen returned to the land of their childhood in October 1994. Here, (from left) Margaret, Marion, Phyllis and Gwyneth pose at the same wall where their father stood in 1981. (Photo courtesy of Dorothea Hoffman Smale of Kanata, Ontario, whose father, Dr. Cecil Hoffman, was Dr. Allen's predecessor at the Canadian Mission Hospital in Chungking.)

DR. ALLEN VISITS FORMER SECRETARY RUBY WONG, 1981. While in Hong Kong in 1981, Dr. Allen went sight-seeing with Ruby Wong, who was his secretary from 1942 to 1945, when he left for Canada. She continued working for Dr. William Service, Dr. Allen's replacement, but by the time he returned in 1948, she had left and her position had been taken by Chang Chi.

THREE SPECIAL FRIENDS, 1982. Pictured here are (from left) Chung Hsui (Susan) Chen, Dr. Marian Chang and her husband, Dr. Dso Li-liang, in the Dsos' backyard in Chungking. Susan Chen had trained at the Canadian Mission Hospital Nursing School, which used the Ontario nursing education program. She had been Dr. Allen's surgical nurse at the hospital before moving to Hong Kong. When he was deported to Hong Kong, she was one of the group of nurses who gave him a special dinner. She came to Canada in 1968, sponsored by Dr. Allen, and worked in the Brockville General Hospital. Later, because of her Ontario-approved nursing training, she easily found work as a surgical nurse in London, Ontario. With help from Dr. Allen, Dr. Dso, the radiologist at the Canadian Mission Hospital, obtained radiological training in Canada at the Royal Victoria Hospital in Montreal. Their friendship endured the rest of Dr. Allen's life.

ENTRANCE TO ALLEN RESIDENCE OF 1947-50. Gwyneth, Marion, Dr. Chen Hong-gui, Phyllis and Margaret stand at the entrance to the family home in the residence compound across the valley from the Canadian Mission Hospital. During the sisters' visit to Chongqing in October 1994, Dr. Chen, vice-principal (superintendent) of the 5th People's Hospital, spoke with them at length through their interpreter. Dr. Chen told them the house was being renovated in preparation for celebration in 1996 of the 100th anniversary of the founding of the hospital.

STEWART AND WINNIFRED ALLEN,
on their fiftieth wedding anniversary, in 1979.

Chapter 7

Denying Collaboration

THE NEXT few days passed without interruption, except when the guard released me, as well as my fellow prisoners Olin Stockwell and Brother Pretat, for exercise or brought my meals. Day and night were the same in my cell with its boarded-up windows and cold, concrete floors. My own body radiated enough heat in that still room to raise the temperature a little above the cold outside air.

A few days after the New Year, the sounds of carpentry work, which I had heard outside my cell since my incarceration, ceased, and soon an armed guard ordered me to gather my belongings—cuspidor, chopsticks, bowl and bedding—and follow him to a new place. A little fearful of where I might be taken, I followed him through a maze of corridors until we came to a still-doorless opening that had been cut through the main wall of the building and a flight of newly-built wooden steps leading down into a separate part of the building on this fairly large property. Then we climbed to the fourth floor where I was shown into my new cell.

Glancing quickly about, I noticed that this room was more poorly furnished. My new bed was a rickety-looking affair, just a woven bamboo mat in a frame, placed on two trestles with very spindly bamboo legs. It did not look as if it would hold my weight. When I said as much, the guard bridled, saying it was the same as what the guards slept on and would hold me. He did allow me to bring to this room the desk-table I had used in the first cell.

The room had its compensations, however. It was open to the light of day. The windows, to the level of my eyes, had been covered over with brown paper, which I had been instructed neither to touch nor remove. Still, to see glorious sunlight, even for the few hours when it broke through the clouds on these winter afternoons, was more than a delight after being twenty-four hours a day for two weeks under the steady light of one 40-watt electric bulb.

I soon discovered that my new quarters were much colder. On examination, I found that one of the uncovered, uppermost panes was absent. Another in the transom was broken. I folded some sheets of heavy, coarse paper made from rice straw and placed them in the openings to stop the cold air currents and so raised the temperature a few degrees.

The following morning investigation of my case continued. Comrade Chu, the man who had been the second investigator during Comrade Wu's interrogation earlier, now took his turn at questioning. He spoke in the local Shantung dialect, which I had found hard to follow in the speech of Comrade Lan, the judge in the Political Court. Chu was quite an unlettered rural man, unlike the educated Wu. His questions were designed to confuse me into altering my previous evidence: Was I sure I had told the truth? Had I told all the truth or were there things I had omitted to say? I had not made enough confessions and always I had defended myself too much instead of admitting my faults.

To all his probing questions I replied I had nothing more to tell. His response was to urge me to "think, think, think," for I had many faults, as evidenced by the thick dossier before him, the fruits of their investigation. I never found out Chu's full name, but somewhere in it there should have been the name "Shiang," Chinese for "to think," for only by much thinking—if Chu was to be believed—could one eventually see the light and make the confessions necessary for true communist redemption.

I did not follow his instructions, since I considered these matters relatively trivial and insignificant. Seeing I could not be drawn, Chu introduced a new subject, one that in our accusation meeting had seemed so ridiculous I had thought no more about it.

"You will not admit that you are a spy, nor that you are a counter-revolutionist, yet the evidence we have before us is that you have had intimate associations with the false government of that traitor, Chiang Kai-shek. How do you explain that connection?"

Aloud I protested my complete innocence and said I had had no special relationships with the Nationalist government beyond what I considered to be rightful ones. Inwardly I acknowledged that while in China I had never spoken out against the Nationalists. As guests of the Chinese, most missionaries felt it was not our position or right to do so. In fact, we had been told by the central government in 1943 that missionaries would remain welcome in China only so long as they refrained from taking sides in any political questions of the day. This did not necessarily prevent us from stating privately to some of our Chinese friends what our personal opinion of the government or its representatives might be.

I told Chu I had co-operated to give the masses the best service possible in a Christian medical institution, meeting their financial needs if necessary. But knowing the Communists' likely misinterpretation of any humanitarian efforts I had made during the war years out of sympathy for the Chinese people as a whole, I kept them to myself. For instance, there was no need to tell Chu that I had permitted the National Health Administration to set up temporary medical headquarters on our hospital property following the famous May 4, 1939, bombing of Chungking. It was best to wait and hear his so-called evidence.

"Did you not permit the Garrison Headquarters to make an air raid shelter on your hospital property in 1939? Do you mean to say that this is not having relations with that rotten Nationalist government?" Chu continued.

I had to admit this permission was given. Representatives of the Garrison Headquarters wanted to tunnel through the rock surmounting the hill to the east of the hospital, joining our already excavated hospital shelter to one they were building on their property on the opposite side of the hill. The through-tunnel thus formed would be thoroughly safe against any bombs. With thousands losing their lives in the frequent raids of that time, who could refuse such a request? But when the shelter was completed, the garrison said all who wished to use this shelter, including hospital personnel and patients, had to buy entrance tickets. We would have to use the garrison entrance all the way around the hill, and ours would be closed. Obviously we had been misled; we had understood the shelter was for public use, without charge, as were other shelters built in the city. Our strenuous objection finally forced a mutual agreement. For a certain sum, paid by the hospital, the portion of the shelter on the hospital side of the hill would be reserved for the hospital's use. Who could possibly take exception to such an attitude?

I was unwilling to say any more, so there the matter ended.

"Now, what about the telephone call you made in 1939 to Chiang Kai-shek? Tell us about that. What business did you have that required his attention?"

Aghast, I could not believe my ears. Just how far back in history, and to what ridiculous lengths, were these people to carry their investigation of me? All I had done was to permit my name to be used in a call made to Chiang's guards to arrange safe passage for a funeral party through the leader's summer retreat property, located between the hospital and the cemetery. The deceased had been a patient in the hospital and a member of our church. I was willing to co-operate in the investigation of *my* actions, but I had decided not to involve others. Nor would I give the Communists any testimony that might sidetrack the investigation or lead to more probing questions.

I told Chu the truth: "I have never telephoned Chiang Kai-shek, either then or at any other time, and there is no one you can produce to state I have done so."

Unsatisfied, Chu persisted, but I remained silent and he was forced to end this line of questioning. The Communists feel they always have the right questions for the answers they expect to receive, so Comrade Chu tried more direct tactics.

"If you will not admit to these associations, will you tell us just what association you have had with Bandit Chiang? Did you ever meet him? If you did, what did you talk about?"

My personal associations with the Chiangs had been most casual, so I unhesitatingly described the three times I had met Chiang Kai-shek. The first was a huge reception for foreigners, including diplomats, military officials, men in leading public positions and some missionary representatives. Chiang had shaken hands with all guests. The second time was at a reception given for the Christian community following the return of Madame Chiang from her first visit to the United States. The third time was in 1944 when, as chairman of the China committee of the Chinese War Relief Fund of Canada, I had accompanied Albert C. Hall of Montreal, who was representing the C.W.R.F., when he was presented to General-issimo Chiang. Through the official interpreter I told Chiang that I had handled funds sent by Canadians to assist the orphanages organized by his wife. I had also directed funds to him from the Chinese Patriotic Society of Canada.

This information, scant and non-incriminating though it was, gave Chu the lead he sought. "You tell me all this and yet you say you never had any relationship with officialdom. You must have done other things for him or you would not have received an invitation to such an affair. Do you not realize that he was giving this reception for favours received from his invited guests?" This last he said sarcastically, as if presuming me to be very stupid.

Ignoring his tone, I answered that my invitation probably arose from the contribution I, as superintendent of the Canadian Mission Hospital, was making for the Chinese people as a whole, a service I was providing under the present regime as well. I added that I had also helped the Communists before they came to power, but he did not like the last remark and cut off the conversation abruptly before I could go further. I would have told him that his own government's foreign minister, Chou En-lai, had been host at an afternoon tea in 1945 to which I had been invited. It had been held to thank the various relief agencies that had co-operated in sending medical and surgical supplies by air to the International Peace Hospitals in Yenan. In so doing, they had gone against the wishes of the Chiangs and acted on U.S. Gen. Joseph W. Stilwell's recommendation that since Mao Tse-tung's guerrillas were taking part in resistance against Japan, they should be assisted and not boycotted, as Chiang was doing rather successfully.

Chu was not finished with his investigation of my supposed collaboration with the enemy. His next question made it clear to me that details of my whole life in Chungking were fully known to my investigators.

"Did not Chiang's representative in Chungking, Gen. Chang Chun, the governor, invite you to treat his secretary?"

I admitted I had examined Gen. Chang's secretary and suggested treatment. In my defence, I said I was trained to give assistance to anyone seeking medical advice without fear of being accused of collaboration.

Probably Chang told his secretary to consult me because I had successfully treated Chang's good friend and my fellow missionary, Dr. Wallace Crawford, then chief of the Public Health Department of the West China Union University in Chengtu. In the summer of 1941, Dr. Crawford had gone to southern Yunnan province to facilitate movement of a considerable amount of mission cargo. It had been side-tracked after a large section of the French railroad between Kunming, in Yunnan, and Haiphong, in Vietnam, was torn up to prevent the Japanese from using it to penetrate South China from the sea coast. Another United Church of Canada missionary, Rev. Wilfred Albertson, had already lost his life earlier in the year from malignant malaria infection in a fruitless effort to salvage this shipment. Just before Christmas I was asked to fly to Kunming to treat Dr. Crawford, who was reportedly critically ill. He, too, had contracted malignant malaria. It had been treated, but before recovery was complete he had fallen ill with typhus fever. I found him delirious with a high fever. As if these two diseases were not enough for a man past sixty to contend with at one time, he also had an amoebic abscess of the liver, which I diagnosed and drained. Anyone but Wally would have succumbed to this combination of diseases, but he wasn't ready to play a harp with the angels. He was brought back to Chungking, placed in hospital, and many months elapsed before he returned to his normal self. He gave me more credit for saving his life than I deserved. I suspect Gen. Chang heard of this incident.

Thinking I had the upper hand in this story, I finished with the parting shot, "Although I did examine Chang's secretary and suggest treatment, the fact remains he did not follow my advice. Since I did not treat him, of course there can be no question of my having given assistance to individuals in official positions."

Quick as a flash he replied, "Whether you treated the case or not makes no difference. The fact you even saw him at all is our present concern."

I could not beat these investigators. No matter how sound my arguments were, they always had a ready answer and it was always right. It was useless to argue and upset them, when all I desired was to complete this investigation quickly and be released from solitary confinement. I presumed I would be sent home, since it would be impossible to work any longer in Chungking after all that had happened.

Apparently I had satisfactorily clarified my relationships with the former head of state and his deputy in Szechuan. Comrade Chu next turned to my relationship with the mayor of Chungking, Gen. Yang Sen, and his family.

Mayor Yang Sen was one of the old warlords. An intelligent sixty-five-year-old military man, he had started the earlier modernization and street widening program in Chengtu. As China became unified, Yang Sen had aligned himself with Chiang Kai-shek. On the whole he was well liked by those he governed, showed no marked anti-foreign sentiment, and numbered several missionaries among his friends, for he was favourably disposed toward the Christian church. He had acquired one wife and twenty-three concubines, each chosen for her beauty or some other special characteristics. He kept all under strict control and, of course, had many children by them, numbering into the sixties. Into my relationships with this family, Chu now began to probe, but his approach was typically oblique and his real objective hidden.

"When did you meet Gen. Yang Sen?"

I had first met him at a reception tendered him by the various Chinese Christian organizations in 1944 following his inauguration as mayor of Chungking. I also attended a reception he later gave in return. But I had had more contact with his secretary, John Chi, a Christian and a Rotarian. I recalled no special associations with the mayor, but I was not allowed to dismiss the subject so easily.

"Have you not had certain active relationships with the American embassy and consulate? Have you not served them in an official capacity?" Comrade Chu asked.

The purpose of this disjointed line of questioning was still unclear to me, but I admitted having given physical examinations to Chinese people applying for visas to the U.S., mainly students or those wishing to join relatives there. I had been asked to help out only because no American physician lived in Chungking and the U.S. consulate had learned that some Chinese physicians had been unable to deny their friends clearance, even when they had illnesses that should have prevented them from obtaining a visa.

"In your medical capacity did you not assist the American government to send Chinese out of China who should have stood trial in our courts?"

I denied this, saying I had not made it my business to ask each person his reason for going abroad. Undoubtedly, some were fleeing the Communist advance, but this they never admitted to me.

"Did you not assist one of Yang Sen's daughters to flee the country in this way? Did not Yang Sen's secretary, Mr. Chi, come to you to make such an agreement to get her out of the country?"

It was astonishing how many facts were at the fingertips of these investigators. Some person or persons had been following all my contacts very closely indeed. But I did not recall any such agreement. Chi came to me for an entirely different purpose: to ask if I could recommend a foreign school where his son could study English. I knew of no school where his son might go permanently to board.

As I was still unable to give evidence respecting Yang Sen's daughter, he commanded me to do some more thinking. To me the matter was a trivial one and my brain refused to act as Comrade Chu wished. Much later on, too late to make any difference one way or the other, I did recall that John Chi had escorted Miss Yang when she appeared for her medical examination, but he had used the occasion for his own convenience. I had forgotten the incident for I had not actually seen the two together.

Chu was bringing more pressure to bear on me in this examination than in any that had gone before. My failure to confirm the evidence they held against me undoubtedly caused them to toughen their approach. Meanwhile, knowing the reaction of the Chinese Communist regime toward Americans, I was not happy that the examination sought to link me with official American consular activities.

"Have you not realized that American consulates in China have been doing everything in their power to assist in the flight of many Chinese we want to investigate or imprison?"

At the risk of appearing stubborn—and in fairness to the American consulates—I had to deny this charge. It was generally known that many Chinese were fleeing the country, but it was a fact that this movement was worrying Washington a great deal. The U.S. State Department put all possible barriers in the way of issuing visas. It required proof of admission to U.S. schools or of the presence of relatives in the U.S. I knew that two lads had been refused visas because their English was so grossly inadequate they failed to pass even the simplest English examination. A mutual friend had requested me to intervene on their behalf, but I had refused to do so. To further check, and if possible prevent, this mass exodus of Chinese to the U.S., applicants for American visas were later required to first secure a visa permitting entry into a second country. The difficulty of arranging this second visa effectively stopped the wave of Chinese emigration from the major cities of China to the U.S. All this I explained to Comrade Chu.

"Who were these children? What was their name? Who were their parents?"

Almost too late I realized that I was in danger of incriminating the two boys. I could have supplied the information, but I parried the question, saying all I could remember was that their last name was Chu. Since there are only four hundred Chinese surnames distributed among the population of five hundred million, and this particular family had left Chungking, I felt the information given would hurt nobody, while the giving of a name was a point in my favour. Investigator Chu, who shared the same surname, changed his questioning immediately.

Abandoning his examination of my possible collaboration with officialdom, Chu now began investigating evidence that I had been critical of the Communist government. In the process he confirmed something I and other missionaries had suspected for some time, namely that the Communists were unofficially censoring the mail.

During 1950, one of our missionaries had received a letter from a co-worker. In the same envelope was a Chinese version of the letter, translated word for word from the English original. Apparently the censor had inadvertently enclosed the translation with the original and both copies had come into the hands of the addressee. Better confirmation of clandestine censorship could not have been secured. In the latter months of 1950, I became certain my own letters were receiving the same treatment. Following the arrival of foreign mail, delivery of pieces addressed to me was almost always delayed by two days while other missionaries received theirs promptly.

"In September 1950," Chu began, "you wrote a letter abroad stating that you were leaving China because our government was not happy to have foreigners here. To whom did you write that letter? Why did you write it? Has not our government always acted fairly and reasonably toward foreigners and toward you? They have never told you that you were not wanted. What reason have you for criticizing our government, which has been protecting you? Even now you are our guest. We are only examining you because your own hospital people demanded that your case should be investigated. Please tell us your reason for writing as you did."

I recalled the letter perfectly. I also recalled that I had spoken frankly, perhaps too frankly, about the new government. After sealing the letter, I had even considered re-opening the envelope and rewriting a portion of the now-incriminating missive, but it was written late at night, I was tired and I felt the chances of its being opened were slight. Hence, without correction of what now proved to be possible damaging evidence, the letter went to its destination: Paris, in care of the Canadian Embassy. Would that I had known in 1950 what I now know as I write these pages. Whatever censorship of my letters there might have been in the first six months of the People's Government regime, I now knew beyond a doubt that during the latter half of 1950 a full and complete censorship of my mail existed, with the possible exception of a few letters sent to my family.

The embassy address obviously had raised the suspicion that I was forwarding information to diplomatic circles, a possible link the authorities could use in making their espionage charges. Only one way of circumventing this implication presented itself. I must be completely straightforward, honest and frank, even if Comrade Chu would not like what he heard. Having implied foreigners were not liked by his government, I had to substantiate my charges.

I told him I had written the letter to explain to a Chinese friend—who had worked for the Canadian embassy in Chungking and was now in Paris—why I felt I could not help her mother with business matters much longer. I told her my return to Canada would not be long delayed. I had reached this decision not, as Comrade Chu suggested, as the result of any action by the Communist government against me, but because it had become increasingly evident that in the not-too-distant future our hospital would be turned over to others for management. My furlough was also approaching, even if still a year or so distant. Only a month after writing the letter in question I had finally become convinced of my inability to co-operate further with the Communists and I had decided to return to Canada within at most six months.

It was true that the Chinese People's Government had offered us its protection. The eighth point of the liberation instructions issued in Chungking on December 1, 1949, was interpreted to read: "Foreigners and their property are to be given full protection. They, on their part, are asked to continue their work as in the past, but under no condition to harbour in their homes, or to assist in their escape, any enemies of the people, or counter-revolutionaries, and to obey the law." I had tried to live according to these instructions. Officialdom had been coldly courteous to me on all occasions, though in the past few months the Foreign Affairs Bureau had displayed a curious interest in learning how long I was planning to remain, before returning to Canada on furlough. Despite all that, I had come to the conclusion foreigners were not wanted in China. Point by point, I gave Chu my reasons.

First, almost immediately after the Communists entered Chungking, many members of the People's Liberation Army who arrived at our hospital refused to be treated when they learned ours was a Christian hospital with a foreign superintendent.

Second (as described in Chapter 1), at a hospital meeting in February I had repeated a statement made to me in May 1946 by Dr. Su Ching-kuan, a medical officer of the Communist Yenan government, that medical workers and other technical groups would be welcomed in Communist territories if they worked with and for the Chinese people. Five of the hospital labour union cadres present smiled behind their hands at hearing this. That led me to suspect foreigners were not wanted after all.

Third, it was becoming increasingly clear that in the new China, missionaries hampered imminent government changes. The May 1950 draft of what came to be known as the "Christian Manifesto" said Christian missionaries were unavoidably tainted with the imperialism of the Western countries from which they came. All imperialistic influences must be uprooted from the Christian church. Missionaries were indirectly informed of a statement by Chou En-lai, foreign minister of the People's Government, to the effect that foreigners could stay in China only as long as their passports remained valid. Ultimately all foreign missionaries would thus leave China, without permission to return.

Fourth, foreign missionaries in stations outside Chungking who wished to come to me for treatment were refused permission to do so. Persons making such requests were forced to accept exit visas to leave China for their homelands. Many missionaries left their country stations for larger cities, with only verbal permission to do so, and then discovered (as also described in Chapter 1) that the Foreign Affairs Bureau in the large city disbelieved them and refused them permission to return home.

Fifth, a missionary nurse[1] had been refused permission to travel to Chungking to nurse a member of her own mission, ill with typhoid fever in our hospital. Even when I explained no other special Chinese nurses were available, permission was still denied. At that time, foreigners were forbidden to leave their homes for more than ten days at a time.

Sixth, movements of missionary workers had been interfered with to the point where they were unable to do the work for which they had come to China. I, for instance, had not been able to visit two hospitals over which I had general supervision. Chinese deputies had to travel there in my stead. In this sense, the government had interfered with our work.

Seventh, former close Chinese friends, who had always been happy to come to our home, were now hesitant to do so for fear official investigations would follow. Organizations with foreign members were embarrassed by their presence. Wishing to avoid this embarrassment of our Chinese friends, we refrained from meeting them openly.

On the basis of all these actions, it seemed logical to conclude government was not sympathetic to foreigners remaining in China. No other reasonable interpretation could be placed upon these occurrences. Again I reiterated that in spite of all these unsympathetic attitudes, I had never received gross official discourtesy at any time, but facts were facts.

---

1 Dr. Allen is probably referring to Isabelle Miller. See Chapter 9.

When I had finished my statement, interestingly enough, Comrade Chu had no comment to make at all. He knew all my statements were true. Nothing he might say could disprove them. Questioning ceased for the morning. The secretary read back the session's questions and answers, I affixed my thumb-print affirming their correctness, and I was returned to my room.

There I marvelled that my investigators could seriously consider any of the evidence yet brought against me as worthy of more than my passing consideration. It all seemed so trivial, but the experienced investigators pitted against me were not fools. They were watching me just as closely as I watched them. Somewhere along the way they might show their trump cards, but as yet I wandered in a maze, unsure where these ploys were leading. Above all, I knew, I must not permit myself to be drawn into a position from which I could not extricate myself. Trivial as these charges sounded, the experience now being gained in combatting them was to be invaluable at a later date. Very gradually, I was learning how the Communist mind works. This morning I had realized for the first time that the most casual contact with someone could suggest a special, suspect relationship. It was my duty to provide convincing evidence that these relationships had no ulterior motives. Only thus could I eventually win my release.

Chapter 8

The Informer

I WAS INTERROGATED frequently through most of January. Sometimes Comrade Wu was in charge, sometimes Comrade Chu. Occasionally both of them took turns in their questioning. The days between interrogations gave me ample opportunity to make complete written statements in English detailing the questions put to me and my responses during the previous examination. Besides being unfamiliar with the political terminology my investigators were using, I also had difficulty following Chu's unpolished dialect. I felt the only reasonable way to protect my interests was to commit my statements to writing and let them be translated by those of the Political Section staff who were very proficient in English. Then none could misunderstand what I meant to say. Preparing and correcting these draft documents also helped fill many hours that would otherwise have been dull and monotonous.

One of the more memorable sessions revolved around a single comment I had made in October 1950 regarding the Korean War. Because I had made this remark to one person only, my assistant surgeon Dr. Tien Bao-liang, the fact that it had come to the ears of my investigators proved that the Communists had indeed planted informers inside the hospital to report on my every move. The session also highlighted the Communists' concern that foreigners were listening to foreign news broadcasts and describing them to their Chinese aquaintances, against expressed government orders.

The session started one morning when, after a review of previously given evidence, Chu suddenly asked, "Who told you that the Korean War was just about finished? We have evidence you made a statement to that effect." My facial expression must have indicated my astonishment, for without hesitating he said, "You surely do not want us to believe you did not make that statement. Take your time and think a little about this, then tell us what you know."

It took no time at all to remember the occasion when I had made the remark. Since the statement had been reported to them, there was no need to evade the truth, so I explained.

"You will recall that by October the United Nations troops had pushed north through North Korea and had almost reached the Yalu River.[1] The North Korean army was fleeing before them. Complete defeat seemed so close that one morning, while scrubbing my hands before operating, I made the remark you have quoted as part of a casual conversation with my assistant surgeon, who was scrubbing up with me."

"As part of a conversation, you say? Do you not know that foreign guests are not permitted to pass Western radio information they hear on to our Chinese people? You realize that most of this information is false and is mere propaganda. We want our people to be protected from such lies."

I admitted I knew this order. "But I did not secure this information by radio," I explained. "At the time, all Chinese knew from the daily papers that the North Koreans were retreating. So, it seemed obvious to any thinking person that the war would soon be over. I said nothing but what most people believed would happen, even though it did not in the end. No harm was intended by my remark."

"How many people in your hospital listen to foreign radio programs or those emanating from Taipeh, the stronghold of the traitor Chiang? How many are discussing what they hear on those programs?"

Again Chu might as well know the truth. "When the Communists came to Chungking, and for the first month or two thereafter, everybody listened to foreign programs and all of us discussed the news together. Later on, your government ruled that Chinese must not listen to short wave programs, and from that time forward, everyone ceased discussing news from abroad. We foreigners have always respected your wishes and we have taken special care to discuss nothing that reaches our ears from foreign radio programs."

---

1 The Yalu River forms the boundary between North Korea and Manchuria, which is in northern China.

With the exception of one more daring individual who occasionally said more than was wise for our own good, as he later learned, all had been very discreet on this point.[2] I had never broken faith with them, except for this one remark about the Korean War.

Ignoring the reference to my assistant surgeon for the time being, Chu pursued his concerns about foreign radio broadcasts, saying, "Tell me all about your radio and the programs you listen to."

I explained that my own radio's tubes had been burned out or somehow it had been damaged the night in July 1950 when I was away in Chungking seeing my family off on their return to Canada. Our cook had slept in the house that night. He had tried to listen to the radio but, having never used ours before, apparently failed to adjust the transformer, thus irreparably damaging the radio. The single radio then left in our own home was not mine but Ian Robb's. However, all of us listened to the programs.[3] In the mornings we listened to the Voice of America before going to work. Sometimes at noon London attracted our attention, but in the evenings we wandered over the dial and heard such places as Peking, Moscow, Japan, the Philippines, sometimes Hong Kong and Australia. On occasion we favoured India or any station offering an especially interesting program.

"Now will you take a little time and tell us what you have heard on these programs, something about what others think of us and our government? What are other people saying about us—the Americans, for instance? You have been listening to them for a year. We would like to know what you have heard."

His questions sounded as vague as another which I had once been asked on an examination paper: "Discuss the surgical treatment of chronic peptic ulcer." A good-sized volume could have been written on that subject. Where, or how, could I start answering this much more vague question, which could easily lead me off into a wilderness of unknown

---

2 Dr. Allen does not say who this was, perhaps wishing not to risk endangering him or those close to him.

3 After my release from prison I learned the Political Section had investigated my radio to secure proof of my story. It remained in their hands until brought out of China in January 1952 by China Inland missionaries Mr. and Mrs. Ellison of Chungking and delivered to me in Hong Kong.

paths from which the return could be difficult? I hesitated before replying. As if sensing my indecision, he began coaxing the answers from me.

"What you have heard cannot be held against you. There must have been many things said about us. Begin your story."

His remarks gave me time to assess the realities of the situation. If I hedged the slightest bit in my answers, Chu would make the going more difficult. If I told him some of the things I had heard, he could be considerably annoyed.

In 1946 I had received a similar request from a Communist government official in the Shansi-Honan-Hopei-Shantung border region, where I had been invited to help with medical relief investigations. Assuming the questioner wanted an honest answer, and careful to avoid distressing him or hurting his pride, I told him exactly what others outside China—and even some of his own countrymen—were saying. As one taking a sudden cold shower, the vice-chairman gasped at my first statement. Then, recovering from his surprise, he settled down to what turned out to be a four-hour conversation. At its close he commended me for being "a very frank person."

I now decided to use the same direct tactics, assuming it was better to be completely truthful, even if I provided information not to his liking. To recall the radio information I had heard against China and communism over the period of a year was a feat of memory of which I was incapable. Rapidly organizing my thoughts, I decided to focus on the important events of the year as they affected China. From these I could build up my story.

I mentioned the reactions of the United States to the seizure of American, French and other diplomatic foreign properties in Peking by the People's Government of China. I discussed the British reactions when their bid for recognition by Red China was not given favourable consideration by the Chinese People's Government. The attitude of the so-called "false, enemy government of Chiang Kai-shek" toward the Communists received due attention. Then came the outbreak of the Korean War in June 1950, when the North Koreans were declared the aggressors. The fighting in Indo-China and Malaya was also considered, since the Chinese, sympathetically, if not actively, were involved in these activities.

After commenting on these subjects, I began a general critical statement about communism, its attitudes and policies. The Voice of America had covered the subject backward and forward, inside and out, many times. In fact, we had heard so much anti-communist propaganda that we frequently switched off the program after the news broadcast. The Voice may have sounded satisfactory to its broadcasters in the United States, but we at the listening end found much of their propaganda inept. It left one feeling angry at the stupidity of some speakers, who made unconsidered remarks in the course of their broadcasts. In them there was none of the subtlety of the London broadcasting speakers. BBC programs were so cleverly prepared that one listened almost to the end before realizing the propagandistic nature of the broadcast. Voice of America propaganda too often repelled, rather than held, its listeners. I well recall what one commentator said when the Chinese government was threatening to enter the Korean War if the "imperialistic war-mongering American aggressors" (as the Chinese always referred to the United Nations forces) did not halt their drive to the Yalu. This commentator, quoting another American hothead, said, "If the Chinese want a fight, then we'll damn well give it to them." Such remarks, in bad taste even at home, can inflame reactions abroad. They do not in the least help the American cause abroad.

I told Chu the Communists were criticized for the people's lack of freedom, the strict government controls, the early morning police raids in people's homes, the unwarranted imprisonment of political "reactionaries," the high taxation, the inability to hold meetings without special police permission, the developing persecution of churches, the Land Reform Program and other such measures.

Expanding on the Land Reform Program, I mentioned the criticism leveled by all freedom-loving peoples: the government was offering the peasants land that had been taken from their "oppressors," the landlord class, all the while planning to take it back, collectivize it, and give the peasants what government felt were their requirements in food, clothing and shelter.

This last thrust evidently struck deeply for Comrade Chu stopped me, turned to the secretary, Miss Liu,[4] who had been keeping note of the subjects I had discussed, and asked, "Is that what the Voice of America has been saying?"

Without a moment's hesitation she replied in her native tongue, "Yes, Liang Tseng-luen is speaking correctly. That is exactly what they said."

---

4 She is not to be confused with Comrade Liu, the man who was Dr. Allen's third and last interrogator.

It was evident that Miss Liu had monitored at least some of the American broadcasts. Her command of English was excellent and the few occasional remarks she made to assist my Chinese led me to believe she had a good university education. However, I could hardly have gone wrong, for the criticisms I had given were those my foreign friends and I, not to mention millions of Chinese, believed were justified against communism and its methods.

Frankly, I was surprised at my failure to elicit any stronger reactions from Comrade Chu, for some of my remarks could easily have been resented. Another time and in other circumstances, I would have enjoyed this unsurpassed opportunity to criticize various aspects of communist ideology. That, in fact, is what I did, while ostensibly making the statement they requested. However, as a prisoner under investigation, I had to watch the reactions of Comrade Chu and his secretary to be sure my extempore statement satisfied them without exceeding the bounds of discretion.

Then the cross-questioning began. "Having heard all this information on the radio, I presume you have been spreading it among your Chinese friends and your staff members? Do not deny what you have done, for we have means of securing the truth. Any falsification or misstatement will be held against you."

Again I asserted that I had kept all these things to myself. I was not one to spread "wild and foolish gossip" (for so they considered all foreign radio reports), "particularly," I went on, "when your government has commanded us not to discuss foreign affairs with the people. We consider ourselves to be guests within your country. As guests we should obey your government."

"Then why did you state the war in Korea was over? You must have known our government would never let the American aggressors remain on Asian soil. They must be driven out. Again, why did you make that statement? Where did you get your information?"

And the whole merry-go-round started all over again.

Finally satisfied I could or would say nothing further about that one remark, Comrade Chu asked, "Who are the people in the hospital who have discussed these matters with you?"

He was asking for specifics and now I was on difficult ground. Come what may, I would incriminate none of my staff. I answered in generalities. If they wanted specific information, they would first have to provide specific names. I was not going to fall into the same trap as Djang Gwei-han, our chief accountant, who had volunteered more than he had to at his struggle meeting and so not only gave his accusers enough rope to hang him, figuratively, but also incriminated others unintentionally.

"I have told you already! Many of the staff discussed these reports among themselves during the first two, perhaps three, months after liberation. Some of them talked among themselves; at times I took part in the conversation. Our hospital staff, on the whole, are, like myself, honourable people. When your government gave orders, we all tried to obey them. When we realized we were offending your officials, we ceased these discussions. No one person could be singled out as having especially violated your laws."

"But," Chu continued, pressing his point again, "if you stopped making these remarks, as you call them, why did you speak about the Korean War to one of your staff members?"

Finally I replied, "The truth is, Comrade, I made the statement because it was a natural comment to make. Everyone knew the North Korean soldiers were running north as fast as they could travel, leaving their arms and equipment behind them. As yet your government had never made any official statement, as far as I am aware, to indicate they intended to intervene in the conflict which we foreigners understood was against North Koreans, not the Chinese people. There is nothing more that I can say in my defence. If what I have done was wrong, and I have offended your government, then I am willing to admit my fault. It is you who must decide if I am guilty. My duty is to state what happened and why."

Apparently satisfied on this point, Chu finally desisted and the logical question to conclude the interview followed.

"You once stated you had given help to our government and to those who befriended it. If that is true, why did you force Dr. Tien Bao-Liang from your hospital? He was a very progressively-minded individual. You should have permitted him to stay and work with you."

Mention of Dr. Tien so soon after our discussion about the Korean War remark confirmed my suspicions he had been planted in the hospital. Since only Dr. Tien had heard my remark, only he could have revealed it to them. How closely Dr. Tien had been working with officialdom against me I never discovered, but I can trace many accusations made against me directly to his handiwork.

"I think your facts are not quite correct, Comrade Chu," I countered. "I did not send him from the hospital. He himself sought a position in a Hankow hospital about the end of August 1950. When he secured this appointment he came to ask permission to leave and it was granted. I would never detain a staff member in my hospital against his will, or prevent one from securing a position of higher rank than we might be able to give him."

On the face of it, these were the facts. I was almost certain Comrade Chu would not know the whole story, because Dr. Tien himself would have preferred to keep it secret. If my short statement satisfied him, well and good.

My strategy worked. Chu had no further questions to ask. The usual thumb-prints were applied to the evidence and I was escorted to my cell, grateful that I had been able to thread my way so easily through an interrogation that could well have been much more pointed and searching.

Exhausted by the morning's interview and safely behind my padlocked door, I mentally reviewed the events of the morning. How crafty Dr. Tien had been! He had remained on the staff just long enough to accomplish his task of undermining me. That done, he had sought a new position seven hundred miles away. It became clear that he was the source of many of the accusations against me. He had put them in the hands of two people—Fung Cheo-wen and Miss Mung—who acted for him when the time became ripe for action.

Without doubt, Dr. Tien had been planted in our hospital by some pre-arranged Communist plan. At the time he applied for appointment we did not especially need a doctor in our surgical department. His persistence and stated desire for further study overcame my better judgment. I engaged him on the agreement he would substitute for a period in our mission hospital in Fuling, sixty miles eastward down the Yangtze River. I also stipulated that if for any reason imminent political changes made it necessary to decrease our staff, he would be the first asked to leave. To this he agreed, knowing full well that when those political changes occurred his position would be safe, for then we would not be allowed to ask him to leave.

We soon discovered the undesirability of this appointment. After the first acute problem caused by Dr. Tien, I discovered he had already been on our staff under a previous superintendent, Dr. C. William M. Service. His work had been found unsatisfactory and he had been asked to secure another position. He remained for two years in a local army hospital's orthopedic service, then came to me. With characteristic Chinese courtesy, no one had mentioned any of this to me.

We first questioned his real ability when after being asked to place a fractured leg in traction, he was seen giving inappropriate orders to the attendants and nurses who were helping. He did not seem to know what was required. Certainly he took no active part in adjusting the complicated extension apparatus. A few weeks later a private case was admitted for re-application of plaster to a tubercular spine. His manner so upset the patient's mother she made many complaints to the admitting office against Dr. Tien. As a result, he was removed from private service. Later, a desperate case whose only possible hope was surgery was scheduled for operation on the following day. Overnight the patient had a sudden change: widespread subcutaneous hemorrhages appeared, which indicated no operation should be attempted. Although informed of this change, Dr. Tien failed to report the incident or to cancel the operation. It was obvious that, in addition to being unable to perform the duties of a junior surgeon, he lacked surgical judgment. All these were pre-liberation faults.

After the Communist entry, two more improperly prepared surgical cases had to be returned from the operating room for attention that he should have ordered previously. Other similarly mismanaged cases continued to occur in the months that followed. In other than the surgical field, too, he had been active. Together with an intern, he had started a campaign against the hospital dietitian concerning the food provided for the staff. Not content with this complaint, Dr. Tien openly went to the kitchen, upbraided the cooks and soon had that department in a furore. There was little one could do to control him except tell him bluntly to keep out of the kitchen and mind his own affairs.

Finally, after he had improperly prepared a patient for an operation, an error that could have resulted in the patient's death, I realized something had to be done immediately. With Communists now in full control of China, I knew that if any patient died through hospital negligence, we could not possibly avoid trouble. I wrote Dr. Tien, reminding him of his agreement. The number of patients was now slackening off considerably. Finances were an ever-increasing problem. I suggested in view of his professional difficulties with us there appeared to be little chance for his future promotion. On receiving the letter, he was obviously upset and requested time to consider his problem.

A week later, our leading Communist, the electrician Tsui Tien-min, and a Communist official tried to enter the women's ward while dressings were being changed. Dr. Tien stopped them in a very undiplomatic and discourteous way. The official promptly hustled the doctor off to his headquarters for an investigation that lasted the rest of the morning. Dr.

Tien returned penitent, expecting me to commiserate with him. Instead he received a letter informing him this present incident was of such a nature we dared take no further responsibility for his actions, suggesting again that he find another position as soon as conveniently possible. He agreed that perhaps this suggestion was the best way to settle his problem, though he had no immediate intention of leaving. He knew I could not discharge him. Under a Communist government I could only remove him by finding another position for him. Three months passed and I heard of such a vacancy. It was agreed that Dr. Tien could fill the position, but he refused, stating he was waiting for another post and would leave when possible. Finally, while I was absent from the hospital one time, he operated on two patients and the complications that followed forced his hand. One of the patients was a Communist official in whom he failed to diagnose an incisional abscess. Obviously, he had been negligent, and after I discovered this, he left for Hankow.

In all this period he naturally did not appreciate my references to his lack of ability. He remained a particular thorn in my side for ten months under the Communist regime, acting as operating assistant surgeon, or as an observer on the ward or in the operating room, watching for the least shred of evidence he might be able to collect to use against me. Such was the individual whom Comrade Chu considered "progressive," while I was seen as a menace. No, I did not force him to leave the hospital. I merely encouraged him, using the strongest possible means of persuasion, to go through the hospital's open door and travel anywhere else he desired.

The whole staff secretly rejoiced with me when Dr. Tien finally took the boat down the river. His Communist nursing friends sent him off with a tremendous reception, during which I had to give the parting address and shed crocodile tears. At the time, I was blissfully unaware of the extent of his traitorous activities. I had been prepared to forgive and forget the past. Dr. Tien had no such intention. Many times he must have smiled to think how little I suspected the stab in the back he delivered at my accusation meeting, though he was miles away at the time.

To the lasting credit of my medical, nursing and business staff, none save Dr. Tien and a junior accountant were involved in making accusations against me.

In such bitter ways as this I gradually became aware of the approved Communist techniques. My pro-Communist friends will point out that no official Communists took part in the activities that led to my accusation meeting. Strictly speaking, that is true. In reality, however, Communist officials not only condoned the destructive activities of the Dr. Tiens in the new China but also made use of all information gained through such sources. With it they conducted innumerable investigations designed to discredit the good reputations of those they wished to destroy. They must therefore, in the end, be held responsible for the results of the accusations initiated by such as Dr. Tien Bao-liang.

Chapter 9

"You are a spy!"

I N THE MIDDLE of January, after I had been the sole fourth-floor prisoner for about two weeks, a second change was made in my accommodation and I found myself placed in the corner room on the third floor. Perhaps a prisoner there had been transferred to the actual prison or, quite as likely, our guards had found more convenient premises for their own living quarters. Whatever the reason, the change was welcome, for I found myself lodged between my two foreign companions in misery—Brother Pretat in the room on my right and Rev. F. Olin Stockwell to the left. Our three doorways opened onto a common stairway and this nearness of friends comforted each of us, even though we were not permitted to talk to one another.

The new quarters were a distinct improvement in position, though cleanliness, size and furnishings remained unchanged. The three windows in the fourth-floor room had opened into an enclosed area with a covered ceiling and only from a small chink to the right had I been able to look on open sky. In contrast, the vista from this new room extended for miles beyond one end of the city. I could see not only the courtyard below, the street outside and many buildings but also beyond these to the distant hills on either side of the river. Officially, as a prisoner in solitary confinement, I should not have been able to look out the window, but, as in the previous room, my short guards had pasted paper over the window panes only to the level of my nose, not realizing the height required to obstruct a six-footer's vision. So I had plenty of opportunity to see much of what was happening about me many hours of the day for several months before the guards discovered their very serious mistake.

Unfortunately, during the first weeks I stayed in the room, outside events did not particularly interest me, for I was engrossed in the task of trying to clear myself as quickly as possible from the many unwarranted accusations restricting my freedom. During the third week in January, I underwent an interrogation that proved to be a turning point in the investigation of my case. It was then I learned of a serious charge against me that I believed until after my deportation was the main reason for my imprisonment. This question period brought all the apparently meaningless and unconnected charges previously made against me into complete focus. For four weeks I had groped in a mental fog trying to bring order and clarity out of what, until that day, was complete confusion.

On this morning Comrade Wu took charge. As usual, he reviewed previous accusations to which I had already given what he should have considered final replies. However, my investigators rarely accepted a single no as a final answer. Through repeated questioning on a topic, they hoped to find some flaw that would nullify my previous evidence, but, since I was always careful to make completely factual statements, they could not trip me up and made no headway. Tiring of these fruitless efforts, Wu finally presented several new problems for discussion and questioning. He went far afield to matters about which I had given little special thought, since they were not raised during my accusation meeting.

"Why did you criticize Wu Yao-tsung?"

It took some moments and a little more explanation from Wu before I realized he was speaking of a man we missionaries had usually referred to as "Y.T." I knew Y.T. as a member of the Chinese Christian church, the former secretary of the Chinese Y.M.C.A. and editor of the *Christian Farmer*, a church publication. I knew he had been appointed by the Communists as one of the five Christian representatives on the People's Political Consultative Council, the organ that officially proclaimed the present People's Government as the legal government of China on October 1, 1949. But Wu Yao-tsung had not been recognized as yet by me or other Christians in West China as the powerful figure he was under this new government. At the time Wu was questioning me, I believed Y.T. entered my case only indirectly. I now know Y.T. Wu, acting as an undercover agent of the People's Government, was the main author of an unholy statement that came to be known as the "Christian Manifesto" (see Appendix C). It was through his and others' machinations that the officials of the Protestant Church in China were forced to relinquish their autonomy and accept the People's Government's overlordship of their churches.

Although I did not know Y.T.'s role, I certainly knew about the manifesto. In May 1950 the first draft of this document was issued and circulated widely throughout the Protestant Chinese church and missionary community for consideration and comment prior to its presentation at a conference of church leaders in Shanghai, which convened later to discuss and officially adopt its resolutions. It was a political, rather than a Christian, statement. I received a copy of the original draft, a much more drastic and uncomplimentary statement than was contained in the final document presented to the government (see Appendix C to compare versions).

Even so, the final draft dealt a heavy blow to Christian missionaries for in its initial paragraph this statement appeared: "Since the principal groups of missionaries who brought Christianity to China all came themselves from these imperialistic countries, Christianity, consciously or unconsciously, directly or indirectly, became related with imperialism." It then went on to urge that "people in the churches everywhere . . . purge imperialistic influences from within Christianity itself." This threw the Chinese Christians into consternation since they had been led to believe that the People's Government welcomed foreign missionaries to remain in China—at least until their visas expired.

Although many Christian groups signed this "Manifesto," one major group, the Anglican general synod, indicated its attitude toward government in a thoroughly and carefully prepared Christian document (see Appendix C). Other Christian groups, who disliked the wording of the final version of the "Manifesto" planned to make their own independent statements. The news about these separate statements had reached us by the grapevine, for which many of us were grateful.

Twice while the "Manifesto" was being circulated for approval I tried to allay our local (United) church leaders' misgivings by mentioning that our own Chinese Church, the Church of Christ in China (of which we formed a synod) would likely prepare its own statement, too. Many Christian Chinese not then being pressured as they are now[1] to sign the "Manifesto" were hesitant to append their seals and few missionaries could conscientiously have signed the original draft had signatures been requested.

---

1 Presumably, by "now" Dr. Allen means 1953 or 1954, when he was writing this book.

Comrade Wu wanted to know just what was so objectionable about the statement Y.T. Wu had authored.

The time had come when I had to voice my frank opinion and attempt to state the position of the missionary community. So, without hesitation I replied, "As far as I am concerned, the leaders of the Chinese Christian Church have the full right to speak officially for their church. In general terms I have very considerable sympathy for much that is contained in the 'Manifesto,' for the Chinese must learn to accept full responsibility for the support of their own church. My own hospital position has been conferred on me, not by our missionaries, but by the medical committee of our church synod, whose chairman is a Chinese. However, when this document states or implies that *all* missionaries are 'imperialistic' in their attitudes, then I must register my opposition to the inclusiveness of such a statement. According to my interpretation of the word 'imperialistic,' there probably are such missionaries, but I and many of my foreign friends do not consider ourselves to be in that category. We have constantly maintained a friendly attitude to the Chinese people. In a land where your government is said to have given the people freedom of speech as one of the eleven guaranteed freedoms, I felt that I was entitled to express my own opinions on this matter to correct any false impressions the statement may have engendered. Those opinions I have voiced to my Chinese friends, but I have never, on any occasion, brought Mr. Wu's name into the argument, nor have I criticized him in any way."

Comrade Wu did not take the matter any further. In his mind there was not the least doubt that any criticism of the "Manifesto" meant criticism of Wu Yao-tsung, the main author. Had I then known the full history leading to its final adoption, I might have spent a great deal more time in answering Comrade Wu, even though my argument certainly would have fallen on deaf ears.

Comrade Wu next asked, "What special relations have you with Dso Li-liang?"

This question was not entirely unexpected, though no reference had been made to Dr. Dso Li-liang, our hospital radiologist, at any time during my long accusation meeting. I expect his good standing as the medical representative on the hospital labour union made Fung and Miss Fan reluctant to bring his name into the proceedings. I denied special relationships with any member of my staff. True, I had helped Dr. Dso secure facilities in Canada for special postgraduate study in radiology, but I had made similar arrangements for others to pursue special study in

Canada, Peking and elsewhere, according to their abilities and facility with English. None had been accorded special or preferential privileges, since I viewed all hospital employees impartially according to needs and ability.[2] My intimacy with each varied according to my business and professional relationships with them. I added further it was always a personal policy never to be so intimate with staff friends that the accusing finger of favouritism could be pointed at me. Wu made no comment, apparently satisfied with my reply.

There was no question that this morning's session was full of surprises on matters never mentioned at the accusation meeting. Still, I had handled them well enough and they did not seem to be amounting to anything serious. But now Wu was about to shake me to my very core. The dramatic change in the session began innocently enough with what seemed an extremely odd question.

"I believe you know a person named Ee Way-deh. Who is he?"

Seconds passed before I comprehended Comrade Wu was referring not to a Chinese but a foreign friend of mine. To make certain before answering, I questioned him in English, since foreigners other than my fellow missionary prisoners had never been mentioned before this.

"Are you referring to Mr. G. R. Edwards of Chengtu?" I asked, all the while wondering where Bob Edwards fitted into my problems. Assured we were speaking about one and the same person, I proceeded to give Bob due credit for his accomplishments.

"Mr. Edwards," I said, " is one of the newly arrived missionaries of the United Church of Canada. He came to China as an electrical engineer to work in mission and other hospitals wherever his services might be needed. He is an expert in the mechanics of radiological equipment. On one occasion last June he repaired a faulty unit at the request of your government in Yaan. We were hoping he would come to Chungking to install a deep-therapy Maximar 250 unit in our hospital. We tried every means but never were able to secure official permission for him to travel to Chungking."

"What sort of person is this Edwards?"

---

2 In fact, Dr. Allen always considered Dr. Dso a close friend, but to admit this was to risk drawing his friend into a dangerous investigation.

"We know him to be a very fine Christian, one who is intensely interested in winning young people into the church, a man of very high ideals. Technically, he is highly qualified," I added, still puzzled why Comrade Wu should display this special interest in Bob.

His next comment supplied a most unexpected answer, and for the first time in all the series of examinations through which I had passed, Wu displayed emotion. Tense with excitement he leaned forward in his chair, his hands tightly grasping the table before him. A remarkable change crossed his features as, with all the vehemence and sarcasm at his command, his voice raised only slightly from its previous calm and even tones, he fairly spat out his indictment.

"You know that is not so. Edwards is a spy! You also are a spy! Why do you still persist in refusing to admit this truth? We all know you for what you are. We have our proof. Yet, ever since you were brought here, whenever we have asked you to confess you keep stating you are innocent. Confess and let us be done with this."

I insisted both Bob Edwards and I were completely innocent of the charge. I was taut and furious at his unwarranted condemnation. It was only with difficulty that I held myself in complete control. This was not the time to lose my temper or to ask on what he based his accusation. With his next words, he supplied the answer.

"You say you are not a spy. Then listen to what I have to tell you. Do you recall that Edwards wrote you a letter last July? What did it contain? You need only think for a few moments and you will realize my charge against you is correct. Any reasonable person must admit that our case is well-founded."

"I received a letter from Mr. Edwards about that time. In fact, I received several such letters during May, June and July. In all of them we discussed our need for his services in Chungking. The question of obtaining official permission for him to travel was mentioned. We were arranging for him to install that Maximar 250 X-ray unit. Every word in those letters was concerned with business matters. What do they have to do with this case?"

"Do you still persist in saying you are innocent? Can you not remember their content? Listen to this." Picking up a sheet of paper from his dossier he began to read, in English: " 'Please let me know what has to be done, and what is the financial set-up respecting the arsenal.' Is not that the correct content of Edwards' letter? Do you not remember it? This statement should be as obvious to you as it is to us. Its meaning is indisputable. If both of you are not spies, then why are you interested in the 'financial set-up' of one of our government arsenals? It is ridiculous for you to deny complicity with Edwards in this scheme."

I sat in stunned silence as I let the full implications of what he had said sink in. The Communists had censored my mail, misunderstood some of the carelessly worded sentences and concluded that Bob and I were trying to spy on the 20th Arsenal. A great deal now became clear to me. The misinterpretation of Bob's remark about the "financial set-up" almost surely explained why Dr. Dso and Mr. Shiung were stone-walled when they tried to get permission for Bob to travel to Chungking to install our unit. I began to think it might explain other official refusals that had made no sense to me.

I needed a few minutes to calm myself and determine the best way to explain what had happened. "Comrade Wu," I began, "what you said is perfectly true. This sentence is written in a way that it can be interpreted as you and the censors have done. I do not blame you for thinking in this way. However, you must realize that the English language is in many respects like Chinese—several meanings may be taken from a given phrase. May I assure you that the interpretation you have made is completely wrong? What Mr. Edwards means is that he is coming to our hospital to repair X-ray equipment and that the arsenal has also requested his services. You see, during the Sino-Japanese War our radiological department had close connections with the one at the arsenal. Their electrician would come to the hospital to repair our equipment, and in return we loaned them some equipment. After the liberation, their electrician left, and since then they have needed someone to repair the equipment at the arsenal. In that letter, Mr. Edwards was asking me whether any arrangement had been made to cover the costs of his work at the arsenal. It is unfortunate he used the terms 'financial set-up.' All he needed to say was 'Are we to charge the arsenal for our services or is it something we are to do freely?' The term 'set-up' can be used in many ways in English. It can mean 'structure,' as you thought, but in this case it only meant 'an arrangement' to pay for services. Mr. Edwards had no thought of spying when he wrote those words, nor did I take that meaning from them when I read his letter. We have no interest whatsoever in the financial structure of that military arsenal or any other."

Comrade Wu had clearly decided the evidence he had against me was so serious that I was in a position from which I could not extricate myself. It was difficult for him to accept my reasonable explanation. So simple a statement obviously could not be true. Grasping the table in front of him with both hands, he glared at me, his raised voice harsh, cold and unyielding.

"Allen, why do you take these serious charges against you so lightly? You know as well as I that your explanation is not acceptable to us. You are a spy. In fact, you are both spies. Why will you not confess? What kind of man are you anyway? You come to China pretending you are here to help our people but what do we find? All kinds of charges against you!"

He picked up the dossier before him. Flipping through the pages he read out some of the charges still to be made against me. "Here I read that you have mistreated patients," he said. "You have pulled them out of bed when they were ill and forced them out of your hospital. You have refused to give treatment to one of the workmen in your own hospital when he was dying. You have tried to force your nurses to give special treatment to your foreign patients while refusing assistance to our Chinese. You have permitted people in your hospital to discharge workmen without justification. Of all these things and other charges I can name, you are accused. Again I say, what kind of a man are you that all these accusations against you have been made by your staff? We know from them and from your persistent refusal to confess to this long series of charges that you are a criminal who has committed many crimes against our people. Again I say, you are a spy. Confess and finish this business."

By this point, Comrade Wu was extremely agitated and in no mood to listen further to any explanation I might make. I, too, was in a cold fury. There was much I would have liked to say, but I kept my lips tightly closed, permitting him to finish without interruption. I could not admit to this long list of alleged faults without giving the necessary explanatory details. As soon as I had opportunity to speak, I was unhesitating and firm in my reply.

"Comrade Wu, I have stated I am not a spy. You are at liberty to believe what you like. You are the judge. I am the prisoner. It is you who must make the decisions. I must tell you, however, that if you sincerely believe I am not telling the truth, you have but one course to follow, according to my interpretation of legal procedure. In peace time, if a foreigner is believed to be a spy, our country would deport that person immediately. I am a foreigner here and you should do likewise. If you believe I am a spy, then send me home. There is nothing else for you to do."

"Liang Tseng-luen, do you really mean what you say, that we should send you back to Canada?" he asked, his manner softening a little.

"If you think I am a spy, you have no other choice. That is exactly what I mean."

Surprisingly, his voice immediately resumed its previous calm, deliberate tones. Turning to his secretary, who had been writing furiously during this lengthy series of rapid charges and replies, he said in the most matter-of-fact way, "Write that down. That is what Liang Tseng-luen states should be his punishment for his faults."

Although he had tried relentlessly to incriminate me, and in fact believed he had succeeded in doing so, Wu appeared quite unconcerned after I rejected his charge. Almost without a break, he continued his investigation as if my remarks had been part of a commonplace conversation.

For me, however, there was nothing at all commonplace about the exchange. A great light had suddenly dawned where previously much had been darkness. This serious charge of spying seemed to provide the key to the whole maze of charges and accusations through which I had been led. For the first time during my month of detention I understood the extreme seriousness of my position. Whether I was innocent or guilty, a charge of espionage, when made in a Communist court, was an exceedingly grave matter if they had any real intention of forcing the issue.

I had no time to ponder this problem before Wu moved on to a new subject. "Will you tell me what you know about Chang Dao-hwei? We are very concerned about this man and the relationship he has to you."

It was not at all surprising that the Political Section should have brought the name of Chang Dao-hwei, or John Chang, into this investigation. For one thing he was a friend of mine and for another he had been under twenty-four-hour surveillance since September, in part because of his connections with me. How seriously my friendship had endangered him I was only now learning. Being associated with a suspected foreign spy would make his every move suspect.

John was the son of Canon James Chang, formerly of Hankow, a pastor of the Shang Kung Hui (Anglican) Church. Canon Chang had come to Chungking in 1938, driven there because of the advancing Japanese army. He had taken a leading part in the activities of the community church located on our hospital grounds. I first knew John as a member of the local Christian congregation. In August 1945, he accepted a position as English secretary to Dr. William Service, superintendent of the Mission Hospital during my absence on furlough from 1945 through 1947. He took a position in a military hospital to the north of the city some time before my return to Chungking in 1948. He was secretary of the Chungking Rotary Club for a number of years, so we had met weekly until the arrival of the Communists in Chungking. After the liberation, he had advised me concerning various problems being caused by the Communists in our hospital compound. About September 1950, a close friend of his on our staff suddenly received a letter saying that John had that day been placed under twenty-four-hour surveillance, though permitted to continue his work translating medical articles and reports from various foreign journals into Chinese for the local medical authorities.

We were shocked to learn in the letter that he had been charged with attempting to help Miss Isabelle Miller, a United Church of Canada Women's Missionary Society nurse, get permission to travel from Chengtu to our hospital in Chungking. I had previously written to John requesting advice on how some suitable arrangement might be made to persuade the authorities to grant this permission. As in Bob Edwards' case, Miss Miller's was no more successful. It appeared evident that my request had been his undoing. Later information revealed that the authorities in Chengtu had put every impediment in her way in an attempt to force her to remain under what was almost the equivalent of house arrest.

Wu, waiting for an answer, amplified his first question. "We understand Chang Dao-Hwei spent much time in your hospital and goes there frequently. What is the purpose of his visits? We know he recently crossed the river to go to your hospital, taking with him a parcel he left for one of your doctors who had just been taken to prison. What can you tell us about this?"

There was nothing suspicious about John Chang's activities. Like myself, he was an innocent victim of circumstances. Only informers in our own hospital could have told the police about that harmless package. It showed how detailed and efficient was the surveillance system adopted to watch the masses. Since so much suspicion attended his movements, it seemed wise to clear him as fully as possible, to remove any misgivings the Communists might have concerning him. All irrelevant matters I omitted and briefly recited this story.

"It is true that Chang Dao-hwei came to our hospital frequently. There were two main reasons for his trips to our side of the river. He is a translator for the Chungking Health Bureau. Our hospital library subscribes to about ten medical journals. He translates various articles of general interest from these journals into Chinese. The hospital librarian is the wife of the doctor you imprisoned after his woman servant secretly brought friends in to listen to forbidden programs from Taipeh on his radio. Word of her action reached the police and she was arrested. Hours later, so was the doctor. Mr. Chang was very friendly with both the doctor and his wife, having known them for some years. The doctor is on a gastric ulcer diet and needs special food, which his wife must bring to him. Mr. Chang's parcel was a gift of special food for his friend.

"The other reason for his coming to our hospital concerned his father, Canon Chang, who had died a few years previously of a cerebral hemorrhage. He had been buried in a temporary grave on our hospital property and his son hoped someday to transfer the remains to a place nearer his ancestors. In filial devotion, John frequently went to visit the grave."

Finally, I told Wu how we had asked John to help us get permission for Isabelle Miller to come to Chungking when we were unable to do so through the ordinary channels. "We felt that the Foreign Affairs Bureau might be induced to grant our request if a government organization would support our application. I asked Chang Dao-hwei to enquire if this was a possibility. He made enquiry without result. There was no relationship between us other than personal friendship. Now that you accuse me of being a spy I understand why the finger of suspicion was directed toward Mr. Chang. You may have thought he was an accomplice. I tell you truthfully he is a very honest man who has given exceptionally faithful service to your Health Bureau authorities. You will find no political fault in this man, nor in any of my other friends or associates. They are all innocent, as I am innocent, of any collaboration against your government."

With that statement, what was to date the most important session of my investigation ended, along with my month-long uncertainty about where the investigation was headed. I now knew that a few weeks' further probing of my case could not possibly dispel so serious a charge as that made against me that cold January morning.

That was the last interrogation over which Comrade Wu presided. He had shot his bolt, and from my point of view had grossly missed the mark. I was not sorry to have him leave the investigation to others, for of the three persons directing the enquiry he was the most to be feared. Every hour spent officially with him was filled with dread and anxiety.

During the next six weeks Comrade Chu continued the investigation. He was the least experienced of them all and relatively easy to handle. Briefly, these later question periods consisted of a series of attempts to extract a confession of guilt from me on the charges of espionage and of deliberately attempting to use my medical knowledge to maim or kill the three Communist officials (see Chapter 5). They also implied I had been bribed to do a particularly successful appendectomy on the son of the Nationalist governor of Chinghai (Qinghai) province, who came to our hospital when another refused to make a diagnosis. In gratitude at having avoided the abscess or peritonitis that would have resulted had the diagnosis been delayed, the patient presented me with a fur coat lining when he left the hospital. I was accused of favouritism. For the purpose of my investigation, this was a perfect case. As they saw it, it proved I favoured their enemies and deliberately withheld my skills when operating on Communists. I explained it was impossible to compare an appendectomy with a chest surgery, but all explanations were unacceptable for no other reason than that I persisted in arguing my case. Try as they might to shake me or make me change my evidence on the many charges, they met with little or no success. Chu continued to instruct me to think, think, think, until I grew to dislike him quite as profoundly as I had Wu during his investigation period.

The wearing down process continued, however, until the climax came one morning toward the end of February. I was still being urged to admit to my spying activities, still unwilling to plead guilty to what obviously were false accusations. During a most trying ordeal when Comrade Chu attacked with more than his usual bullheadedness, I burst out in anger with all the passion I could command.

"How often must I tell you that I am no spy? Will you never cease trying to urge me to confess to what is false?"

Whether from loss of strength and weight, the result of insufficient food during those weeks,[3] or because of the intense strain of bearing up under Comrade Chu's persistent efforts to force a confession, or both, I cannot state, but suddenly to their amazement and my consternation my eyes streamed with a flood of tears. The session closed until I was able to get my crying under control enough to continue. I then apologized for disrupting the investigation. Chu replied, "You are not the first who has broken down in tears during our investigations."

---

3 Dr. Allen describes these and other physical conditions of his solitary confinement in Chapter 10.

"I have told you the truth. You must believe my interpretation of Ee Way-deh's letter. You must! You must! If you will not, then you must make the decision of guilt yourselves. If you decide I am a spy, then I have no recourse but to accept your decision."

This was exactly what they would not do, for every accused prisoner who is judged guilty must himself confess to his faults. Thus the court is saved the necessity of proving the defendant guilty. Only abject confession will suffice. They could easily see their efforts might soon bear fruit; that I might yet confess what I still continued to deny; that I was near the breaking point. Or were they beginning to believe my statements? I did not know. Whatever their thoughts, they decided I had received a sufficiently severe grilling for the day. The usual thumb-printing closed another difficult session.

Feeling depressed, I returned to my room. I was fast approaching the belief that the well-publicized, proven Communist methods of extorting confessions from prisoners conceivably might be used against me in the near future. This impression was not lessened by my having been informed on more than one occasion that the Political Section had such means available to make me speak truthfully. They may only have said that to exert what they considered suitable pressure on me to yield to their demands. Perhaps they never intended to use those means in my case, but elsewhere they assuredly did.

Assailed by thoughts of a forced confession, I began to be plagued with a ferment of self-questioning that now arose to break down my resistance to these gruelling investigations. Why should I, innocent of these charges, be called upon to suffer all the miseries that forceful methods would bring? Why not confess to spying, satisfy their demands and complete the whole unpleasant business? I had no special fear of serious consequences to my own person from such a confession. I had been informed on good authority a year earlier that the Communists wished to avoid becoming seriously involved in diplomatic complications involving foreigners who might decide to remain in China. My personal experience up to that time had convinced me this was the truth. The government might be difficult, but the possibility of losing one's life seemed slight. Anything would be better than staying alone in this room day after day. Oh, to be released and to return home without further delay! Too much of my own company was surely affecting my thoughts that afternoon.

The hours dragged with increasing monotony toward evening. The days were lengthening and it was still hours before bedtime. I paced my cell, my mind in torment and dejection, while I tried to determine what my course should be. The guards outside frequently came to my door, watching me through their slit of a peephole. Finally, worn out, I got into bed. Sleep was long in coming on this, the most depressing day I had yet experienced.

Morning came after a tormented night of broken rest. Breakfast and exercise, usually keenly anticipated, brought no change in my mood. The scant reading matter in my possession offered little help in whiling away the hours until noon. My thoughts were far afield and words, though read, failed to penetrate my distressed mind. Pacing the floor again and again, I kept asking the same question: Shall I confess? Shall I confess? Get it over with! Get yourself out of here! Anything at all, anything but this!

After the longest of many dreary mornings, the guard finally opened the door to announce dinner was available. Whether the meal was better than usual, or the long hours of strain had ushered in their opposing reaction, I do not know, but after more than twenty-four hours of acute mental agony, I finally forced myself to think with integrity and reasonableness about this new situation. I began to question what would happen if I made this contemplated false confession. What would my employers, the Board of Overseas Missions of the United Church of Canada, say if my name was blazoned in headlines over all the Canadian papers: MISSIONARY ADMITS HE IS A SPY. And what will happen to Bob Edwards. He, too, will be charged with spying. Bob is just a newcomer to China. He has not been well. He is not yet able to endure an investigation such as I have had, conducted entirely in Chinese. Further, the investigators do not like to use English on such occasions. Bob might break under the strain of the whole ordeal. Why should I wrongly involve another so that I may be released from my present difficulties? Was it right he should become so seriously involved by so trifling a matter as that one short sentence misinterpreted by the censor in an unfortunately-worded letter? These and many other similar thoughts soon forced me to a final decision. No matter what the ultimate cost, I would not falsely confess to such a charge. To ensure my decision would remain unchanged, I sat down immediately, seized a piece of rough grass paper and, while shreds of the coarse straw fibres were pulled off by my pen, causing me much difficulty in writing, I drafted these not-too-legible words as my final position on the charge of spying:

Repeating your charge that I am a spy, based on no other evidence than the unfortunate wording of a sentence contained in a letter from Mr. Bob Edwards to me, I must make the following statement. I have explained to you what I believe Mr. Edwards meant when he wrote this letter. I have made repeated declarations to this effect. I have told you many times what I believe Mr. Edwards meant. Without his prior consent I am unprepared to admit that he had other than quite innocent thoughts when he wrote the letter referred to.

Apparently you are unwilling to believe me. When this investigation began you asked me to tell you the truth. I have constantly and consistently tried to do so. If I state Mr. Edwards and I are guilty of spying, I am telling a falsehood, something you have specifically urged me not to do. I will not perjure myself in this way. Further, my mission board has sent me here for a specific purpose, and has placed me in a position of trust, to engage in medical work in this land of China. If I state falsely that I have been involved in espionage activities, what will be their attitude toward me? Again I must say I am not a spy. This statement is final and irrevocable. I will have nothing more to say on the question. I have quite decided to make no further assertion on this point. This letter must be accepted as final. There is nothing further to say.

The draft having been composed and corrected, it was a mere matter of detail to prepare a suitable official declaration. I appended my signature, called the guard, and requested him to present the document to the proper authorities. That done, I felt my spirits rise as if a great weight had been lifted from my shoulders. With temptation swept aside, my despondence left me, never to return.

Whether this action forced the Political Section's decision to cancel further investigations I cannot say, but neither Comrade Wu nor Comrade Chu ever called me to attend another official investigation. The enquiries ceased completely as of that day in late February until one evening in late May, when I was roused from my bed to meet Comrade Liu, the third and last of my investigators while I was held in solitary confinement. Until that night, however, I had three long months to while away. Instead of being wasted, they turned out to be more important to my future life than I could ever have anticipated.

Chapter 10

Life in Solitary Confinement

WHEN ACCIDENT or disease suddenly deprives a person of his freedom to work and support his family, the immediate physical and mental reaction can be disastrous. Forced to be dependent on his family or his government or charity until he has recovered, he may temporarily break under the strain.

The hundreds of foreign missionary and business men and women who have been thrown into Communist Chinese prisons or placed under house arrest without warning have each experienced a similar dislocation in their normal lives. Statistics have not yet been released indicating their numbers, but combined figures for both Roman Catholic and Protestant missionaries and some business men number from three to four hundred souls. At least fourteen of my friends have been imprisoned for periods ranging from five days to well over three years. One of them, imprisoned since January 1951, is still unreleased as I write these lines.[1] Eight of us were confined in the prisons of Chungking during 1951. A ninth is now there and may have been brought to Chungking during the same year.

Each of these prisoners has probably had reactions somewhat similar to mine during his or her period of confinement. Some imprisonments have certainly been more difficult and few, I suspect, have been easier than mine. There are those who have reported being shackled by the hands or feet or both, who were tortured in various ways. There is evidence, as reported in *The China Bulletin* (a newsletter published by the Division of Foreign Missions NCCC/USA in New York City), that one,

---

1 Dr. Allen was probably writing in 1954.

Dr. William Wallace, was bruised by beating and killed, perhaps unintentionally. There is more than a suspicion that his body was hung by the
neck with strips of torn sheets to make it appear a case of suicide to those
called upon to view the body.

When I was led to confinement, I expected to be sent to the type of
local prison I had seen in 1940 and 1941, where prisoners lay on the dirt
floor in part of an unfurnished room barricaded off from the remainder
by a glorified picket fence. The ragged, dirty prisoners had little bedding
and the strong ammoniac odour of stale excreta permeated and polluted
the dank atmosphere. Rats and other vermin entered freely and overran
the prisoners at night.

Anticipating this, I asked Ian Robb to send me bedding and a single
change of full-length woollen underwear. As it turned out, however, Rev.
Olin Stockwell, Brother Pretat and I were taken to relatively superior
quarters. This is not to say those squalid conditions did not exist in
Chungking or elsewhere in China.

One friend, a single woman missionary imprisoned in Honan, reported
that she, a single male missionary and a young married couple had been
placed together in a single dirt-floored room that lacked adequate—let
alone separate—toilet facilities.

Another friend, Frank Cooley of the Y.M.C.A. and minister of the
Student Centre at Shapingpa, was imprisoned in Chungking on October
18, 1951. He reported being placed in a four-by-seven-foot cell. It had a
twelve-foot high ceiling and a fourteen-inch-square barred window, walls
of stone or plaster and a floor of thick planking two inches above the dirt.
Its door had a slit for observation or passing food in to the prisoner. Cooley
wrote:

> I was not supposed to wash the body, but I often risked scolding from
> the guard by washing myself with a teacup from the pint of boiling water
> provided after the noon and evening meals. Not being able to wash
> adequately was one of the unpleasant parts of the experience. Once a
> day I was taken out for three minutes, in front of a fixed bayonet, to
> empty the slop jar provided in my cell. I had a cell to myself, or to put
> it another way, I was in solitary confinement. Three rice bowls and
> chopsticks were provided, no furniture whatsoever. Some cells contained
> as many as five prisoners.

For three weeks he remained in this condition, catching pneumonia
for which he eventually was treated with sulpha drugs. Then he was given
his Bible, previously refused, other reading material and a pencil and

paper from his baggage. Sometimes it was light enough during the day to read. Lights were on at night when reading was forbidden.

Cooley and my friend in Honan were classified as criminals from the beginning of their incarceration. That point should be emphasized when comparing their accommodation with that given to Stockwell, Pretat and me. We three were undergoing preliminary investigation. This latter category officially gave us a certain status denied to already condemned prisoners. While the first room in which I was placed was not pleasant, I at least had a bed. (The guard advised me very early in my stay it was wise not to take a daily nap, as it might interfere with sleeping at night—a good idea perhaps, but he underestimated my desire to keep warm, as well as my capacity for sleeping.)

The rooms that Stockwell, Pretat and I were moved to in mid-January were newer, better lighted and much more pleasant. They may not have been as comfortable as our own homes, but the walls were of plaster on brick and the floors of varnished wood. Theoretically we were in solitary confinement. However, during the winter months and until nearly the end of May, I was able to watch what was happening in the world about me through the unpapered upper portion of my windows. I watched the Chinese prisoners (nine, at most) at their exercise in the courtyard below me. One very dejected individual whose head was always bent toward the ground was the picture of apathy. He had been admitted to a room below mine. During much of the first day doleful moans came from his room. Finally, a guard went to his door and vehemently ordered him to cease his noise immediately. He obeyed and we again returned to the peaceful routine of finding something else to occupy the lonely hours.

I watched the gradual reconstruction of parts of the property belonging to the Political Section of the Public Safety Department. A house nearby was cleared of its tenants, torn down and replaced with a kitchen to serve the department's large staff. It was completed by the first of April. Then the retaining wall was torn down and replaced and extended down the street to enclose another property, for what purpose I did not discover until June, when after a fourth move to a basement room we were permitted to make use of the courtyard. Then I saw that a huge cement tennis, volleyball and basketball court had been constructed to provide recreation for the staff, who never left the premises after their work, so tightly supervised were they. Rallies and other pep meetings were also held on this site. Last but not least some other buildings were torn down, excepting a latrine, and the whole converted to a staff shower. This was opened toward the end of June. Public funds were used unstintingly for these purposes. Government workers must have their needs attended to as never before in the past. The masses provided the money, but there was no reason why they should object to this use of taxes. Previous governments always used money to build for government, but this new magnanimous government's construction was for that newly-honoured group called "the people," even if the people never had the opportunity to use it.

In August as I was being transferred after eight months of solitary confinement to prison for a further two months, I discovered that what had been a filthy dirt road was now paved. Elsewhere, many other public properties had received extensive face-lifts during 1951. It seemed money was never lacking for government purposes.

On the street outside my solitary cell's windows, people constantly streamed past, especially at certain hours of the day. Here I watched smallpox vaccinations and cholera-typhoid inoculations being given. Some accepted, others did not. As the weather grew warmer, housewives did their washing and cooking on braziers on the verandahs opposite. A training centre for government cadres was held in a home opposite, and I spent many an hour listening to the teaching of political slogans and propaganda manoeuvres. At other times I listened for hours on end to groups marching or learning the various Communist dance movements to the dizzying monotony of regular drum beats—tum-tum, tum, tum. But worst of all were the frequent public demonstrations passing on the main street, out of sight but only a short distance away. The slogan shouting from these so vividly recalled my experiences of December 20th it took months before I could hear them with equanimity and maintain normal blood pressure. On Sundays and other special occasions the loud speakers were on and many were the political propaganda meetings broadcast for the edification of the public—and me. Many of these were markedly hysterical. Watching and listening to such events occupied many hours that otherwise might have been empty or dull.

Maintaining our physical condition was very important to us, and that was dependent on our diet. All of us were accustomed to frequent meals of Chinese dishes, and some Catholic missionaries ate only Chinese food. But few Protestant missionaries were in the habit of eating that diet three times a day, week after week or month after month. A few of our missionaries had advocated this policy of living *à la Chinois*. Most believed such a policy unwise because they did not think a strict Chinese diet would maintain adequate health and resistance against the many widespread infectious and contagious diseases in China. Already, as a physician, I had noted serious dietary deficiencies in the missionaries in Chungking during the later years of the Second World War. Many were financially crippled by the gross disparity between the rate of exchange of foreign currencies and the purchasing power of the dollar and could not afford food for a proper diet. Here, during my confinement, was a first-hand opportunity to test the result of a prolonged local diet. To this end I was careful to observe the quantity and quality of our food over a more than ten-month period.

Breakfast was a special concession to us as foreigners. We each received about six ounces of scalding milk of excellent quality and at first two pieces of dry toast. Sharp at noon we received a dinner as good as that fed to a few of the more responsible individuals and families who ate on the premises. The underlings and guards had their meals at a Buddhist temple until the new kitchen was opened. Our noon meal consisted of two or three small bowls of steamed rice, with small helpings of four vegetables. Two of these servings contained bits of chopped meat, egg or eel, very occasionally fish or chicken. A bowl of soup containing bits of vegetable, liver, blood sausage or egg washed down the meal. Supper about five o'clock was a similar meal. Usually the food was tastily prepared, adequately spiced, with onions, leek and garlic the main flavouring. The only faults we could find in the quality of the diet were its undesirable proportion of local vegetables with low nutritive, mineral and vitamin values and its insufficient protein. Far more serious was the inadequate quantity of food. We were given the same amount received by the average Chinese, but Olin Stockwell and I each weighed at least fifty percent more than our Chinese brothers. Long before the next meal was due we were hungry and actually perishing from the lack of sustenance. Brother Pretat, on the other hand, was a smaller man of about 135 pounds, so he fared a little better in this respect. He realized that both of us were gradually losing weight on our diets and when he could, he courteously took the smallest helping of the three servings brought to us.

The old Lunar New Year, a feast day for the Chinese, fell in the first week in February. That morning Olin surprised Brother Pretat and me by bringing into our rooms, with permission of the guards, a large basket of oranges and handing fourteen of them to each of us. Never was fruit so eagerly received as that morning. Delighted, I spoke to him in Chinese. This was the first opportunity I had had to speak to him openly in more than six weeks, although we had been communicating secretly at the latrine for some time, as I will describe later in this chapter. I asked him to convey my thanks to his wife, whom I suspected had sent this gift. He promptly informed me he had made the purchase himself. This bit of information was quite the best news I could have received. Later in the day, when both of us were at the latrine, I mentioned how lucky he was to have money. When imprisoned I had had currency equivalent to about $2.50 Canadian, but I had already used some to buy a wash basin and a large enamel cup, items not provided by the government for its guests. There had been so much difficulty in getting these it had not occurred to me that other articles, especially edible ones, might be bought. Olin informed me that not only did he have enough money on his person but he also had a large cheque that could be cashed when needed. As soon as he had a chance, he secretly passed me the equivalent of five dollars. My first purchase was a kilogram of shelled peanuts with which I treated my fellow prisoners. Brother Pretat, also in holiday mood, provided a variety of Chinese biscuits for us. From that time onward we each made purchases, through the guards, of oranges, candy, peanuts and dried spiced meat in moderate quantities, which helped greatly in alleviating our hunger pangs. Still, we continued to lose weight. Late in February, Brother Pretat was taken from his cell and we never saw him again.[2]

About this time, after the investigations had eased off somewhat, I had an informal visit one evening from Investigator Chu. He wanted to know all about tuberculosis, and I finally discovered he was worried not only about himself but also about the personnel of the Political Section. After I had given him all the advice I could, we chatted together informally for a short time. Unwisely I had left the receipt for my kilogram of peanuts lying on the table. This finally caught his eye. Picking it up he thoughtfully perused it and then asked its meaning. I explained it was a holiday purchase and each of us had treated the others to something. He made no comment but resumed his chatting.

When he rose to leave he tried to give me a bit of advice, the same he had given me many times before: "Think, think, think about your faults and then confess them all to us. When you do that adequately we will

---

2 After my release from solitary confinement, I learned that Brother Pretat had been taken to the Chungking Municipal Prison before being deported to Hong Kong about July 1951.

release you." I replied that I had thought over my problems very carefully, that I had already confessed all the faults of which I was aware, and that I was not the kind of individual they thought me to be. Then I asked if it would be possible to write a very short letter to my wife to let her know that I was well. I had not expected to receive permission to do so, but I was interested to hear his reply: "Not just yet. I think your wife will be much happier to get a letter later on stating that you are away from here." With that terse comment he left.

Meanwhile, Olin and I continued to lose weight. I was also losing strength. As the weather became warmer the fifteen-minute periods of exercise we had been allowed after each meal were reduced to only twice a day and later to only once. These became more tiring and after climbing the two flights of stairs to our rooms I was short of breath for longer than normal. About this time, I found I could not control my emotions. The first breakdown occurred during one of the many interrogations we were forced to endure. On several other occasions in my own room I suddenly broke into tears for no apparent reason. Then one Sunday morning without warning I had an attack of cardiac irregularity and dropped heartbeats. It lasted for about two hours and was relieved by rest.

For some reason unknown to me, Comrade Wu appeared at my door one morning in the beginning of March, a few days after this episode. I happened to be reading while munching a few of the peanuts I now used to supplement my breakfast of hot milk and bread, the toast having been deleted as a luxury some weeks earlier. He was as surprised to find me eating as I was to receive his visit. He had come to me privately once before, asking for medical advice for treatment of Job's ailment, an eruption of inconveniently located boils that were causing him great discomfort. On that occasion he had asked if I would give him the required injections and "guarantee that there would be no untoward results." I said I would be glad to give these if that was his wish, but "I would not guarantee anything. Practitioners of foreign medicine never guaranteed they could cure patients or prevent complications." I was not going to take the chance of using a needle that someone in his group might have sterilized inadequately. Taking the hint, he found treatment elsewhere. I had not seen him since then.

"What and why are you eating? Have you not had your breakfast?" he asked curtly.

I explained my reasons, and without further comment he turned and left the room. A day or two later, on our usual purchasing day, part of my request was brought but peanuts were missing. The guard stated he could not get any. Next morning I again asked for peanuts, placing the required money in his hand. It was taken away but was brought back by the head of the guards. There were to be no more purchases of peanuts.

In a few days Wu had determined on a course of action and came again to my room. As usual, a guard was in attendance, since no interview could be held between a prisoner and others without a witness. Business-like, he lost no time in preliminaries.

"Liang Tseng-luen, I want you to be quite frank tonight. Tell me exactly what you think of your living conditions."

A direct question demands a direct answer, if possible. I had nothing to lose by being frank, but still my reply was guarded until I understood why he was asking such an innocent-sounding question.

"Respecting our living quarters and furnishings I have nothing to say. We are living in the same kind of rooms and using the same kind of furnishings as you and your comrades. Likewise we are eating the same kind of food as you, except for the morning meal of bread and milk. While we are receiving such treatment we cannot complain. But there is one matter I believe you have overlooked in your consideration for us. Those who are responsible for our food have forgotten that the comrades weigh on average 120 pounds, while we weigh about 180 or 190 pounds. We are receiving the same quantities as you. This situation cannot continue indefinitely. See?" Here I pulled up my sleeve and grasped the loose skin of my arm from which the underlying fatty tissue had largely disappeared. "This is how much weight I have lost in the past two and a half months. We must have more food but we need not have better food. Personally, I am satisfied with its quality."

He listened patiently. Outside of the interrogation room he was an easy person to talk to. Sometimes a smile would even crease his usually expressionless face.

Then he passed on to other things, trying to persuade me to tell the truth about the charges against me. For a long time we talked back and forth. Finally I told him very plainly: "I have always tried to tell you the truth every time I am asked a question, but to me it seems as if the more I try, the more unwilling you and Comrade Chu are to accept my statements. I have no interest in lying to you or to anyone else. I have no gross or serious faults to hide. There is no good reason why I should be held here indefinitely for more investigations since I have already told you all I know."

Changing the subject, he said, "Liang Tseng-luen, when you said some time ago that you wished to be sent home to Canada, did you really mean what you said?"

In all honesty I had to reply, "No, I have no wish to go home at all. What I would like to do is to prove to you people that I am neither the oppressor, collaborator nor spy you believe me to be. I would like to return to our hospital and continue working with my colleagues there where I believe I can be of assistance to them and to the Chinese people. If you will not believe me to be an honest man and insist that I am a spy, which I am not, then I have no option but to return to Canada."

Then he made an interesting proposition. I had heard of it but never expected to avail myself of it, for in the acceptance one in reality admitted one's guilt and condemned oneself beyond recourse.

"You may not know that you have the choice of suggesting your own punishment for what you have done. What then is your suggestion that it shall be?" asked Comrade Wu.

Even at this point I tried to play along with my investigators and answered, "I am aware of your procedure. Personally I feel that in my circumstances about three months here should be quite enough time for any transgressions I have made against your government and I should be released as soon as possible to proceed to Canada as a free man. Or if the hospital needs my services, I will continue my duties there, for I believe I have succeeded remarkably well with most of its staff members."

At this last remark Wu laughed. "Do you really think they would have you back again after they have made so many accusations against you? And do you realize that three months is only ten days away? Do you really think that would compensate for all your faults: your deliberate attempts to harm our officials; your statements against our government; your oppression of many people in the hospital; your concealment of supplies that belonged to our government; your assistance to the wife and family of a counter-revolutionist? Do you think that period would suffice to repay all these and other charges that have been laid against you?"

Wishing to make it appear that I considered these charges less serious than Comrade Wu thought them, I replied without the least flicker of an eyelid, "A maximum of six months should be entirely adequate for all practical purposes." Long before this time I had roughly calculated the possibility of six months to a year before I could free myself from their clutches. Voicing my opinion to Comrade Wu that half this anticipated period was acceptable to me could not make matters worse than they were. Perhaps he might even accept my suggestion at face value. However, he left, saying no more.

The following morning, just after our return from our daily quarter of an hour's exercise, the captain of the guard came to my room and asked me to tell him exactly what was wrong with our food. What changes did I wish to have made either in quantity or quality? It was clear he had been sent as a result of my interview with Comrade Wu the previous evening. Perhaps, after all, he really was adopting an unnatural fierceness during interrogations, for certainly he now seemed determined to give us his assistance through his intermediary.

Briefly I stated what I believed were our minimum requirements. I did not desire a change from the milk and bread for breakfast. For one thing we needed the vitamins from the milk and the smallish breakfast could be made up by increases in the other two meals. Olin, some months later, suggested a change to a larger volume of soybean milk instead of cow's milk and a large bowl of rice gruel in place of the bread, and to this I agreed. For lunch and supper I suggested as adequate quantities four small bowls of rice, instead of the previous two or a little more, at each meal and about double the amount of vegetables and meat we had been receiving. I asked for nothing more.

Promptly at noon that day in mid-March, for the first time in almost four months for Olin and three months for me, we had all the food we could eat. From that day onward we had no special food problems while under the Political Section's jurisdiction. Fortunately for our health, there was another change early in April. The new kitchen being built under our eyes was opened. Since many of the comrades were from Shantung where they were accustomed to use flour rather than rice, we received hot steamed bread, the consistency of rather firm dumplings, for one of the meals. Instead of white rice, a much less milled variety with much higher vitamin B content was substituted. Thus our symptoms of vitamin deficiency, which was bordering on an acute form of beriberi, diminished considerably. Nevertheless our physical stamina gradually decreased due to the inadequate protein, vitamin and mineral content of our diet. Yet, it is a fact that we lived at least as well as our guards and, from what we saw of their food, sometimes fared better. This did not change until I was removed to the regular Chungking prison at the end of August. Olin, our able prison muse, produced limericks such as these about our food:

> We eat white rice, cooked to the minute
> With vegetables, and meat within limit.

> Soup with a savour
> An Oriental flavour,
> For the guard always sticks his finger in it.

> Onions do not smell like roses
> And leeks offend our western noses
> But in Chinese food
> They're very good
> Quite worth the risk of halitosis.

While it was all very well to crack jokes about the food, we had other problems to face in our prison life. Probably the matters of room temperature and washing facilities were the most difficult and serious. Our rooms were unheated and none of us had an abundance of clothing. Throughout January we all suffered to some degree from the cold. Occasionally I caught a glimpse of Olin with his blankets wrapped about his shoulders in order to keep warm. I used mine to wrap up my legs while sitting at my desk.

We were allowed one wash basin of cold water which we secured following our exercise periods and emptied twenty-four hours later along with our double-duty cuspidors. Again the muse states:

> When you are prison-wise,
> You must learn to economize.
> One basin of water
> Surely had oughter
> Wash face, clothes and floor—contrariwise.

In a forty-degree Fahrenheit room, it was not pleasant to take off one's clothing and use cold water to bathe. During the cold months, Olin had to wear his pyjamas constantly. I was more fortunate. Imprisoned a month later, I had come better prepared with full-length woollen shirts and drawers. We learned why the Eskimos sewed themselves into their clothes.

> A little smell
> And dirt as well
> Was better far
> Than to be froze.

Only once during the eight months of solitary confinement did we receive a hot bath. This occurred one warm March day. Each of us was taken in turn to a small outhouse containing a shallow iron *go* (a kind of wok) under which a fire is built and in which the Chinese do all their cooking, boiling of large quantities of water and the like. We were told to collect all our dirty clothing for boiling in the *go*. This we did eagerly and really had a clean-up afternoon. We stripped before the fire and used towels wrung out of the hot soapy water to get the equivalent of a hot-water bath. In June, when showers were installed, we were allowed to use them twice weekly or oftener. Olin, the irrepressible rhymer, wrote of this situation:

> Three months without bathing you stink,
> And clothing once white has turned pink,
> But why worry your head
> The jail is in red,
> So they ought to turn pink, don't you think?

Drinking water was adequate, brought two or three times daily in steaming kettles directly from the kitchen. On each occasion I filled a large enamel cup, holding about ten ounces, and the one free rice bowl made available to each of us. With careful use, this also provided enough water to brush my teeth.

Shaving was always a problem, for we were denied our razors. The guards decided when we were sufficiently uncomely. They themselves grew very little facial hair. Some at least did not appreciate our ability to do so and disliked our beards. As much as five weeks would elapse before they provided us with a razor blade and, what was even more delightful, hot water. Olin, determined to grow a beard, managed to avoid shaving on the first two occasions, after which he was finally ordered to remove what was about a three-month growth. I am certain the beards did not improve our appearance and indeed during their first two weeks of growth they were distinctly uncomfortable.

As barbers our guards were a signal failure. We started wondering whether we might not ask for a hairdresser to give us permanents. Just what two bald-topped men with hair becoming long and curly at the sides and back would have looked like in a few more months we never discovered, for at the end of five months (six for Olin) the guards finally decided we should have haircuts, and the flowing locks were shorn.

During the first weeks we were rarely offered a broom to sweep the floor and then only one so badly worn out it did hardly any good. In early February, just before the Chinese Spring Festival, formerly called the Lunar New Year, the Communists decided the whole building must be cleaned. A day or two before the event, in an effort to demean us they suddenly brought buckets of water, mops, wash cloths and dusters and ordered us to clean all wood and glass surfaces. This meant windows and their frames, doors and their sashes, and the wooden floors. The three of us set to work with a will, enjoying this opportunity to do something different. It happened to be a nice day and the water was not too cold. The improvement in our rooms was incredible. The grubby wooden floors now were shown to be varnished, save for those parts that had been worn bare by the passage of many feet. Twice a week thereafter, I made a habit of washing the floors before throwing out the morning water, thus keeping quarters respectable and clean.

Mending clothes also required some effort. Early in January I received, among other items, some darning wool and a suitable needle. I kept the latter for four months, but long before that time I ran out of wool. My requests for more wool were denied, and I grew desperate. Anticipating such an eventuality, I had carefully husbanded the string that had been tied around the packages we had purchased in previous months. The need for food purchases had lessened since our food allowance had increased, but we were still permitted to buy such necessities as soap, paper, ink and tooth paste. Finally I was reduced to ravelling the string until it could be threaded. Eventually my socks began to resemble sacking as the darned portions grew larger and larger. I still possess one such pair, which I occasionally display to an interested visitor.

We used all manner of tiny, insignificant means to while away the time. We recorded the passing days and checked the record on Sundays, which were markedly different, to correct possible error; we entered notes in such a manner as to convey no information to our guards; we checked the progress of the sun northward by the lengthening rays pouring through the window on the side wall until finally the beams were strong enough to provide a short sun bath.

Each portion of the day was carefully mapped out in a prearranged program that included watching the activities outside my window, until one morning a rain storm came from an unusual direction, flooding the floor of my third-floor room and soaking the paper on my windows so that it came off. The captain of the guard then discovered the window panes had been placed on the inside of the frame without benefit of putty. This called for prompt action. He rushed off, brought what appeared to be a putty-like material, and assigned me the task of setting the panes. Then came paper, which the guard insisted must come higher than my head. Thus cut off from viewing the outside I was more completely isolated than I had been for some time, but this period did not last long.

The weather became warmer, the cuspidor's scent stronger, and the unventilated room stifling. I stripped to my shorts one Sunday morning. Two days later, either out of malice or more probably to give us relief from the coming summer heat, the guards moved Olin and me to semi-basement rooms on the first floor. Mine was below the level of the ground behind it, as I soon discovered when other summer storms delivered their torrents of rain and a perfect flood of water flowed across the floor on each occasion. Here I spent three more months until the end of August. It was the coolest summer I had spent in Chungking since first arriving there in 1938.

This room had other advantages apart from its coolness. Outside the guards sat, and there they all ate their meals. We overheard their conversations, and on Sundays we heard snatches of radio programs from time to time. Sometimes Chinese, sometimes Russian music and even American jazz came through to us from Moscow, Peking or Chungking.

Our guards worked rotating shifts, new personnel appearing from time to time. Many of them were from eastern China, mainly from the provinces of Shantung, Hopei and Honan. It was easy to recognize them from their dialects. Occasionally a local Chinese was brought in for political or police training. Each guard carried a rifle slung over one shoulder, though some were provided with revolvers carried in holsters attached to their broad leather belts. Shod in leather boots, a far cry from the grass sandals provided before liberation, these government support-ers, male and female, were outfitted in ill-fitting, grey, cotton-filled, quilted uniforms for winter wear. The women in particular were most unattractive in this male clothing, an impression not helped by their not-too-well-kept straight, black, bobbed hair. With the entry of communism all the glamour and individuality of women's dress disappeared. No one bothered to give the women a second glance.

Except for the two or three guards assigned to watch us during our exercise period each day, most took almost no interest in us. Toward the middle of April, however, something happened. They suddenly appeared with drawn revolvers, closely escorting us each day as we went to empty our cuspidors. This period of intense watching over us we found decidedly unpleasant, but like all things it came to a close, for which I, at least, was most grateful. It was not likely the guns would be used against us, but we never knew when a finger too handy to a trigger might slip, with disastrous results.

Occasionally a guard would show himself to be friendly or even considerate, when he could do so without causing problems for himself. On the March afternoon when we were given our first hot bath I attempted to talk to the guard while I boiled my clothing in the *go*. He was a sociable fellow who would have enjoyed talking with me under other circumstances. I began the conversation by asking him where his home was. Instantly he put his hand to his lips warning me not to speak. Then he answered my question in typical Chinese fashion by tracing with his finger on the palm of his hand. He was under the strictest controls, yet he dared to be human when alone in my presence.

I remember two special occasions when another guard showed his friendly concern for me. One night, probably after one of the more severe examinations, I was unable to sleep. Only a light army sleeping bag and my McGill University sweater, suitably folded and placed to support the lumbar curvature of my back, cushioned my body as I lay on my bamboo frame. My bed was located in the corner immediately opposite the door. A hole had been bored in the door, and through this the guard could watch me any time of the day or night. (As explained earlier, the room was never dark. In fact, one prisoner facetiously remarked that "prison was like unto heaven for there was no night there.") Noting my restlessness the guard finally opened the door and came to my side to ask kindly if anything was wrong and to offer his help.

Another time, after I had received an inoculation of typhoid-paratyphoid-cholera vaccine, this same guard came to my assistance. Some of the vaccine must have been carried directly into my bloodstream, for after a very short time I was seized with a terrific chill. Piling on all the bed coverings and extra clothing available, I got into bed, but that night was agony. I had a high fever and a splitting headache. Our last drinking water for the day had been given about five o'clock in the afternoon. I was parched with thirst. Finally at my call, the guard came. Although it must have been midnight, he bestirred himself to find hot water for me, which he finally secured from a thermos flask belonging to Olin. This I emptied into a bowl and rationed as best I could until the fever abated toward morning. His kindness that evening was more than cursory and I gave him my special thanks at a later date.

The day following the inoculation, however, I had a run-in with an entirely different kind of guard. Still feeling unwell, I left my first meal almost untouched. This second guard gruffly asked why I did not eat, was the food not good or was there some other reason? His tone of voice implied he thought I was beginning a hunger strike. I assured him I was only temporarily indisposed, but he made no effort to relieve my discomfort in any way. The first guard had shown kind concern for my personal well-being, but the second thought only that I might be trying to resist their discipline.

Sundays were different both for us and our guards. Our breakfast of milk and bread was served about seven o'clock, followed about an hour later by our second meal, normally served at noon. Following this meal, all departed save for the skeleton staff left on duty. Most were free for the day and returned about four or five o'clock to serve supper. For us the day was always a long one and we were glad to see its end. Olin speculated about what the guards did during their free time but could only come up with another limerick:

> Sunday was a quiet day,
> Guards and staff were all away.
> Where they go
> We do not know,
> But not to church to sing and pray.

One summer Sunday I overheard an enlightening conversation between two guards outside my basement room. One was a newcomer whom the senior guard was instructing in the theory and practice of communism. At first I paid little attention as I paced my 120-square-foot room for what exercise one could get in so small a space. But as the senior guard repeated one phrase I stopped near the door, under the open transom, to listen just a little more carefully.

"Remember, this business of ours is a world problem, not just something happening here in our China. We are out to win the world and some day all the world will become comrades with us." This was the point he intended to impress upon his pupil, for in true Communist style he repeated this sentence so many times in one form or another it could not fail to penetrate the densest human skull.

The Communists' sense of mission is equal to that of the most ardent Christian missionary. God-fearing people who try to deal with the threat of communism and its ideology of false gods must understand and fear the missionary zeal of communists. Communists are taught that not even the sacrifice of life itself is too dear when the all-encompassing faith of communism is in any way threatened with extinction.

As prisoners we had no illusions about our guards. We knew they took their duties seriously and would brook no nonsense from their prisoners. Nevertheless, the most anticipated period of the day was our exercise time, not so much for the chance to exercise as for the opportunity to communicate secretly with one another. Though forbidden to talk, we managed to exchange a few discrete sentences if the guards happened to be looking away. We turned the lavatory building into our communication centre, for although it was under the scrutiny of the guards it was also sunk five feet below ground level. It was here I received my first written message, from Brother Pretat. He wrote that he was concerned about how to pay for his lodging in the government prison, as well as his trip to Hong Kong.[3]

It was also in the lavatory that I began my written communications with Olin Stockwell. Olin fully expected to be released in late February or early March, after completing three months of confinement, and he had managed to convey that much to me during our snatched exchanges in the exercise yard. That expectation was responsible for the start of communications between us that continued at intervals during the remainder of my time under investigation. After the charge of alleged spying was made against me, I finally gained the courage to write the initial letter to him. Believing he had a chance of early release, I informed him of my predicament. I told him the Communists did not believe my repeated assertions of innocence and I urged him, when free, to tell Bob Edwards or someone of our mission about the serious charges being laid against Bob and me. I also informed Olin early in February 1951 that I could see no hope of my own release in less than six months and that probably a year might elapse before I was given my freedom. Olin appeared to have the advantage.[4]

---

3 He might have saved himself the worry, for both his prison lodging and his trip to Hong Kong were paid for by the Chinese Catholic Church. After confiscating much if not all Catholic property, the Communists turned over such portions as were required by the Chinese Catholic Church for its use, and that money at least provided for the courtesy to Brother Pretat. Protestants were less fortunate. I, for one, paid for both the food I ate during my two months in the municipal prison and the costs to travel to the Hong Kong border.

4 In fact, Olin was doomed to disappointment. My release ultimately preceded his. After fourteen months in solitary confinement, he was sent to a counter-revolutionary prison several miles from Chungking. There he remained until November 1952, when his Communist teachers finally considered him fit for release. He arrived in Hong Kong later that month.

I expected long dreary months of confinement. My library had increased by only two books—a novel, *Captain Margaret*, and a copy of *Preoperative and Postoperative Treatment*, so I asked Olin if he had other books at his disposal or if, once free, he might secure and send in to me copies of the Bible and works by Shakespeare. He took my request to heart immediately. He wrote a letter to his wife, Esther, who was in Chungking awaiting his release, asking for these, but no answer came. Then he offered me his air mattress, thermos flask and wrist watch, the mainspring of mine having broken.

From that time on we kept up a steady, surreptitious correspondence, each fully acquainting the other with his situation. Olin soon discovered that other charges—false, of course—were still outstanding against him and he described them to me in March. He had been falsely accused of writing a letter containing a secret code. He did not know it, but the Communists were badgering his wife, outside prison, trying to extract incriminating evidence from her against her husband. This I discovered when I arrived in Hong Kong and could piece together both Olin's and Esther Stockwell's stories.[5]

Our messages were usually passed on the stairway while the guard was leading us out, or in the lavatory, or outside as we were emptying our receptacles. If one of us wished to pass a note to the other, he would signal the recipient to stand at the first emptying spot, facing the guard, who could not see us below our waists. Then the giver could slip his note into the recipient's back pocket. We fumbled a few times but were never caught, though on one occasion I am certain the guard must have seen me put my hand over a gate. Without question he was suspicious, for the guard was immediately tightened and temporarily we had to use extreme care.

Getting these messages written in the first place was much more difficult than passing them. We never knew when guards might stealthily

---

5 Esther Beck Stockwell describes this incident in her book, *Asia's Call* (Stockwell Press, San Francisco). She writes that "Lucy" from the Foreign Affairs Bureau once brought a paper with numbers, dots and dashes and asked her what it meant, whether it was an embroidery pattern or a code such as Mr. Stockwell used when writing to America. Mrs. Stockwell writes that she denied both interpretations. Dr. Allen, in a report written in Hong Kong in January 1952, concludes that the "coded" letter was deliberately planted in Olin Stockwell's mail by someone who had access to his correspondence and wished to get him in trouble with the authorities. *Ed.*

approach their peepholes in our doors and watch us. On one occasion it seemed important to write a note that, if discovered, could have caused considerable trouble for me. To avoid being seen I took a book and placed the sheet of writing paper within it while I penned my message. I made certain I was out of the guard's line of vision and kept an ear cocked for footsteps. I was busily engaged when suddenly the key turned in the lock, the door flew open, and there stood one of our most feared guards. As brazenly as possible, in order to avoid rousing the suspicion that I might be doing something against instructions, I said, "What is the matter? What has happened? What do you want?" He made no reply at first, but he had one of the most interesting expressions I had ever seen on a Chinese face—a mixture of fear, bewilderment and relief at finding I was still in the room. He had clearly opened the door expecting the room to be empty, since I was nowhere in view. My disappearance would have caused him very serious difficulty. Obviously relieved, he said quietly, "Perhaps in future you had better stay out in the middle of the room where you can be seen." Apparently he was so relieved that he suspected nothing further.

Early in our communications, Olin was eager to learn the latest December news, now two months old. He was particularly anxious to discover what had happened to his two missionary associates, Luella Koether and Janet Surdam. Both women had been under suspicion. Indeed both had had a difficult time with the authorities, who forced them to study Communist dialectics and propaganda daily. The last I had heard was that they were about to return to their homeland, the United States. Yet for some months of our confinement, Olin and I had noted one peculiar, inexplicable, almost daily occurrence. While we were exercising, a certain door leading to the exercise ground was always kept closely watched. Only on the signal that all was well were we ordered back to our rooms. After my return to Canada I learned the secret: both Luella and Janet had come to Chungking en route home and had been arrested and placed in rooms on one of the two floors below us. One of them caught sight of us once. Seeing five cups of milk brought regularly, they guessed correctly that three male prisoners—ourselves—were keeping them unwitting company. The charges against them, among others, were collaboration with the American spy, F. Olin Stockwell.

Time passed and Olin and I continued indulging in our clandestine correspondence. He began sending me a series of crossword puzzles he had created. I provided the answers, which I often noted were not at all complimentary either to the Communists, to the conditions under which we lived or to the guards. At the time, I detected what I thought was a trace of bitterness. This may have been all in my imagination, however, for in his writings penned in prison and published following his return home to Chicago there is anything but a note of depression.

After the puzzles, a series of some forty of his limericks came to my hands. Some, such as the samples above, were humorous, but others were in quite the opposite vein. When the guards discovered he was making these puzzles and poems, transmission had to cease. Then to while away the time I composed my own.

Olin also had a few books which he passed to me. He had managed to bring with him a dog-eared volume of Moffatt's translation of the *New Testament*. I borrowed it for three weeks, reading it from cover to cover many times. That, together with my medical books, Elizabeth Goudge's 1936 novel *A City of Bells,* Dr. Carpenter's *Paraphrase to the Book of Philippians* and Stanton A. Coblentz's *The Music Makers,* an anthology of over a hundred pieces of verse, formed our library until mid-July, when I received a welcome addition of several copies of the *British Journal of Surgery,* two recently published volumes of the noted orthopedist Dr. Jones (*Surgical Diseases of the Bones and Joints* and *Surgical Operative Procedures*), and a government issue edition of *The Loon Feather,* a delightful best seller. This latter volume I left with Olin on the day I departed in August. I hope it was given to him to brighten the months of solitude he must have endured until January 1952, when he was transferred elsewhere.

As long as we could command a sense of humour under our living conditions, life was not too difficult. But that sense of humour was put to the test when, as the days grew warmer, we discovered we were not as solitary as we had supposed. Our new companions began pouring from the beds and walls, and hunting these insects became an absorbing pastime.

One night, my suspicions about the permanence of my bed proved well founded. Bamboo furniture made at certain seasons of the year tends to become worm eaten and finally collapse. My bed was no exception to the rule. One midnight while heaving myself from one side to the other, I heard the terrific sound of splintering bamboo. I landed on the floor in a shower of bamboo dust. Immediately there were shouts from the guard below, who tore up the two flights of stairs demanding to know what had happened. I told him it was nothing serious, but he went off to get help, for he was not sure. His courage bolstered by two others, he then flung open the door. In the dim light stood a short, trembling guard with a drawn revolver, followed by his partners similarly armed. I laughed the matter off to put them at their ease. Seeing I was making no serious attempt to do anything foolish, one of them departed to find me another bed.

Eventually my second bamboo bed suffered the fate of the first, only to a more serious degree. I was ordered to throw the whole on the scrap heap, which I was thrilled to do, since its insect inhabitants were many. To ensure that no further furniture collapsed under my weight, my guards gave me a huge frame of solid wooden boards, one-and-a-half inches thick, to place on two heavy trestles. Although the bamboo bed had seemed hard, these boards yielded not in the least. By this time I had been moved to my basement room. Meanwhile I had developed a neuritis of the right shoulder, which constantly gave trouble so that ultimately I had to forego using that arm and hand for such work as washing the floor. Many were the nights when between my painful arm and the pressure of the various bony parts on the hard wood bed I was most uncomfortable.

Along with the first replacement bed had come a piece of wire, which the bed's former occupant had used to probe for bedbugs. From then on the hunts and the slaughter increased daily. But alas, the use of that wire ceased one day, the result of the visit of an inquisitive guard. He was looking through one of my medical books, which was profusely illustrated with intriguing pictures of operative procedures, when he discovered my darning needle. Shocked that I had such a thing in my possession, he demanded to know where it had come from. I said the guard had given it to me and then failed to ask for it back. Indicating this was a most dangerous weapon to leave about, he said he must take it away and would only return it when I needed to use it. That put him on the lookout for other secreted objects, and one day, as I was busily digging out bedbugs, he opened the door and took a second weapon from me, the dangerous piece of wire I had found attached to my bed. Just what damage I could have done with three inches of copper electric wire or a needle I do not know, apart from possibly opening a vein or some such foolish move.

Fortunately, the guard did not think to look further, so he did not find several other small pieces of wire another guard had given me earlier in my confinement. Walking downstairs to the exercise yard that spring day, I was carrying a wash basin of dirty water in one hand and a full cuspidor in the other. Suddenly, the two ends of my plastic belt parted company. Holding up my trousers while using both hands to carry my load was not easy. When I started back to my room, I put my hands in my pockets and thus managed to carry my washing water and control my sliding trousers at the same time. Safe in my room I explained my predicament to the guard and asked how I might mend my belt. Obligingly he brought an instrument to pierce holes in the belt, pliers and a length of copper wire. In half an hour I had repaired the belt well enough to last until I was able to buy another in Hong Kong eight months later and still had several wire clippings left over. Every prisoner knows that such things may have their uses. Those wire clippings, several inches long, like the string which came to us on our parcels, were set aside for emergencies. Interestingly enough, nobody thought of the possible fatal use to which string could have been put. I for one had quite enough to hang myself had I so desired, but I never entertained such thoughts.

Though my basement room was cool, it had no view and the sun never shone in it. But I did not discover its most serious drawback until one day when the sky darkened and a deluge of tropical rain poured from the heavens. The rear wall of my room, although of cement, became a veritable sieve through which a stream of water percolated. The next few hours I spent on my bed until the storm withdrew. It was while contemplating the rising waters on the concrete floor, my legs dangling idly over the edge of the third and hardest bed, that I made my discovery.

I felt some irritation at the back of my knee and on investigation found it covered with many bedbugs. Like the first two beds, this frame, presumed to be fresh, was also inhabited. A search soon revealed the insects' rendezvous was the set-in cross bar holding the frame together. They had emerged when the rising flood waters threatened their home. From that day onward, I whiled away many hours engaged in battle with the bedbugs. Using my thumb as bait, I lured the attackers from their den one after another and killed them with the wire. While outside the Communists were waging their war against the landlords in the Land Reform Program, in which close to two million people are known to have lost their lives, I was enjoying my private massacre. I kept accurate records on the plastered wall, using a nail that had somehow come into my possession. By August 27, 1951, when I was transferred to the prison attached to the Chungking Law Courts for final official trial and arraignment, my records showed 656 killed, none wounded.

In such trivial ways we were forced to occupy much of our time. Try as we might, it was not easy to fill increasingly long and tedious hours with constructive thought and activity. Thus are those with weaker minds reduced to the point where they are prepared to accept almost any conditions to better their circumstances. Literally hundreds of foreign missionaries and members of the business community, together with millions of Chinese, both Christian and non-Christian, have passed through experiences similar to or worse than those I have described. That none of the foreigners subjected to these indignities (except possibly Dr. William Wallace) suffered gross mental aberrations because of their experiences is a tribute to the intrinsic stability of their characters and their powers of endurance. How our faith helped fortify us for these ordeals I shall now try to explain.

Chapter 11

Faith

Your living is determined not so much by what life brings to you as by the attitude you bring to life; not so much by what happens to you, as by the way your mind looks at what happens. It may be that this cross which you are now bearing is the means by which you may come to know a closer and better relationship with life and with God who makes all things possible.

AUTHOR UNKNOWN

S HORTLY AFTER MY RETURN to Montreal, Canada, in February 1952, I found the above words printed in our church's weekly bulletin. They express the very essence of the attitude of the missionaries who remained in China, hoping their presence might favourably influence the Chinese under the new Communist regime. These words were also true for the ordinary American prisoners of war who suffered so severely under their captors, the North Korean and Chinese Communists. In press dispatches printed when the first prisoners of war were released, certain unnamed individuals voiced their conviction that in their severe trials God made his presence felt in a very personal way.

Missionaries tended to have more individualistic, intense and deeply spiritual reactions under the severe strain they experienced while awaiting their unknown fate, whether in prison or not. Most of the imprisoned missionaries who understood communism and its methods even slightly realized that the confessions the Communists wanted to hear would eventually be forced from them to some degree before they could expect release. How quickly an individual appreciated this aspect of his situation as he went along with the Communists as much as he dared was a definite factor in securing earlier release. At least one particularly stubborn individual is still in the hands of the Communists more than three years after the start of his incarceration in January 1951.[1] He must confess to those things demanded by the Communists before he can be released. It is no easy thing for a missionary to confess falsely that he is guilty of espionage. Nevertheless, no final clearance is possible without confession of some kind and no other path to freedom is open to him. Depending on the conditions used by the Communists in the area where he is incarcerated this may be a long-drawn-out procedure.

It must not be concluded that only those individuals confined to prison had special problems to face. All those who were held in China from at least the beginning of 1951 had to wait long weeks or months until official permission to secure exit visas was granted. All that time, they were reluctant to enter into the life of the community or were prevented from doing so by being placed under house arrest. Those who voluntarily separated themselves from the surrounding community did so to avoid inconveniencing or endangering their Chinese friends, who inevitably were investigated if they had contacts with foreigners.

A correspondent in East China wrote me on March 5, 1954, with news of a Chinese woman I had asked after, saying, "I was not able to contact her but did it through some Eurasian friends. I wish I could see her personally but that is impossible these days."

Similar isolating conditions were mentioned by another correspondent, the Chinese widow of a Swedish merchant, whose daughter, Ingeborg Andersen, was a naturalized Canadian. The widow, who suffered from crippling arthritis, had waited almost two years before being allowed to leave Chungking for Hong Kong. Previously befriended by all because she was a sweet and generous woman, she wrote that in Chungking "people did not come to see me probably because they were afraid to do so."

Isolated from former friends and often from each other, foreigners remaining in China had to find other sources of help and companionship. For many this help came from their faith in God. The words of Dr. Joseph G. Sutton, superintendent of the Essex County Mental Hospital in Cedar Grove, New Jersey, seem particularly apt in describing what happened to

---

1 Dr. Allen is probably referring to a Conservative Baptist missionary, Lee Lovegren, known to be still in prison in March 1954.

people like me in China: "I believe a person with strong religious beliefs has something that will sustain him longer than a person who has not. Someone who has a cause greater than himself undoubtedly will not break as soon as one who lacks it."

Hugh W. Hubbard was a missionary friend of mine who left Chungking late in the spring of 1950 to live in the vicinity of Peking. There, however, he was detained under house arrest until the end of 1951, around the time I too was released. In his first letter after release, written on April 1, 1952, while en route to Hong Kong by ship, he described his long period of house arrest with his wife, as well as the general situation, things he had not dared to mention while still in China. He named people under house arrest and others in prison. He also described the rising anti-American feeling:

> The propaganda against America is unbelievably terrific. . . . No Chinese can afford to appear friendly to any American in public. No Chinese friends dared to say goodbye or see us off at Tunghsien or Peking station, or Tientsin wharf, though many did in private when they could. Every American is under suspicion as a potential, if not probable, spy.

Hubbard's revealing letter ends with a statement that echoes the words of many who have left China:

> Yet in the midst of these events that sadden the heart and at times fill it with mighty wrath, the last fifteen months of waiting have been—you will find it hard to believe—good months for us personally. Never has God seemed so real, so near, so comforting, and loving.

A second friend, Frank Cooley (mentioned in the previous chapter), who continued working at the Y.M.C.A. and as a minister at the Student Centre at Chungking University until some months after liberation, was arrested without warning on September 18, 1951, and held in prison for fifty days, then released to be escorted to the Hong Kong border. In a letter dated August 5, 1952, he described how after three weeks in solitary confinement with nothing to do, he was given his Bible, Augustine's *Confessions* and paper and pencil:

> During these next weeks I found the study of [Saint] Paul's letters particularly helpful and stimulating, especially the prison epistles! . . . I will only say that this was a precious time for me, a time during which I was repeatedly blessed of God richly with more than enough patience, faith, strength and grace. I am grateful to Him and to the Chungking Military Control Commission for putting me to the test, slight tho it was,

for the results in my life, I believe, have proved very worthwhile. I wouldn't exchange those weeks for any others in my life.

I had one fleeting glimpse of Frank on November 8, 1951, the one day he was in the same Chungking hotel where I was awaiting deportation after my release from prison.[2] He looked an unkempt, long-haired, bearded individual such as only comes from a Chinese prison. He wrote me on September 21, 1952, that "my heart soared when I saw you in that hotel in Chungking. When I got back to my room and closed the door, I just literally jumped up and down singing for joy!"

I need not continue quoting the faith-strengthening experiences of others, since this would mean describing one for everyone detained in China from 1951 through 1954, when almost the last of the missionaries were released. I cannot pass on to my own experiences, however, without mentioning again my fellow prisoner, Rev. Olin Stockwell. While imprisoned and in solitary confinement he wrote a book, *With God in Red China*, which contains a great deal more than I would have considered putting into writing under such conditions. In this he tells of his experiences, but something he has omitted I feel should be told, since he, like me, is now, enjoying highly-valued freedom in a country where people can think, speak and act within the law without fear. I have mentioned we started a secret correspondence that kept each informed of the other's main problems. In reply to my first letter he wrote something like this:

> If the ordeal does not last too long, I am most grateful to God that he has put me into prison, for in these [twelve] weeks I have come to know God as I have never known him in the past. He is here with me always. I have been able to write the skeleton of a book of prayers, about forty of them, which I shall entitle *From a Chinese Prison Window*. They are replete with Chinese illustrations. Further, I have been able to study my New Testament with a new insight such as I have not had in the past. Things which formerly I did not comprehend, now I have been given, by God's grace, to understand.

Imagine anyone being grateful for being put into prison. That is what both Frank and Olin have said independently of each other.

---

2 Dr. Allen's experiences at this hotel are described in Chapter 14. He was not permitted to talk to any fellow foreigners while staying there.

I have always hesitated to reveal my personal thoughts about my own spiritual experiences. The Scriptures tell us to enter a closet privately and there have our devotion alone with God. That aloneness was given to Olin and me for long hours each day, week after week, month after month. But even though we were at times reduced to the activities mentioned in the last chapter in order to pass the time, it was rarely that I could truly say the hours dragged unduly. No more than once or twice did I spend a sleepless night, and on one of those I was ill. For someone whose days had been filled to the brim with hospital duties and whose evenings had been spent completing correspondence, I suffered very little from my enforced inactivity. The reason was that I, too, came to realize how very close God was to me.

I first sensed this closeness immediately after returning to my room in a torment of anguish following the Political Court's preliminary investigation the night of December 22. I paced my cell, seeking consolation and peace of mind. Gradually, as I tried to subdue my turbulent thoughts, a verse from the hymn "In the Cross of Christ I Glory" came to me and I marvelled at how appropriate it was on that occasion:

> When the woes of life o'ertake me,
> Hopes deceive, and fears annoy,
> Never shall the Cross forsake me
> Lo! it glows with peace and joy.

After spending a further hour in quiet song, I prepared for a refreshing sleep to meet my future, whatever it might be.

As music played an important role in my prison experience, I should explain that from my youth until my late twenties, I had been interested in picking out tunes on an old family organ and learning snatches of sacred and operatic music to my own (if no one else's) satisfaction. My vocal practising ground was the family orchard in Naramata, B.C., where I yielded to my inmost feelings while tending the trees and gathering their fruits. Choirs and choral societies provided an outlet for this, my single special interest at that time. This interest extended through my years of study at the University of British Columbia, in Vancouver, and, later, McGill University, in Montreal, where I served as president of the Choral and Operatic Society and the Musical Association. In China this interest had waned to some extent. Yet now, in confinement, it was natural to find my expression in music.

The deep depression I felt on Christmas Day in prison, so alone and far from family, lifted only when I began to sing some Christmas carols, then "The Star of Bethlehem" and finally a special setting of "Jesus, Lover of My Soul." I started singing the second verse

> Other refuge have I none;
> Hangs my helpless soul on Thee;
> Leave, ah! leave me not alone;
> Still support and comfort me.
> All my trust on Thee is stayed;
> All my help from Thee I bring;
> Cover my defenceless head
> With the shadow of Thy wing.

but before I had completed the stanza, the full force and meaning of its words struck my consciousness. Many times I had sung this hymn. Familiarity had made me lose sight of the deep meaning it contained. But that Christmas, this hymn had a very personal meaning, as had the hymn I sang my first evening in the prison. I left the verse unfinished. With extreme clarity I saw that despite my predicament there was no need for the worry that had beset me the past three days. My family was fairly cared for at home. All I needed to do was to place myself fully in the hands of God and his Son, a Man crowned with thorns, whom his enemies had nailed upon a cross. He surely would carry me safely through every future trial.

My mind turned back the pages of the years until it stopped at another critical period of my missionary life, nearly twenty years earlier. In 1932 our hospital in Kiating had been filled with wounded soldiers, casualties of a series of conflicts between the warlords Liu Hsiang and Liu En-hwei. Every bed was filled with officers, while the men lay on straw-filled ticks scattered over the floor. There was just room enough left between patients for the doctor and orderly to change the dressings as necessary. When these ordinary soldiers were ordered to leave hospital for other parts, their commander paid the hospital charges. Officers were expected to pay their own accounts. Our hospitals always had difficulty collecting these charges from any of the military. One officer stated he was leaving on the same day as the soldiers, whose accounts had been already been settled by the commander. Unfortunately, the accountant was away from the hospital and I had to present the officer with his account. Not only did he refuse to pay but he defiantly pulled out a large roll of paper currency, transferring it from one pocket of his overcoat to another. Then from his bed he raised himself enough to deliberately strike me with his fist. Being young, angry and inexperienced in the ways of the Chinese, for no patient had ever done that before, I pushed him back into his bed, refusing permission for him to leave until his account was paid.

Desiring revenge, the officer dispatched certain friends to his commander. They falsely reported that I had refused to give permission for his soldiers to leave. Furious, and unaware of what actually had happened, the commander ordered the informants to teach me a lesson or two. They gathered a mob and went that afternoon to the hospital. Destroying chairs and benches and using the debris as clubs, they and others with rifle butts started to drive me backward up the hospital stairs. News of their plan had reached the ears of a local dignitary who dispatched one of his armed guards with instructions to see that I was not harmed. During the fracas this guard stood with drawn revolver close to my side as I parried the thrusts of rifle butts and clubs. It was a serious affair, the aftermath of which, when all facts were properly reported, caused the dismissal of the commanding officer. As for me, I decided never again to insist on payment from military officers. Better to lose the account than risk my own life. I also decided that if there was a possibility my life might become forfeit in the pursuit of my missionary activities, I should make suitable arrangements for the care of those I might leave behind. At that time, I settled once and for all the question of possible death and fear of death.

Now, alone in my cell and brought face to face with an uncertain future, I experienced an overwhelming feeling that the spirit of God was ever-present. From this I gained the strength, courage and confidence to conduct myself in a manner befitting a Christian missionary, with sufficient humility where necessary, never showing an outward trace of fear, keeping a serene countenance, leaving no possible opportunity for criticism of my attitude by my Communist contacts. I further gained the faith that all problems would be successfully resolved and that I would eventually be permitted to leave my chosen work and China without carrying away rancour or bitterness against those who had caused my arrest and imprisonment.

That never-to-be-forgotten Christmas experience shaped the entire coming year for me. Though not wishing to repeat such a loss of freedom, neither I nor any other imprisoned missionary has ever been heard to express regret for having been thus incarcerated. The democratic world owes a debt not only to us, the missionaries who were so unjustly imprisoned, but also to the many prisoners of war who have been held in Communist prison camps. Without the experiences we have had, the rest of the world could not know the nature of the ideology with which it has to deal. Now each of us knows the strength and character of the Communist forces that oppose us as a free democracy and as a Christian church.

But beyond this, our personal experiences have been such as to put new meaning into the words of the hymns we sing, the scripture we read and our sources of spiritual power. To us God came alive as we communed alone with Him through no intermediary. These are experiences we prefer to keep within ourselves rather than discuss openly. Yet, in prison, who could help but react strongly to such Bible verses as these, from Jeremiah, chapters 30 and 31?

> Why criest thou in thine affliction?
> Why mournest thou in nightly watches?
> Sing ye aloud with gladness.
> Thy mourning is turned into joy.
> For I the Lord am with thee and will save thee.
> I have loved thee with everlasting love and have
> redeemed thee.

It was during the first three months of confinement, when I was being interrogated, that I integrated into my own personality the message of the soul-inspiring music of the Christian church, from hymns to oratorios. The simpler songs learned in childhood and grand and stately works such as the tunes of Jerusalem ("And Did Those Feet in Ancient Time") and the Welsh Cwm Rhondda ("Guide Me, O Thou Great Jehovah") became part of my spontaneous daily singing. My repertoire contained great hymns such as "Abide With Me" and the many versions of the Twenty-third Psalm through to several magnificent oratorios, culminating in the emotionally thrilling Hallelujah Chorus from Handel's *Messiah*. While under the severe strain of the investigation period, I constantly turned to singing religious music, to the almost complete exclusion of secular songs, when other exercises palled and I needed additional physical activity.

Friends have asked, Did the guards not interfere with your singing? They did, just after I was removed to the fourth-floor cell, very early in January, and then again in the month of July. On the first occasion I had indeed become excessively exuberant and one of the more surly guards bluntly told me, in the suitable Chinese equivalent, to can the noise. On the second occasion, I was apparently interfering with the noon rest hour when some of the Political Section cadres and officials wished to take their cat naps. Usually I was discreet and sang only when it was most likely the guards were not nearby. Perhaps hearing my voice was evidence enough for them that I was still in my room, if it was not actually a factor in keeping them at a distance. Though not as dramatic, my singing reminded me of the night when Paul and Silas had sung in prison and an earthquake had opened the prison doors and unfastened their chains (Acts, 16:26). Olin wrote an amusing limerick along that line:

> Paul and Silas shook a prison of stone
> They sang so lustily of Christian song
> Oh me, oh my,
> I don't know why
> The Lord gave me no such baritone.

I soon began listing each new hymn as it was brought to mind, for I had neither musical scores nor hymnal for guidance. I had listed more than two hundred religious titles before the guards took away the book in which I had entered them. As the list grew longer, it became clear that most of them used the Cross as the central theme. It was logical that this should be so, but here, alone with my thoughts, my awareness of the image of the Cross intensified. In this I was not alone. One day, while exercising, I discovered that Olin, as he paced to and fro, was quietly whistling to himself "The Old Rugged Cross," a well-known hymn about the symbol of suffering and shame upon which Christ died for all mankind.

Reading was also an important activity during my solitary confinement. Although my original prison library consisted of only two or three books, it expanded when Olin began sharing some of his books with me. We will never forget the experience of reading, in his dog-eared New Testament, the Acts of the Apostles and the activities of Paul both in and out of prison, when we ourselves were in similar circumstances. Only in such a personal way could we and others similarly imprisoned or detained fully realize the trials and difficulties suffered by those who have carried Christianity down from its earliest days to the present. For me it was also more than a novel experience to read the whole New Testament from cover to cover, as one would read any other book. This I did a number of times in the three weeks Olin's volume was in my hands. (The guards were unaware it was a part of the Bible.) Thus we gained a new appreciation of the truly marvellous story it contains and the hope it gives to those who place their whole trust in it.

One day, by hand of the guard, Olin passed me the *Paraphrase of St. Paul's Epistle to the Philippians*, by Dr. Carpenter, Bishop of Exeter. In his inimitable manner, Carpenter paraphrases the letter as a twentieth-century Paul might have written it. Particularly meaningful to me was a passage about the Cross:

> Surprise is expressed sometimes that Christians think so much and speak so much about the Cross. Why drag it in? The answer is too long to set here in full, but in essence it is this. The Saviour came from heaven to destroy the works of the devil and to use no other means of doing so than the weapon of sheer love. That, in an ungrateful, devil-ridden world, means that suffering, the extremity of suffering, is inevitable. Christianity without the Cross would be unrecognizable. It must be added that just because it contains the doctrine of the Cross, Christianity fits life at all points. The cult of Apollo, young and beautiful, crowned with roses, may seem well enough for a day of spring and sunshine, but life is not all like that and the only thing which can take the poison and bitterness out of the suffering which is bound to come to all is the knowledge that God is there too, on the Cross, understanding it all, enduring it all.

Meditation, singing and reading filled many hours, but I also spent considerable time keeping a diary. Into the diary went many things, such as planning for my future medical and extra-professional work after release.[3] I copied into its pages Olin's sixty-two-page version of the New Testament, so that we might share in meditation on it. The diary also contained excerpts from a few other available books that seemed especially appropriate at the time, as well as seemingly irrelevant remarks intended to refresh my memory later but so written as to be meaningless to my captors. Eventually the diary, which I hoped to bring home with me, filled two large booklets, and included the more interesting poetry from *The Music Makers* by Stanton A. Coblentz and from Elizabeth Goudge's novel *A City of Bells*.

One other diary entry described a mystifying experience I was able to explain only after my return to Canada almost a year later. On a certain day in March, shortly after returning from our morning exercise, I strongly sensed, almost with the suddenness of being hit by a bullet, that something involving me had occurred in Canada. Immediately I feared that some

---

3 With minor modifications, that plan was fulfilled within a few miles of the location he anticipated. Dr. Allen began private practice in Cardinal, Ontario, on the St. Lawrence River, about thirty kilometres east of Brockville, where he was on the staff of two hospitals, Brockville General and St. Vincent de Paul.

member of my family at home had fallen ill or had some accident. But this impression did not satisfy me for long. All along, except in moments before sleeping, I had studiously avoided thoughts of my family on the other side of the globe. Pondering on them and their possible welfare was useless and could have been devastating in its effect on my morale. They would be well cared for during my enforced absence. The Communists strictly warned prisoners against thinking about their families. Their arguments were very much to the point: "The family cannot help you, nor can you assist them in any way. Your present business is to use this opportunity for study (indoctrination or 'brainwashing') so that you may be made a new man, fit once again to associate with society." On the day of that strong sensation, I made an entry to investigate what had happened that day, once I returned home. Surprisingly, I learned it was on that day the news of my imprisonment had been broadcast in both the Canadian press and the *New York Times* in the United States. All over the continent, in personal meditation as well as in public prayer, I was remembered by friends and fellow Christians. Any doubt I may have had about thought transference (of which I have experienced many less powerful instances) or the efficacy of prayer has been dispelled by my experiences during those eight months of solitary confinement.

April came. As the days passed and nothing happened, it seemed to me the interrogators had indeed listened to my refusal in late February to talk further on the subject of spying. If my calculations were correct, I had nine more months before a likely release. (As I mentioned in an earlier chapter, although I had told Comrade Chu my sentence should be no more than six months, I expected it to be closer to a year.) Olin, too, saw the days pass with no obvious sign of an early release for him. There were times when our spirits were far from lighthearted. Sometimes I saw traces of moisture about Olin's eyes, when the sun happened to touch his face at the right angle. As each month drew to an end, I could see he was making plans in anticipation of imminent departure. But each month passed without release and his apparent disappointment seemed deep, or at least I thought it did, since he had envisioned at most a three-month detention. At such times I did my best to indicate by a smile or solicitous words that hope was not yet dead. Likewise, Olin's account of his experiences tells of his concern for my position. There evidently were times when it appeared to him that I, too, was in the slough of despond. Thus each of us tried to help the other to bear his troubles in silence.

One of the reasons we tried to show the appearance of calm stoicism was to bear witness to the power of our faith. Initially, of course, every Christian prisoner had the same thought at heart. During the long months, Olin and I sought ways to bear witness to our strengthened faith. Olin expressed our concern aptly in another limerick:

> When in Rome, the apostle Paul
> Had guards and friends upon his call.
> But we have none;
> How under the sun
> Can we bear any witness at all?

"God moves in mysterious ways His wonders to perform." While we were wondering how we could fill our time and what we could conceivably do to reach our guards and the political staff through some Christian witness, unknown to us events were already moving in that direction.

When I had filled two booklets, each four by six inches and one hundred pages long, with writing, the captain of the guard suddenly entered my cell one morning and said, "Will you please show me what you have been writing during these many days? You seem to be very busily engaged. What is it that interests you so much?"

"I am sure there is little there to interest you," I said. "Part of it is poetry, some of it is religious writings. If you wish to see what I have been doing, here are these booklets." I handed him one.

Having glanced through it, he asked for the other. Then he asked if I had written on the coarse grass paper normally used for toilet tissue. Opening the desk drawer and drawing out a few sheets on which I had recently prepared a draft statement for the investigator's office, I passed them to him. He made no attempt to search for other evidence but gathered these and left the room. Presumably the same thing happened to Olin, whose room the guard entered after leaving mine. There I know he secured, among other material, the abbreviated script of Olin's projected book of prayers.

I knew all the voluminous material collected must inevitably be translated into Chinese for the official records. (This was the task of weeks and I wished them luck, for already on several occasions I had been asked to rewrite my reports more legibly. Olin's handwriting was only slightly better.) Only one of the quoted passages in my writings gave me cause for concern. This was a prose passage I had copied from Olin's only novel, Elizabeth Goudge's *A City of Bells*, which he had loaned me. It talked of belief in the existence of God and of the human soul and was the antithesis of Communist doctrine, which denied both.

At the end of the novel, the narrator asks Ferranti, the villain of the story, why he did not commit suicide. Ferranti tells of some arguments put forth by the narrator's father, a church canon:

> One [argument] was that nothing whatsoever, not even the existence of God to his lovers, can be proved, but that every man, if he is to live at all finely must deliberately adopt certain assertions as true, and those assertions should, for the sake of the enrichment of the human race, always be creative ones. He may, as life goes on, modify his beliefs, but he must never modify them on the side of destruction. It may be difficult, in the face of the problem of human suffering, to believe in God, [said the canon], but if you destroy God you do not solve your problem but merely leave yourself alone with it—a ghastly loneliness. The same, he said, with your belief in your own soul. To deny it is to degrade yourself to the level of an animal and to lose your reverence for the human race, for if a man's existence is to be measured by the span of this life only, then is he a paltry and inconsiderable thing. What he said about creation haunted me when I wanted to "shuffle off" this mortal coil for I had flattered myself that as a writer I was a creator, if an unsuccessful one, and it seemed to me that in crushing out my life I should be denying all that my life had hitherto stood for—his parrot-cry of "never destroy" was like a bell ringing in my head and I didn't kill myself.

I wondered how the local Communist cadres would react to such a comment. I waited somewhat impatiently for several days, but no reaction came.

Then, what I believed at the time to be a brilliant thought crossed my mind. I called one of the guards, for it was a Saturday, one of the days on which we could purchase our few necessities. On my list was another exercise book. (The guard returned with one of the most expensive he could find, for which I had to pay from my small cash reserve.) My thought was this: If the guards were going to read everything we prisoners wrote, then why not do a little writing especially designed to address the areas in which they claimed disbelief? Thus began a series of articles written on the one hand to occupy a few more of my solitary hours and on the other to give a Christian answer to some aspects of the Communists' ideology. I seized upon this task with zest. I would enjoy needling my captors just a little, even if they rejected my efforts as worthless.

My investigators had been trying without success to force me to confess to deliberate attempts to inconvenience, maim or even kill their cadres and officials. Perhaps they might the more enjoy an article I entitled

"The Triumph of Love." This briefly gave the true story of a Moslem sheik who, hating Christians and after killing the friend of a missionary doctor in Arabia, found himself afflicted with a disease requiring surgery. This surgery could only be performed in the hospital of that very missionary doctor. Using an assumed name the sheik was admitted and successfully operated upon. As he was preparing to be discharged, he called the medical missionary to his room and admitted to having given a false name. The doctor replied that all along this fact had been known to him.

"You mean," said the sheik, "that before you operated on me you knew who I was and you did not kill me when you had me in your power and held a scalpel in your hand?"

"Yes," replied the doctor, "I could have done so had I wished. But neither the religion I believe in nor the profession I practise permits me to take a life, even if the opportunity presents itself. Our religion teaches us that we should love our enemies and be kindly to those who abuse us."

To the Communist, the idea of loving one's enemies is anathema. In a 1977 document commemorating the twenty-eighth anniversary of the founding of the Chinese Communist party on July 1, 1949, Chairman Mao Tse-tung wrote: "The army, police and court of the state are instruments for classes to oppress classes. To the hostile classes the state apparatus is the instrument of oppression. It is violent and not 'benevolent.'" The "hostile classes" were the reactionaries, the landlord class and the capitalists. In the same paper, Mao quoted the Sung dynasty philosopher Chu Hsi who wrote a still-remembered maxim: "Do unto others what others do unto you." This is the exact antithesis of the Christian precept: "Do unto others as you would have others do unto you." While Chu Hsi sanctions retaliation for wrongs done to one or kindness only in return for kindness, Christ says that anything we do to others should be what we would like done to us; Christ tells us not to retaliate for a wrong done to us.

I wrote an essay on this subject and asked how there could be peace in a world where there was no demonstrable attempt at love and forgiveness but rather an accumulation and intensification of hatreds.

In another, closely written, three-page essay I sought to shake their own non-belief in the existence of God. To use spiritual concepts was useless. Instead, I recalled a lecture on the physics of water, given by a Professor Davidson while I was a freshman in the University of British Columbia. Forcefully and dramatically, he discussed the various properties of this essential substance, a combination of the elements hydrogen and oxygen, without which life could not exist. He said:

> Consider what would happen if water was not volatile and did not rise as vapour to form rain which could descend on most parts of the earth to help produce vegetation for food. Water expands as it freezes at zero degrees Centigrade, thus permitting ice to float; if the reverse were true and ice sank, it would not be very long before life itself would be extinct. If water did not have the property of absorbing tremendous quantities of heat in comparison to other types of matter the tremendous increases of daytime temperature caused by the sun and the increasing coldness during its absence would again cause such marked variations of temperature that life as we know it could not exist.

He concluded his lecture, which I am sure no student ever forgot, with the statement, "Water to me is the greatest piece of evidence I know proving the existence of God."

After further elaborating the subject for the edification of my would-be scientific Communist friends, I pointed out that it was inconceivable such physical conditions as I had mentioned could exist and be operative without some orderly mechanism or mastermind that was controlling all matter, inorganic as well as organic, including life itself.

How useful my efforts were in permanently changing the thinking of those who read and translated my writings I cannot say. Certainly there were no gross reactions to my comments that I could detect as the months wore by.

With the exception of the severe depression I experienced in late February, following the four or five weeks of investigations in which I was repeatedly accused of spying, on only one other occasion did I become in the least despondent. For most of my months in confinement I had successfully conditioned myself to meet any eventuality in the manner described above. But in July I suddenly realized that the six months I had suggested to Comrade Wu in early March as being the maximum length for my incarceration had passed some days earlier. Yet still I remained in their clutches, no evidence of release within sight. Then another great Christian hymn, "How Firm a Foundation," came to my relief, reviving my rapidly sinking spirits. For more than six months its bars had never entered my consciousness, but now given vocal expression they met my need in an immediate and remarkable way:

> When through the deep waters I call thee to go,
> The rivers of woe shall not thee overflow;

For I will be with thee, thy trials to bless
And sanctify to thee thy deepest distress.

When through fiery trials thy pathway shall lie,
Thy grace, all-sufficient, shall be thy supply:
The flames shall not hurt thee, I only design
Thy dross to consume, and thy gold to refine.

As I sang the last stanzas, I asked myself why I should worry any further. The hymn set me to thinking whether there was any way to hurry my Communist friends in coming to a decision concerning my ultimate disposal. Thereby hangs another tale, the story of how I got a single bit of information beyond my prison walls to my friends and loved ones, indicating that I was alive.

After some thought about how to contact the outside, I remembered that a large amount of penicillin belonging to the hospital had been stored in the attic of our home in the residence compound. In a short time its expiry date would come and go. The authorities would not want this medicine to become outdated and useless. I wrote a signed and dated letter to Rev. George Rackham, business agent for our mission, telling him this and asking him to investigate the situation. I also asked for some vitamins to supplement my Chinese diet and a new supply of yarn for darning my socks. The clever part was what accompanied the letter, a note to Comrade Chu which I hoped would be the means of telling me whether I was about to be released:

> To Mr. Chu: You will note by the enclosed letter that the supply of penicillin in my attic must be nearing the date of expiry. If not checked and put into circulation, this will be a serious loss to the hospital, which I am sure you could not wish to occur. I would appreciate your assistance in forwarding this letter to Mr. Rackham for his attention, unless, that is, my release is imminent, in which case I can care for the matter myself. Yours sincerely, A. Stewart Allen

Nothing happened for ten days. Then came a note from Chu asking me to write another letter for him to forward to Rev. Rackham, which I did. Obviously, they did not wish to present a ten-day-old letter to Rev. Rackham, whose residence was only minutes away by their courier. I received the vitamins and yarn, and deduced from all this the important, if discouraging, information that investigation of my case was not yet complete. My family, however, learned through my stratagem that at least I was alive and presumed well in July. This was the only official evidence they ever received that could help them deduce my condition.

I had had good reason to hope by July that I would soon be freed. A second round of investigations, begun in May, had clarified the charges that would be raised during my official trial. These investigations were different from those held in the winter. I wondered if all the essays on Christianity that I had been preparing for my guards might have suggested the novel, written means of investigation used in the spring.

Chapter 12

The Rotary Club Comes Under Suspicion

A FTER I denied in late February that I was guilty of spying, almost three months passed without interrogation. Then one evening in late May, just as I was falling asleep, a knock came on the door. A guard came in and told me I was wanted by the investigator. He asked me to get dressed and said he was taking me to the interrogation centre. I began to wonder, of course, just what was going to happen. I had read of night investigations, and these usually were rather difficult sessions to deal with.

In the interrogation room there were two seats and a table. The interrogator, Comrade Liu, sat in the seat behind the table. He motioned me to sit in the chair facing him. Conversationally, he began the session.

"Allen, I would like to hear what you have to say about peace. What is your attitude toward peace?"

This was a new approach. I thought a moment and then, being a Canadian, referred to the relationship between the United States and Canada, two countries whose common boundary was unguarded the five thousand five hundred miles of its length. People were free to cross from one country to the other at certain points. If we wished to go to the U.S., we stopped at a customs house and registered our names, where we were going and when we expected to return. People crossed both ways and there was rarely a problem. This state of affairs had continued for one hundred years, and I could see no reason why other countries might not assume the same attitude toward each other and make arrangements between themselves that would avoid conflicts.

We talked in this vein for some time. I finished my comments by stating my opinion about the Korean conflict. The Chinese Communists had entered the conflict a month before my imprisonment began, claiming the advance of United Nations forces into North Korea was unacceptable to the security of the Chinese People's Republic. "It seems to me," I said, "that if the armies of the countries originally involved, namely the U.S. and Russia, had come into their designated areas after the Second World War and contented themselves with disarming the Japanese and sending them back home, there would be no war now between the United Nations on the one hand and China and North Korea on the other. Instead, both the U.S. and Russia had stayed and attempted to develop the areas they had entered. Moreover, China need never have been involved in the issue, as its territory was not crossed by any of the opposing forces."

We went on to other subjects. Liu wanted to know something of what the American Red Cross was doing in China. We talked about this for a little while. He was also interested in Rev. George Rackham, manager of the Canadian Mission Business Agency, whom they found unwilling to follow orders promulgated by the government. They did not seem to understand him and their associations with him were difficult.

We had a very amicable meeting. Neither of us raised his voice and the situation seemed much improved over previous occasions when a group would question me and seem unwilling to accept my statements. It was a welcome relief to talk with someone who seemed willing to listen patiently without trying to correct me.

After a congenial three hours, he said, "Tomorrow morning I am going to send you some questions I wish you to answer in as much detail as possible."

I waited for his questions to arrive the next morning. There were three. First, he wanted to know, in writing, what the American Red Cross was doing in China. I had told him the evening before that I was willing to describe the activities of not only the American but also the Canadian and the British Red Cross, with whom I had also had intimate contacts some years before. Second, he asked for a detailed statement on Rev. Rackham and his relationship to the mission and everything about him that I could tell. Third, he asked me to "please give in detail the counter-revolutionary activities of the Rotary Club."

I did not know what I could say to answer that last question. It was a very unusual one, as far as I was concerned, because the Rotary Club was, among other things, a leader in promoting peace among nations. As far as counter-revolutionary activities were concerned, I could think of none by our local Rotary Club, of which I had been the president when the People's Liberation Army entered Chungking on December 1, 1949.

After much thought, the only thing I could remember that might be considered counter-revolutionary was our invitation to the general in charge of the Nationalist Southwest Military Command, the forces loyal to Chiang Kai-shek. At the time he spoke, the forces were retreating before the P.L.A. I had felt it unwise to have this guest speak to the group. Rotary rules stated plainly that individuals in political activities involving strongly opposing factions should not be invited to air their views in open meetings of the club. Try as I might, it was impossible for me to think much beyond that particular item on our agenda.

I sent down my report. It was immediately returned. "We want to hear more than that. There is much that you should be able to tell us." Again, after more thought, I sent back what additions I could.

In a day or two, Liu called me in to what turned out to be the usual type of investigation. The matter of the Red Cross was quickly disposed of when I stated that during the war years the materials supplied by the American, British and Canadian Red Cross agencies for hospital use were distributed to all hospitals in Nationalist territory.

Questioning then turned to George Rackham: "What does he do beyond what you have stated?" I had mentioned he was in China as a business agent for the mission. He received goods and supplies that were coming into Szechuan from abroad. He was there as both a Canadian and a representative, as I was, of the United Church of Canada. Part of his job was to help the people disembarking in Chungking to arrange their affairs before they proceeded to their assigned stations. His business had nothing specifically to do with the missionary effort but was entirely a business side of the United Church of Canada Mission. His services were available to other missions.

"But," they objected, "you haven't said anything about where he gets his money to carry on his business. Why haven't you mentioned that?"

"If he is doing business, he must have finances for carrying on his work," I answered.

They wanted me to be more specific[1]. "Where does he get his money? Does he deal with the black market?"

---

1 Dr. Allen did not volunteer any more than he had to, because he was concerned that he might say something that could bring Rev. Rackham under investigation. Presumably, Rev. Rackham's work was financed at least in part by the United Church of Canada.

"He has been instructed—as we all have—never to deal with the black market. Everything must be aboveboard and handled through the proper channels at banks. You can rest assured that he is not involved in any way with the black market."

That settled the Rackham matter.

Then Liu went on to the question concerning the Rotary Club. "We cannot understand why you have been unable to answer this question. You were in charge of this Rotary Club for some months, and yet you cannot or will not supply us with details of what has happened. Who was the chairman of your program committee?"

I replied with the name of one of the committee members, an American. "He was the one who arranged programs for the meetings, along with his committee."

"And what was he?"

"He was a member of the American Embassy."

"And what was his official duty in that office?"

"He was in the Bureau of Information."

"Can you not appreciate what was happening?" said Liu. "You had a man come to the Rotary Club meeting and he was asked to talk about the railroad between Chungking and Chengtu, which had been partly constructed before the war. This American asked this man to come and speak on this subject. Can you not see what he was doing?"

I looked blankly at him.

"He was planning this program," continued Liu, "in order to gain all the information he could and then pass it on to the U.S. State Department. They will use that information in the negotiations for financing to help China complete construction of the railroad. The roadbed has been ready for rails to be laid, but the war prevented the government from securing rails from Hankow, which was under the control of the Japanese at that time.

"Can you not see, as an intelligent person, that this was the purpose of his action on that occasion and that other people who came to the Rotary Club each week were selected for this purpose? In other words, he was using your organization for his purposes and therefore these actions are against the government of the day and this is a counter-revolutionary activity."

Looking at the situation from his point of view, I could understand their suspicions.

He then went on to describe other topics discussed at our Rotary Club meetings, and I agreed that he was correct. "Then why didn't you write that down in your report? We asked you to give us details of what was happening in those meetings."

I had only one comeback: "You asked the details of what was happening at these meetings. On previous occasions when we have been talking about my problems, you must remember that many times I have had to stop and speak not Chinese but English to get across to you what I was trying to say. I am most familiar with Chinese medical terminology. If you will pardon my saying it, when a Chinese speaker comes to the Rotary Club, he uses a Chinese vocabulary that I am unable to follow. If you ask me to give details of what he said, I am at a complete loss, except that I know the general topic of his talk."

Liu listed other topics that had been discussed at Rotary Club meetings, and it seemed to me as he went along that he knew a great deal about what went on there. Finally he said, "At one particular meeting you discussed the question of communism."

I did not recall such a meeting and told him so. When I said no such subject had ever been discussed when I was there, he said, "You are supposed to be at all of the meetings. This is one of the things you promised when you joined the club, that you would have regular attendance. This meeting did occur and if you did not hear it, where were you?"

"I recall I was in Chengtu once on mission business and missed the Rotary Club meeting that day. Another time I had business in Chungking that took me away from the meeting. There was one other time."

"Where were you?"

"I was in Shanghai."

"When were you in Shanghai?"

I tried to remember the exact weekend I was there. I told him, and he agreed, rather crossly, that I had been there for that week and had missed the meeting at that time.

"You mean to tell me," continued Liu, "you were in Shanghai at the beginning of May 1949, when everybody was trying to get out of Shanghai and paying much higher fares than normal? They were trying to get out, and you were there then? How did you get there?"

"I went by one of the mission planes stationed in Chengtu."

"And how did you get home?"

"They waited for me and I went home by the same plane."

"Why did you go to Shanghai at that particular time?"

"I was asked to go by the International Red Cross, because they had recently received a shipment of medical supplies I had previously ordered. They suggested that if I did not get them out right away, they could be lost and we would never get them when the Communists took over the area."

(What I did not tell Liu was that I had also picked up a donation to the hospital of gold bars valued at $1,000 (U.S.). It was to be used to repair our outpatient department, which had been damaged by Japanese bombing.)

Satisfied with my very complete answers to this rather ticklish question, he proceeded with another. Midway through it, however, he suddenly stopped and then said, "You do not need to answer this. You were not president at the time."

Throughout his detailed questioning, I had been wondering how Liu could list off week by week the subjects that had been dealt with by the various Rotary Club speakers. A flash of insight came with his last statement.

In a February 1950 meeting, as the speaker talked about the road to be constructed between the Chungking region and Tibet, four uniformed women from the local Foreign Affairs Bureau walked in the door. I invited them to take a seat until the meeting was over. After adjournment the group's spokeswoman asked the executive to remain to answer some questions.

"Why are you carrying on meetings? Do you not know you must have permission to do so from the government?"

Somewhat tongue in cheek, I replied, "We have been carrying on our meetings expecting that the district governor of the Rotary Club would inform us as to what we should do."

"Your district governor has no authority over you at this time. You must get permission from the Foreign Affairs Bureau if you wish to carry on your meetings as you have done."

We were all instructed to go to the bureau the following Tuesday and bring our Rotary Club books and documents. When we did so, we were asked the name of our organization. On hearing it was the International Rotary Club, the official said, "International? Nothing international can be allowed. Please let us see your books."

We turned them over to him and he gave us a receipt. No permission was ever given. That was the end of the Rotary Club in Chungking.

Now I realized that Liu was able to question me in such great detail about the Rotary Club because he had seen the minutes of the meetings.

I believe my investigators used the Rotary Club questioning solely to test how accurate and straightforward I was being in my statements during earlier examinations on other topics, especially when I was considered a spy. I have often wondered just what might have happened had my replies deviated in any way from what was contained in the minutes of the Rotary Club during the time I was president.

The experience impressed on me the desirability of being very frank and direct in my answers. We finished the session without any reference to the spying activity with which I had been charged months before. It pays to be truthful at all times. To the Chinese investigator, *t'ai du* (attitude) is all-important. Indirect replies, excuses and argument lead only to prolonged detention.

The session dealing with my Rotary activities was the last in the official investigation of me, and I was left to occupy myself in other ways until the Communist system of justice arrived at the next step, my confession.

Indeed, soon after the last session, I was told I should prepare a statement of my faults, particularly what I had done with the J.C.R.R. medical supplies I had been responsible for before the arrival of the P.L.A. I described in full detail what had happened from the time we received the supplies to the time they were distributed and finally returned to the Foreign Affairs Bureau. I wrote that there had been no official repercussions at all once I had taken to the Foreign Affairs Bureau the documents indicating where supplies had been delivered and showing that they were being returned to the government. I made this statement very complete so there would be an accurate record of what had been done.

The authorities, after perusing the report, told me it was much too long and asked for a shorter statement. I was well aware, when writing this second statement, what they wanted, for when they said they only wanted a few words, I had feigned a bit of surprise and said, "Oh, it's a confession you are requesting, is it?" and they had said, "Yes, that is what we want." I wrote a few sentences saying I had been responsible for taking these supplies in hand with every intention of helping those who were to receive them, both the mission hospitals and the government hospitals.

There were no further examinations in the interrogation room after my short statement was received. But, as is usual with Chinese affairs, quite some time passed before the authorities finally took the next step.

I awoke the morning of August 27 with a song from the popular Rodgers and Hammerstein musical *Oklahoma!* going through my head. It surprised me, because it always seemed hard for me to sing any songs that had no relation at all to the church. But this morning, my heart sang "Oh, What a Beautiful Morning" and that made me wonder whether something was going to happen that day.

At mid-morning a guard came to my room and said, "Pack up all your belongings. You are going to be moved." He did not say where. Elated, and hoping for release, I did as I was told.

After a few hours, another guard came in and took what I had gathered. We walked for some fifteen or twenty minutes—but not to freedom. Instead I was taken into the Chungking court prison and an unknown future.

Chapter 13

Brainwashing

MY FORMAL investigation was over and I had been permanently discharged to the Chungking prison located next to the court building and not far from the Chungking airfield. This move, I knew, represented progress toward a resolution of my case. After an official court trial, I would undergo the required Communist re-education and then sentencing by the court.

Chinese prisons were not noted for comfort or special cleanliness. However, recent improvements had been made under the Nationalist (Kuomintang) government. My escort led the way to the admitting station, where an officer proceeded with the necessary documentation. Then my person, clothing and belongings were checked. All those items that seemed unnecessary for me to take to my room were set aside and listed, to be held in storage until my ultimate release. When it came to taking off my glasses and turning these in, I objected, stating that I could not see to read or do anything accurately without them. "Never mind," said the attendant, "you will not need these, and it is much safer for us to look after them for you so there will be no possibility of them being damaged." In the end, I was allowed to keep only my bedding, soap and towel and the clothing I wore.

I was then taken to the first of two very similar rooms I was to occupy during my prison stay. About fifteen feet by eighteen feet, it was one of several rooms along either side of a one-hundred-foot-long corridor. The corridor's walls were actually slats, allowing the guard who paced the corridor to look into each room and easily see and hear everything that was going on. The lights in the corridor provided the only night lighting for the prisoners' rooms. In the far wall of each room was a single window which opened on an outside court.

Each room was expected to accommodate twenty-four prisoners. There was no furniture of any kind, but in the rear corner was a huge jar to serve as privy. As we had no beds, we lay on our blankets or sleeping bags at night, placed head to foot with a passage between the two rows on either side. Occasionally, when the prison was overcrowded, extra inmates would have to sleep between the two rows.

The room I was brought to that first evening was almost completely filled with Chinese inmates. I arrived just after meal time and found that no food would be served again until the next morning. Someone managed to find me two *mantou*, cylindrical pieces of steamed bread that had by this time cooled and more or less solidified. These were plentifully supplied at meal times, but as they were now hardened, I could not enjoy them at all. I folded my sleeping bag and lay down for the night.

The next morning I was given an identification number by which I was known for the short time I stayed in that first room. We all rose at about seven o'clock. Two or three prisoners would stay to wash the floor, thus keeping it free of vermin. The rest of us marched out to wash ourselves in water provided for bathing. We each took our towels, rubbed them with some soap and went out to the tub of muddy hot water from the silty Yangtze River. We were also given a glass of clear cold water for brushing our teeth. Newly-arrived prisoners were sent to the prison barber to have their heads shaved, a further protection against vermin such as lice. We then returned to the room for the rest of the day.

Breakfast, which was served immediately on our return, consisted of plenty of hot steamed bread and a bowl of rice gruel for each person. To this was added, at the mid-day and evening meals, a larger bowl of vegetables to be shared by five persons. Meat was served only once a month, in the form of several slices of bacon for each group of five.

Every person had the chance at least once during the day to be taken, singly, to the latrine. This consisted of a number of channels some five or six feet below the planks on which we stood while performing our duties. There was no privacy and I was able to see that many prisoners had amoebic dysentery. We were not allowed to speak to anyone from another room who might be present in the latrine. To do so was to court trouble. River water was used to sluice the channels, and the waste water went directly into the river several hundred feet below.

Between breakfast and the mid-day meal, and between that meal and the evening meal, re-education classes were the order of the day. I discovered there was a room similar to mine at the end of the corridor. We prisoners were taken there for about half an hour every few days and told what subject was to be discussed, as part of our indoctrination, when we returned to our room. As the guard paced the corridor, he checked to see that everyone was discussing the day's subject matter.

However, on August 28, before I had become accustomed to the daily routine, I was called to appear officially in court, which was presided over by a judge, assisted by a secretary. The judge perused the evidence against me and noted that I had made my confessions. He enquired carefully into the two charges that had been laid against me: that I had been guilty of "seizing, concealing and illegally distributing without permission" some medical supplies at the time of the liberation (described in Chapter 6); and that I had failed to pay taxes on certain sales of medicines.

This second charge needs some explanation here. Some medicines had been donated for us to sell to raise money to assist in rebuilding the bombed-out outpatient clinic of the city hospital. Actually, two sales of medicines were made, one before the Communists promulgated new tax regulations, the other immediately afterwards. The new tax was retroactive to January. We did not know of the official announcement of the new tax until nearly two weeks later, as the government habit was to advertise for one day only and it was easy to miss such poorly advertised regulations. Proceeds from these sales were placed in a separate account held by me, so they were inadvertently overlooked when, in April, tax officials came to check hospital accounts. We had not been separating taxable from non-taxable items, so the officials suggested a flat overall tax, equivalent to $300, as a reasonable settlement for the three months' transactions. This was paid.

I explained to the judge that if the two medicine sales had been remembered, they would still not have been reported later, as the sales tax was only a matter of eighty-nine cents. Addition of other taxes brought the total up to about $20. In either case, the sum was too small, we had felt, to make any substantial difference on a flat tax of $300, especially when donated articles were involved.

Before I left the court, the judge made an incidental comment that interested me. The personal history I had been required to supply, which he had before him, indicated I had once worked as a farmer. "If he was formerly a farmer," he said to his secretary, "he cannot be too strongly a counter-revolutionary," to which I inwardly smiled.

The session was short and I was returned not to the cell I had occupied overnight but to a new one, to which my bedding and other belongings had already been moved. I soon learned no person who attended court was returned to his previous cell. In my new room I was prisoner Number Twenty. Here I remained until my final release.

The purpose of the daily re-education sessions soon became clear. They were intended to orient each individual into a common denominator of "correct" communist thought and action. To achieve this, each individual was taught to observe the actions and words of his neighbours for the presumed benefit of society as a whole.

Re-education operated this way. Gathered in one place and seated on our bedding, we listened to our "teacher" discourse on the subject we were to discuss for the next one, two or three days, depending on its importance. After returning to our quarters, each prisoner was expected to repeat what he could remember of the lesson. During discussion, everyone had to participate, even if he only repeated what someone else had said. The subject could be positively expanded but never debated. If someone's thinking was "faulty," another prisoner could quickly interject his comment, without breaking the speaker's train of thought.

Some subjects were interesting and helpful to all, and in these I was vocal, adding relevant information when I could. A few times topics on the history of China were discussed. Most of my fellow prisoners were illiterate and it was news to them, for instance, that China had developed the use of paper and gunpowder during its long history. Subjects on public health and medicine also were useful to these people. On these subjects I spoke often enough to show my interest and, more important, approval. Always I had to remember that the eyes and ears of every other prisoner were trained in my direction. When communist ideology was the subject of discussion, my interjections and repetitious comments were less frequent.

Participation was mandatory, and there were ways to ensure that everyone joined in. One day a poorly-dressed and uneducated middle-aged prisoner joined our group. He sulked and refused to enter the discussion. On the third day, while he made his visit to the latrine, our group chairman asked for ways to make the man join in. All agreed some action must be taken. When the man returned, he was called to the front of the room. In severe tones the chairman asked him why he had not yet spoken. The man made no reply. "You are a criminal. Don't you understand? If you were not a criminal, you would not be here. You must change your attitude or you will never leave here. You have got to talk." After more exhortations along this line, the man finally pleaded abjectly for a little more time and he would talk. The intimidation worked.

Every month each of us had to prepare a written confession of his faults and misdeeds. What could we do wrong with twenty or so people constantly observing us? More than you would think, for these were not major confessions of the kind expected by the authorities before a prisoner's case could be processed. They were instead confessions of trivial faults. I apologized for sticking my knees in my neighbour's back when turning over at night; for spilling soup on the floor, which meant it had to be cleaned up next morning; for thinking of my family in Canada.

We then made our confession aloud. All other prisoners took turns criticizing the confession. One observant prisoner began his criticism of me as follows: "Have you ever noticed Number Twenty when he retires at night? If you watch him, you will see that he stretches out, then takes several deep breaths and turns over and goes to sleep. This suggests to me that he is not taking full advantage of our daily discussions and suggests, "Thank God, this is over for another day." There may have been some truth in his observation, although the breathing was really for relaxation only.

In these sessions there was also an element reminiscent of the investigations all prisoners had undergone before coming to the prison. The best example of this was an investigation that went on intermittently for three days. It began when a guard reported that Number Ten had met and spoken with a former cell mate when both happened to be at the latrine at the same time. Speaking to anyone else in the latrine violated expressed orders. "When he returns," said the guard, "make him confess his fault."

"Haven't you something to confess, Number Ten?" began the chairman. "No," stated Number Ten. After repeated questioning, however, he admitted he had talked to a prisoner in the privy against regulations. "What else do you have to confess?" probed the chairman. He was not satisfied with Number Ten's denials of any further wrongdoing.

"What about all the garlic you have been receiving lately? This must bring some taste and variety to your meals."

"Oh, no. I get this to alleviate my diarrhea," said Number Ten.

"Are you sure that is why you are given it daily?"

"Oh, yes, yes. I could be in great trouble if I did not have it."

"Well, you know that's very interesting," said the chairman, whose duty it was to inspect everyone's evacuations in the privy. "Every time you have used the bucket at night, I have checked your movements and I have never noted that you have diarrhea."

Faced with the irrefutable evidence of the chairman, Number Ten finally had to admit he secured the garlic to give him a more palatable meal.

It is this insidious training of prisoners and ordinary Chinese citizens to spy on others and then report to the authorities any activity they deem to be against authority and the state that is considered so despicable by the Western world.

How closely I was being watched became clear one day when the guard appeared at the open slats of our room and said to me, "I have never seen you on your knees praying." I was startled by his remark and assured him that it was not necessary to assume that position to pray. Praying could also be done while lying quietly in bed after a long day of discussion.

I had to be on my guard constantly against apparently innocent questions that were really intended to trap me. Out of the blue one day, I was asked, "Do you know there is another foreigner, a Western woman, in this prison?" Unsuspectingly I replied yes. Asked how I knew, I answered that I had seen her through the back window.

That was the trap. "Don't you know you are not supposed to look out the window to see what is happening there?"

I had to do some quick thinking before coming up with this tongue-in-cheek reply: "You see, it was this way. All of you know I am deaf in one ear. I take a seat right in front of our teacher so that I may hear what he says. If one of you at the back speaks, I must turn my head to see the speaker. When I turn my head, the window is right before my eyes and there is no way I can avoid seeing what goes on in the courtyard outside."

Similar questioning of others interrupted our discussions from time to time, giving the group the chance to indulge in collective and sometimes quite devastating criticism.

I recall one interruption that was almost amusing, however. One time, when the weather was very hot and we were all sweltering in our room, the Chinese prisoners decided to remove their shirts in an effort to cool off. Naturally, I did the same. The remarks my Chinese companions made immediately after my shirt came off were very interesting. They had never before seen anyone with a hairy chest and mine was quite liberally so. They remarked on the extent of my hairiness—and for a very short time everything else was forgotten but the discussion of the hair on the bodies of Westerners, both male and female. I mention this because it was the only time everyone forgot about the indoctrination class and became spontaneously interested in something else.

Toward the end of my incarceration a topic of special interest to me came under discussion. When the "teacher" talked about "the imperialistic reasoning for the Christian missionary movement," I saw the missionary work I had been engaged in from a new perspective. Some of his points were valid, but on the whole the picture he gave for our next discussion was very distorted. He also stated that the flood of immoral films being shown in Shanghai and other markets was an attempt by Americans to weaken Chinese society's moral fabric.

That evening while lying in bed I pondered what my own contribution should be vis-à-vis the false picture that had been presented. The acknowledged rule was that each speaker could talk without interruption for an indefinite period, so I resolved to be the first speaker of the day. When discussion began the next morning, I started by reviewing the whole missionary enterprise. While admitting that certain groups may have had ulterior motives, I pointed out that basically our intention was to improve the standard of living for the Chinese themselves. Then I talked about my own activities as a physician. Not only had I attempted to relieve illness and suffering, but I was also helping to train Chinese personnel to continue the work I was doing. Already most of the thirty-five thousand registered physicians trained in Western medicine were the product of missionary activity.

The mid-day meal interrupted my dissertation, but afterward I went on to explain the film industry problem, saying our teacher had not understood it. I said there was no effort on the part of the U.S. government to systematically undermine the morals of Chinese society by showing cheap pornographic movies in Shanghai and other Chinese cities. Rather, there were unscrupulous people in the film industry who were prepared to sell these films simply to reap financial gain for themselves.

After elaborating my thoughts for more than five hours, speaking all the while in Chinese, I concluded my observations. Immediately the chairman spoke: "Do you realize, Number Twenty, what you have been saying?"

"Yes," I replied, "I think errors in thinking should be corrected."

When the report on that day's discussion period was made, it read as follows: "Number Twenty used most of the time defending the Christian mission activities and purposes." There were no official repercussions.

One final incident that happened while I was in the court prison is worth noting. Early on, I had promised one of the prison officials that if there was a medical emergency, I would be willing to be summoned to help. One day a prisoner fell off the roof of a low prison building on which he had been working. The prison authorities were concerned that he might be seriously injured, so they asked me to examine the man. At the accident scene, I checked him completely and told the authorities he had no broken bones and was suffering from nothing more serious than shock. He would be feeling normal in a few days once his bruises disappeared.

On October 15, 1951, I appeared again in court, this time for sentencing. Two other foreigners were sentenced with me: the mother superior of the Catholic Mission Hospital, and David A. Day, an Australian member of the China Inland Mission. Each of us received a written judgment detailing our official offences. Mine listed the medical supplies charge and the tax evasion charge. Because the second offence was not intentionally committed, I was asked to pay the amount of the taxes said to be due, only about $20, and assessed a nominal fine of about $90. For distributing medical supplies to the mission hospitals for which they had been intended—supplies to which, in all fairness, the Communist government could not lay claim—I was to be expelled from the country.

All three of us were ordered to be permanently deported from China as undesirable persons. Then we were discharged back to our respective cells in the court prison to await official release. Although we had the right of appeal, if dissatisfied with our sentences, none of us took this option, so pleased were we that at last our ordeals were over.

Chapter 14

Freedom at Last

W HEN I was released from the court prison on October 23, I was taken to an inn close to the dock used by the ferry that crossed from Chungking to the south side of the river. All missionaries who were leaving the area stayed at this inn while awaiting passage from Chungking. While there, I was almost as strictly guarded as if I were still in jail. I was not free to leave the place.

My appetite on arrival at the inn was huge. For the first time in months I was able to select my own food, and I immediately added fruit to my diet. I celebrated my birthday, on November 26, by ordering a special fish dish that cost me almost a dollar in gold.

While I was at the inn, a group of missionaries from our own mission, including the secretary, Rev. Howard Veals, came through on their way back to Canada. They all had orders, as I had, that there were to be no communications between us while they were there. Nevertheless, I did have the chance to speak surreptitiously with one or two of them, Howard Veals in particular, to clear up some of the financial affairs of the hospital. I watched, and whenever I saw somebody heading to the lavatory, I made it a point to have business there also so I could speak with him.

During my nearly two-month stay there, I began to attend to outstanding hospital and personal business. This was a slow process, for my affairs had been left as they were at the time of my arrest nearly a year earlier.

One day I had a visit from Comrade Kao, an official of the Foreign Affairs Bureau. Kao and I had had a number of official dealings in the months before my arrest. My relationship with him had been good and his attitude had always been kindly, even during the complications that arose over the distribution—and eventual return to the government—of those fateful medical supplies. Kao asked me to go across to the hospital with him. Most important to the Bureau was to get the hospital safe opened in order to examine its contents. No one had been able to open it, although George Rackham had given them the safe's combination when he left Chungking to return to Canada.

We said little on the way across the river. When we arrived at the hospital, we were taken immediately to my former office. A group of hospital people, including Fung Cheo-wen, still chairman of the hospital labor union, were waiting there for me. After several unsuccessful attempts to open the safe, I remembered an initial setting that was not included in the instructions. The safe was opened, but there was actually little of interest in it. I was also allowed to go through the contents of a desk drawer to look for anything I wanted to keep. Nothing seemed to have been touched in my absence. Among the papers I kept was a letter from Madame Sun Yat-sen, thanking me for helping to provide relief during the war period. Finally, I had to settle a bill for the hospitalization of our cook, who had been discharged from the hospital just before my arrest. Chairman Fung argued that I should be charged the current, higher rate for the treatment the cook had had, but Kao refused, and the matter was quickly settled.

Our business concluded, Kao and I returned to Chungking. While at the hospital we had talked quite freely and openly, but it was interesting that when we boarded the ferry to cross the river, he took me to the stern of the boat, where we were alone and he could state his own feelings.

"Dr. Allen," Kao said at one point, "your attitude is good. It is unlike Olin Stockwell's, which is very bad. I am sorry you have had to go through this trouble, and I want you to know that we realize what has happened to you. We are sorry and we hope you will not hold it against our government."

"No," I replied, "I will not hold this against your government, but how much easier it would have been had you come to me with your problems. We could have solved them in your office without difficulty."

I accepted his words as an apology for what had happened, and logically I could not have expected more from him.

The first week in December the hospital sent me a statement indicating that matters had been duly settled, as far as they were concerned, and I was free to leave.

Curiously enough, the morning of December 17, I woke with that same refrain from "Oh, What a Beautiful Morning" in my head, just as I had on that August day when I was transferred from solitary confinement to the prison. Could it be, I wondered, that at last I was going to leave Chungking and head for the coast?

Indeed, that was so. Later in the morning I was told to prepare to leave for Hong Kong. The ten-day journey would take me by ship east along the Yangtze River to Hankow, by train south from Hankow to Canton and thence to Shumchun, by foot across the bridge at the river border there and over to Hong Kong's Kowloon Peninsula and finally by train to the city on Hong Kong Island.

That evening I was led to the door of the inn, where I was joined by a French priest, Brother Ouvrard, who was to be my companion on the journey out of China. With him were two P.L.A. soldiers, armed with rifles and bayonets, our escorts for the trip to the border. We all left the inn together and headed for the ship. Brother Ouvrard and I were heavily laden with our luggage, which we were supposed to carry without help. Arriving on board, we were shown our deck beds and were told the guards would sleep in the lower bunks and we would occupy the upper ones.

Next day we found an abundance of peanuts being sold on board and bought some. Out of courtesy, we offered some to the guards. They refused, which of course we expected, since they were not allowed to receive anything that might be interpreted as a bribe. Throughout the trip to Hankow we often offered to share snacks with them but they never accepted.

We were free to go anywhere we liked on the ship and to talk with anyone. Several church people on board wished us well and thanked us for the time we had spent in China in our mission work.

Arriving in Hankow, we disembarked and spent the night in the city. Our guards stayed with us as we strolled about. For the first time in several years we saw bananas and bought some. Again, the guards, who had never seen bananas in their lives (none grew in Szechuan), refused a taste.

Next day we crossed the river and boarded our train for Hong Kong. At our last overnight stop, in Canton, we had to change our silver money for paper currency, as there were no exchange facilities at the border. On my way back to the hotel I purchased more bananas. I reported my return to the hotel to one of our two guards, but the other was absent. Alone with the guard, I asked him again to share some bananas with me. "Oh, very well, thank you," he replied. Together we enjoyed the fruit, now that he was alone and could not be charged by his partner with having accepted a bribe. In other words, it takes two people to make a

Communist, and he was quite willing to share bananas when it was safe to do so.

As we boarded our train the next day, the chief guard explained that when we arrived at Shumchun and the border they could no longer help us with our luggage. We would be on our own as we took everything to be checked prior to leaving China. We thanked them for having been so helpful during the first part of our trip.

That long walk from the end of the train to the checkpoint just before one gets to the bridge—nearly a quarter of a mile—was almost the death of me. During my two months in the court prison, I had had no exercise and after that I had only walked up and down stairs and along the inn's verandah, so my muscular condition was poor. My baggage consisted of clothing, a bedding roll, a typewriter, three books and a suitcase I bought in Hankow. I should have carried less. When I finished that walk, my arms were just about paralyzed and ready to let everything drop.

Our money was confiscated and we had to leave instructions for its disposition. Then we were given ten Hong Kong dollars, which was considered adequate to cover our train fare to the city and to get a few necessities on arrival there.

We crossed the border bridge into the British crown colony of Hong Kong on December 28. Throughout the ten-day journey I had had the feeling that I would never be on safe ground until I got my foot across that line at the bridge over the Shumchun River, that something might even then happen to delay my escape to freedom. When at last we crossed that line, I looked up at Brother Ouvrard and his face had spread from the vertical to the horizontal. I could not see my own smile, but that was the way my heart felt. Freedom is a pretty precious thing; you do not realize how precious it is until you have lost it.

After crossing into Hong Kong and going through Hong Kong registration, we took the train to Kowloon. There I was expecting to be met by Miss Margaret Brown. She was a W.M.S. missionary at the Church Guest House on Hong Kong island, which was where I was to stay. But Miss Brown could not make it, and we were met instead by a French priest, who said he had been greeting people crossing from China every day for the past ten months. He took us for sandwiches and beer (although I asked instead for an orangeade) and began at once putting our minds at ease regarding how we, as deportees and, in Chinese eyes, "criminals," would be viewed by the Western world. He said hardly a day went by without the arrival of deportees and they could now be numbered in the hundreds. When we informed him there were others behind, he laughed and said, "The criminals always get through first. I'd better go along now and meet them." Then he footed the bill for our drinks and sandwiches and went off. A second priest joined us and after I had explained what had happened in my case, he laughed, "I'm a deportee, too." So our spirits rose and worries about our reception took wing forever. The second priest bought tickets to take us into Hong Kong (Victoria), even though we assured him we had enough money to pay our own way. As we approached the city, Brother Ouvrard and I said our farewells. At the station, I collected my belongings, hired two rickshaws to carry them and headed for the address to which I had been directed, the Church Guest House.

By the time I had climbed the long hill to the guest house I was puffing like a grampus, even walking slowly. Again I realized how much my physical condition had deteriorated. I walked into the building just before tea time and immediately sent off a cable to my church and to my wife to lift the suspense for her of what I knew must have been a heavy nervous and emotional strain during all of that long year. When I went into the dining room for tea, I met a man who was just on his way to the daily prayer meeting. He later told me that he reached the meeting room in time to hear people asking if there was any news of me before they started the prayers. He reported my arrival and there was a prayer of thankfulness for my release. It made me feel humble that so many hundreds and probably thousands of people had been keeping me and other prisoners in mind in their prayers.

That first night, I visited Esther Stockwell to tell her what I knew of her husband (see the epilogue). Later, at the guest house, I read through all my waiting mail and started to catch up on the news of family members, friends and events in the world and in Canada during my imprisonment. I was too excited to sleep more than three hours, but I slept well the following night.

The morning of December 30, I went to the Union church for the year-end service. It was good to be at regular worship again. For the first time in 1951 I was able to let myself sing out in church. Several times I was almost at the breaking point from nervous reaction to my release. I kept a handkerchief in hand in case I cried, but I managed to keep myself in check. In the evening I saw a Nativity pageant, so I got just a little touch of Christmas, too. It began with "Comfort Ye" and "Every Valley," and several others pieces from Handel's *Messiah*, as well as Christmas hymns and readings from the well-known Christmas story. The whole thing pulled pretty heavily at my heart strings. Both of the above songs were ones I had sung many times while pacing my solitary room. The contrast between that time of imprisonment and this new freedom was almost too much for me emotionally.

For the first time since my incarceration 373 days earlier I could finally allow my thoughts to be with all my family in Canada.

Epilogue

D R. ALLEN remained in Hong Kong until January 18, 1952, using the intervening time to clear up hospital and personal financial matters. He wrote many letters to family and associates, describing his experience. He also began preparing official reports for the United Church's Board of Overseas Missions and the Canadian Department of External Affairs. Mr. Fletcher, the Canadian trade commissioner, acting for the Canadian government in his case, had also requested a report from him. He wanted to record his impressions of his experience, while they were still fresh in his mind and before they were "colored by the outside world" and reports he was getting about what had happened to others.

The state of his health also concerned him at the time. During his imprisonment, he had had little exercise, his diet had been restricted, his hearing had been affected by an ear infection and his teeth needed treatment. Penicillin and sulpha powder soon improved his hearing to the point that he could hear someone speaking conversationally fifteen feet away, and a trip to a Hong Kong dentist stabilized his dental condition enough to allow him to arrange a flight home.

He was even concerned about his hair, which, having been shaved off in prison, was growing back out. By early January it was beginning to look entirely satisfactory and he felt he looked somewhat like a "respectable" person once more.

Much of his time was taken up with escorting Miss Margaret Brown, who acted as hostess for the Church Guest House where he was staying, to the Kowloon station where retiring missionaries were daily arriving. This station held a great attraction for all those who had left China and wanted to know how friends and colleagues still there were faring.

In a letter to Winnifred he wrote, "This period also has given me the chance to get in touch with what has been happening during my incarceration. Hearing the experiences of others, including those of our own mission, is bringing me into proper perspective again. It would have been a much more difficult matter to accomplish had I gone home immediately, which of course I was unable to do, as you know. My main aim is not to get myself into a state of bitterness, which could well happen after this kind of an experience."

Dr. Allen's Hong Kong letters are filled with references to the friends with whom he was renewing acquaintance. "It is a real thrill," he wrote, "to be received as [I] have been since coming out of China. It just seems . . . as if the whole world has been thinking of us, especially [those of us] who have been so unfortunate as to fall foul of the authorities. This is a new experience in so many ways. One almost feels the welcome could not be greater if one rose from the dead." The man whose only "conversations" had been with Communist interrogators, during the months of solitary confinement, or with fellow prisoners undergoing strict "re-education" suddenly found himself in the midst of genial gatherings. He mentions visits with the Holths; Dr. Hensman; Miss Sayre from Chengchow and Miss Deene from Shanghai, both of whom had been imprisoned; Bob and Fran Edwards; the Honnors, who were with Standard Oil; Mr. Durdin and his wife Peggy; Marven Dunn; the Fletchers and Mr. and Mrs. Hart (Margaret Hosie).

In Hong Kong there were a number of former graduates of the nursing school in Chongqing who had left China to escape the Communists. One of them was Susan Chen (Chung Hsiu Chen), who had been his surgical nurse at the Mission Hospital. When they heard Dr. Allen was in the city, they arranged to have a special dinner prepared so they might come and talk with him and learn what had been happening in China since they had left.

Shortly after his arrival in Hong Kong, he learned that Esther Stockwell, Olin Stockwell's wife, had been waiting at the Church Guest House for some months in the hope that she could talk with him and learn more about her husband's condition. He went immediately to see her and they had a long talk in which he reassured her that Olin was in good health when last seen in August. He told her he did not know why the authorities were detaining her husband; even Olin could not think of any good reason. Then Esther explained what she thought had happened. She said Olin had been "having difficulty" with the Chinese pastor with whom he worked. One day he gave the pastor a letter to post for him. She believed it was opened and inside it was placed a paper that looked suspicious to the censors. (Dr. Allen remembers her as saying they were ordinary crocheting instructions.) After her husband had been imprisoned, the authorities came to her and showed her the letter and the paper, which they believed was a particular type of code Olin had been using. Olin, of course, knew nothing about what had been done and could hardly confess to any fault connected with it.

Dr. Allen also wrote a statement on Olin Stockwell's position as he then knew it and visited the American Consulate in Hong Kong to report on him. He was told that at least thirty Americans remained in Communist jails or under house arrest in China.

It was not until more than a year later that Olin was released. Realizing a confession must be forthcoming before he could be freed, he began to draft a false confession to explain the mysterious paper he had never seen. All situations or incidents in his story that his captors could not check he gave in "great imaginative detail," but all they could check was written as vaguely as possible. Then, being a minister, he had pangs of conscience about lying and went to the interrogator saying the confession was a fabrication. He was told to finish what he had started, so he did. Soon he was released for indoctrination and returned to the United States. There he had to overcome some criticism from members of his home church, who did not understand the pressures Olin and other prisoners endured. *With God in Red China*, a book he wrote about his experience, was soon published by Harper and Brothers of New York. Olin toured the country, giving lectures and enlightening Americans on the nature of their Communist foe in China. A few years later, he and Esther returned to missionary work in Southeast Asia.

Almost immediately after arriving in Hong Kong, Dr. Allen had a chance to speak with Bob Edwards, whose innocent phrasing in a letter had been the source of the spy charge levelled at Dr. Allen in prison in early 1951. He realized Edwards could not possibly have known Communist censors were reading all of Dr. Allen's correspondence. Nor could Edwards have guessed that his (Edwards') simple written request for information on "the financial set-up respecting the arsenal" would be so disastrously misinterpreted by those censors. In a letter to his wife, Dr. Allen described how he explained the mix-up to his friend: Edwards "took the shock of his involvement in this thing well, as I broke the news to him . . . in a jocular way which . . . took off the sting somewhat." Edwards was only too glad to carry letters and to look up Dr. Allen's mother and sister in Vancouver on his arrival there the first week in January 1952.

One of the most important tasks Dr. Allen set himself in Hong Kong was to have an accurate translation of his court judgment and deportation order prepared. He already knew it was a false accusation, for while still in prison awaiting release after the court passed sentence, he had asked a Chinese fellow prisoner to translate the gist of it for him. Now he needed to know exactly what the judgment contained so he could make accurate reports to the Board of Overseas Missions of the United Church of Canada and the Canadian Department of External Affairs in Ottawa.

The translation, made by two qualified scholars of Chinese, shocked him. The facts of his case did not conform to the statements in the judgment; in fact, they differed markedly from it. "Only when this (translation) was completed could I state firmly and positively what at last I had been forced to believe: no matter how sincere, suave and seemingly honest might be the attitude of Communist officials, when their own purposes required it, they were prepared to distort non-incriminating information in order to condemn those they wished to punish." (The translation appears in Appendix A, with a related discussion there and in Appendix B. A photograph of the original Chinese document appears with the other photographs in this book.)

On January 18 Stewart Allen finally boarded a plane that took him home to Canada. He was met at the Vancouver airport, as he had expected he would be, but his reunion with his wife was delayed momentarily by media attention. "Halfway down the gangway, I was accosted by a reporter. He said, 'Please stand there for a minute while I take a picture of you.' On the tarmac were my wife and Drs. Gladys and Ed Cunningham, who had come to meet me at that late hour of the night. I proceeded after the picture was taken and went immediately to them and received their very warm welcome."

A two-week holiday with Winnifred followed, a gift from the Allens' home church, Dominion-Douglas United Church in Westmount, Quebec, near Montreal. A good friend, Ewart Everson, owner of the General Motors dealership in downtown Montreal, saw that the couple had the use of a car in British Columbia. Although Dr. Allen made a few public appearances while on the West Coast, his wife insisted he should use the time to rest. He did not argue, for, as he wrote to Constance Ward on their return to Westmount, "Win's own reaction since my return home tells a story in itself. I have never seen her in so fine trim . . . nor so happy in a long time."

On the way home they stopped in Toronto, where Dr. Allen met with the United Church's Board of Overseas Missions, explaining exactly why he had been taken into prison and what had happened to him there. Also in Toronto he agreed to be interviewed later by *Maclean's* magazine. Finally, he and Winnifred attended the annual dinner meeting of the West China Club, where he again related his experiences. Some in his audience were concerned that many of the imprisoned missionaries had absorbed much of what they had been told during the indoctrination phase of their incarceration. "I made it very clear that, as far as (my) indoctrination was concerned, it did not take very well. They were very grateful to hear this."

The Allens travelled by train to Montreal on February 6, 1952, the day King George VI died and Elizabeth II succeeded him. They were welcomed by their minister, the Reverend Dr. A. Lloyd Smith, who had sponsored them in China. It was arranged Dr. Allen would speak to the congregation at the evening service the following Sunday. When the time came, the place was packed to the doors. "It was a joy to be back again," wrote Dr. Allen, "among the people that I knew and loved and who had been so kind to us during the period that we represented them in China."

To the church that night came Dr. Wilder Penfield and his wife, who wanted to hear him talk, though they were not members of the congregation. Dr. Penfield, who was a famous neurosurgeon and a friend of Dr. Allen's, sent word to him by an usher that they had been there but would not disturb him during that reunion service. Dr. Allen was touched by their thoughtfulness. Later the Penfields invited the Allens to a private dinner.

About two weeks later, Dr. Allen went to Ottawa to meet with personnel from the Department of External Affairs, which had tried unsuccessfully to contact him during his year in prison. In this session, "I went into detail about what had happened and why it was that no one was able to do anything at all about the situation. I was completely cut off from everyone, as far as Canada or China was concerned." While there that day he also was debriefed by the Department of Defence and had a five o'clock meeting with Lester B. Pearson, then minister of external affairs. He had been told Pearson had only ten minutes to spare, but, as Dr. Allen wrote, "Mr. Pearson had very many things on his mind and the ten minutes went to thirty before I was permitted to leave." Pearson's interest gave him some clue to how much importance the government placed on clarifying information that was coming from China.

The interview with *Maclean's* took place shortly after the Allens' return to Westmount and the story appeared on newsstands in mid-April, the same week he gave an important address to the Montreal Rotary Club. The membership of between four and five hundred people included members of his church, businessmen, financiers and professionals. "I spoke, as usual, in a low-key way," wrote Dr. Allen, "because I did not believe in any other way as being a satisfactory method of informing the public of my experiences. Almost at the end of the speech, someone leaned over and said in my ear, 'Your story is out on the street today and people are learning more (from it) than you are telling us.' "

The church's mission board, meanwhile, had granted him a furlough during which he could speak to various church groups and other organizations. He accepted an invitation to give a week-long lecture series at the Naramata (B.C.) Training School in July 1952 and had to prepare a large number of addresses and check all his information, "so I could give the full statement on both sides of the question." Following the week at Naramata, he visited a number of churches in southern British Columbia and Alberta to which he was invited as a missionary speaker. He found that often he had been billed as an anti-communist speaker, but it was not his way to get people worked up against communism. Instead, he tried to educate his audience about the work of missionary doctors in China and gave a balanced view of the changes wrought by the Communist Party.

As 1952 drew to a close, Dr. Allen turned his thoughts to writing up the events of 1951. His correspondence shows that he had completed a large portion of his manuscript by 1954, when he asked former missionary colleague, Rev. Howard J. Veals, to review it. Rev. Veals' reply arrived in September 1954.

Dr. Allen wrote many letters and had many conversations in an effort to learn the fates of people who played some role in his story.

Dr. Ian Robb wrote him with details of his own activities after Dr. Allen's arrest. Wondering why Dr. Allen and Constance Ward were gone so long, Ian went over to the nursing school. There he saw the serious trouble they were in. He quickly returned to the house and began destroying anything that could be incriminating. Late that night Fung Cheo-wen sealed Dr. Allen's hospital office and his and Constance's rooms. Next day Ian burned a book critical of communism that he had taken from Dr. Allen's room the night before, but he failed to stir the ashes in the kitchen stove. The house servant reported that a book had been burned and Fung confronted Ian about it. Ian, all innocence, got out of that trap by saying he did not know there was any law against burning books. The only other help he could give Dr. Allen was to send along some medical books and a warm McGill University sweater. Meanwhile, Constance Ward was kept under guard in the hospital for ten days. On January 2, shortly after her release, both she and Ian were called to the same building where Dr. Allen was being held. They were questioned separately. Ian was asked about operations Dr. Allen had performed on certain Communist patients. The investigators wanted to know whether the post-operative infections these people developed could have been avoided. Ian replied that only some very sophisticated ultraviolet radiation equipment could have prevented the complications. His investigators demanded to know why the mission hospital did not have such equipment and Ian replied that not even many Western hospitals had it. Both Ian and Constance were allowed to leave late that night. Constance had to make weekly visits to the Public Safety Department for a month. Shortly after his investigation, Ian followed the advice of Chinese friends and ceased his medical practice. He left China in March and Constance left in August.

A letter from Constance Ward, which detailed what had happened to her, also mentioned the fate of Chang Tsen-hwa, the man whose arrest Dr. Allen had been called to witness: "The head of the laborers at hospital who was imprisoned in January 1950 was released in Jan. or Feb. 1951. I saw him a couple of times near the stall at which his wife sold oranges, etc. He looked well and so did the family."

By November 1952, Dr. Allen had retired from the United Church of Canada and accepted a position in charge of the outpatient clinic at the Royal Edward Laurentian Hospital in Montreal. Later he became medical director of the Grace Dart Hospital in Montreal, which specialized in the treatment of patients with tuberculosis. In 1959 he began private practice in Cardinal, Ontario, remaining there until his retirement in 1978.

His interest in China continued, however, and although he was officially outside the missionary work of the church, he still maintained his Chinese contacts.

In 1981, Dr. Allen at last returned to the China where thirty years earlier he had been a prisoner. He left Toronto on May 21 with a three-generation tour group led by Jack Mullett, under the auspices of the West China Club of Toronto. Those in the group were either former West China missionaries or the children of missionaries, many of whom had gone to the Canadian School in Chengdu; two sons of one of these children also came along.

A partial account of the trip, written by Dr. Allen, describes his reunion in Hong Kong with Ruby (Chak) Wong, who had been his secretary at the hospital until he returned to Canada in 1945. They spent a long, delightful day of sightseeing together. Over tea, Ruby told him that "the older folk worry about what the future might bring to their children. Having passed through the difficulties of the Cultural Revolution, they fear that the present lull may not last and that present and perhaps other controls will continue." The account also mentions that he dined with Dr. and Mrs. Au, the daughter of the deceased Mr. Tang, one of the three men who had been forced out of the Mission Hospital's administration during 1950.

Dr. Allen found much that was just as he remembered it fifty or thirty years earlier. Rice was being transplanted as before, "no different from the China we knew, including the [water] buffaloes." But he saw evidence of the passage of time in the shabby condition of the residences and churches he had known decades before.

In Chongqing, he was entertained by his good friend and former associate Dr. Dso Li-liang and his wife, Dr. Marian Chang. On June 5 he wrote to Winnifred: "Dr. Dso is organizing a party this evening. Seeing old hospital this afternoon and Dr. Dso has notified them of our arrival. Chang Chi [his secretary during the liberation period] is lost from sight."

On his way to the Canadian Mission Hospital in Chongqing, the changes were evident. The Yangtze and Kialing Rivers and the line of hills on the south bank were the same, but the streets had changed and a bridge had taken the place of ferries. Fortunately, when Dr. Allen's taxi came to the hospital gateway, that, at least, was recognizable. A crowd gathered and soon he was with hospital staff people.

That afternoon Dr. Allen caught up on some of the hospital's recent history and learned what he could of the people who had been there. According to Erica Chow, a Brockville public school student who interviewed Dr. Allen and wrote a biography of him which he treasured, "When he was there, he heard about people that are still living because of the operations done by him." For a doctor, there could be no greater tribute.

Describing his return to Chengdu and Chongqing, Dr. Allen wrote to Winnifred: "No signs of hostility." It must have been hard for him to believe that everyone would now be friendly to him and other foreigners when what he most remembered about his departure from Chongqing was the shame of being deported as a criminal and of seeming to be shunned by those who had known him. It took the visit thirty years later to lay to rest any fear that animosity toward him still existed—if it ever really had, except for a few zealous Communist sympathizers and officials.

Dr. Allen believed he was successful in keeping himself from feeling any bitterness toward his captors that might poison his life after release. There is no doubt, however, that he felt one or two unnamed individuals had been particularly intent on engineering his deportation. During his visit to China he attempted to ascertain who this person or persons might have been, but he left no record his daughter or editor could discover to show whether he had found what he sought.

Certainly he was frustrated that the final official charges against him had nothing to do with the many charges made during his accusation meeting. A letter he wrote to all his friends in May 1952 summarized his experience and ended as follows:

> On not one of the charges contained [in the accusation meeting] was I found guilty and sentenced by the court. . . . The two charges of which I was said to be guilty were already under investigation seven weeks prior to the accusation meeting in December and had nothing fundamentally to do with it. The first item respecting taxes would have been handled normally through the Tax Bureau, the other [regarding the medical supplies] was not likely to have been handled in court at all. Since the political section was only an investigating body which sifted the charges made at the accusation meeting, I was never officially pronounced innocent of all these charges, since they never reached the court. Thus there was the maximum of publicity—all detrimental—at the time of my arrest, but the public was never informed to the contrary at any future time.

It is interesting to note, therefore, that in 1989 or 1990, the Chinese government made a move to clear Dr. Allen's name and offer an official apology. In early 1994, his daughter Phyllis Donaghy wrote the following in a letter to her sister Margaret Williamson:

> The story I related at Christmas [1993] was one Katharine Hockin told me about three years ago. Bishop Ting of the Church of Christ in China or the Catholic Church (I don't remember which, but think it was probably the former) was invited to receive a Ph.D. from the U of T and came to Toronto for the Spring Convocation, I believe. Dad received an invitation, but gave it to me because he couldn't go, encouraging me to attend. Unfortunately, it was at night and away downtown, so I did not go. The invitation included a reception afterwards. Among the invited guests were Katharine and the Chinese Consul to Canada. The consulate

was in Toronto. During the reception, the Consul was enquiring if anybody knew Dad [Dr. Allen]—where he was, if still alive. Katharine volunteered she knew and was told the Chinese government wished to write Dad apologizing for the treatment he had received in China in 1950-51. Katharine gave him the address (in Brockville, I presume). About 3 months later I was at a function with Katharine and she asked me if Dad had received such a letter. Apparently shortly after that reception, the Consul in Toronto was replaced. The upshot was that Dad never did get such a letter. That was why I was pleased to hear that Richard received the royal treatment when he was in China last fall—it made up for the neglect or oversight in Toronto.

"Richard" is Dr. Allen's nephew, the Honourable Richard Allen, Member of (Ontario) Provincial Parliament for Hamilton West (New Democratic Party), who visited Chongqing on September 29, 1993, during a two-week trade mission to China for the Ontario Government. At that time, he was Minister without Portfolio, Responsible for International Trade. He and his party went to the Canadian Mission Hospital, now called the 5th People's Hospital of Chongqing, where they met the current superintendent, Dr. Guan Ren-long, as well as several doctors who had worked with Dr. Allen forty-three years earlier. They were Dr. Fong Yao-xian, Dr. Guo Cheng, Dr. Lü Jia-yu, Dr. Li Zhoa-xing, Dr. Xu Chang-yu and Dr. Liu Huo-ling. "They all lit up at the memory of Stewart, and spoke with genuine and deep affection for him. But younger and older staff alike greeted us with a warmth I and my staff will never forget," writes Richard Allen in an October 13, 1994, letter to the editor of this book.

After returning to Canada, M.P.P. Allen received a letter from Dr. Guan. In addition to encouraging "friendly cooperation . . . between the medical organizations of your province and our hospital" as a means of updating the Chongqing hospital, the superintendent also wrote:

> Through the visit, we believe that you have had a preliminary under-standing of our hospital, which is one that has already had a history of almost a hundred years of friendship with the Canadian people; espe-cially during the World War II, the Canadian friends, such as [Dr.] Alexander Stewart Allen . . . etc., despite all kinds of difficulties, had, with noble humanitarianism, treated and cured lots of the sick and wounded, strongly supporting the Chinese people's fighting against the fascists. We will always cherish the memory of these Canadians.

This gratitude toward Dr. Allen was evident to his four daughters during their visit to Chongqing in October 1994. As Margaret mentioned in her introduction to the book, the vice-principal talked with them at length about plans for the hospital's centennial in 1996 and emphasized the importance they placed on Dr. Allen's work there. His daughters saw clearly that the Chinese want to forget what was bad in the past, in order to move on to a prosperous future.

Indeed, the China of today has changed from the China the Allens knew in the late 1940s. Some things may have been untouched by time—the water buffaloes still work in the rice paddies, as they did half a century ago—but in ways both small and large, China in 1994 is unlike the newly-liberated China Dr. Allen left in 1951. The sisters noticed the bomb shelters along the highway leading into Chongqing from the north. They had once sheltered Chinese during the many bombings by Japanese planes during the Second World War. Now they were being used as private shops. The villa of "that bandit Chiang Kai-shek," the Nationalist leader hated by Dr. Allen's Communist investigators, is now a first-class hotel furnished in 1930s style. Chiang's Chongqing residence is featured on postcards. Subtly sweet bananas, so rare in Sichuan in Dr. Allen's day that his guards saw them for the first time when escorting him south to the Hong Kong border, were now abundant in the province. The unisex quilted Communist Chinese uniform, which Dr. Allen found so deplorable, especially on the women guards, has given way to smart Western-style uniforms. In general, the people wear Western dress in all but rural villages, where old people still wear the traditional clothing the four sisters remembered. Today's modern business women are fashionably dressed, even to the high heels worn while bicycling to and from work.

Whereas once the Communist Chinese leadership used extreme measures to eradicate any trace of Western influence in their country, the current government actively courts Western investment and institutions. A renewed interest in the West is evidenced by the strength of the Chinese Christian Church, the widespread use of English, the increasingly entrepreneurial economy and even talk of the eventual return of such institutions as the Rotary Club.

The Christian Church is alive and well in China today. The sisters attended a Sunday morning service in the Sishengci Church in Chengdu, founded by Canadian missionaries. The church was destroyed during the Cultural Revolution of 1966-69, and Dr. Allen saw it in ruins in 1981. It has been rebuilt and now seats a thousand people. On the day of their visit, there was standing room only. The church is now the site of the Sichuan Theological School.

Dr. Allen had to answer his interrogators in Chinese, with occasional help from an interpreter when he had trouble understanding or being understood. Today, the English language is far from shunned in China. Many Chinese, especially in the big cities, now speak excellent English. It is taught very early in school and in many places the Chinese, particularly young children, practise English by greeting Westerners on the street and engaging them in friendly conversation. The *New China Daily*, the newspaper Dr. Allen's staff member had to peruse each day for new announcements from the People's Government, is now published with a full English translation for the benefit of foreigners. It seems an excellent paper, says Margaret, equivalent to any major Western paper, with good coverage of international news as well as Chinese political and social issues.

The Communist leadership has permitted a gradual move from the communal system toward a measure of capitalism. The country is enjoying a thriving economy and massive construction is taking place all over. Private enterprise can be noted in the farming system and in the prevalence of private stores and markets. In the 1940s, farmers lived in mud houses with straw-thatched roofs; now they live in their own two-storey brick or concrete houses or in multi-family communal housing. The land, however, still belongs to the government and farmers must give twenty-five per cent of their crops to the government. They can sell the rest of their produce on the open market and they are doing very well. The Allen sisters saw street-side stalls filled with fruits, vegetables and meat; they saw enclosed "supermarkets," where fresh foods were sold, as well as well-stocked Western-style grocery stores. They saw no bread lines, as in Russia, where food is scarce.

The Chinese Government's increasing openness holds out hope that one day institutions such as Rotary International will once again operate in China, as they did just over forty years ago. A Rotary International workshop (described in *The Rotarian* of June 1994) was held in Hong Kong in January 1994 to discuss a strategy for re-introducing Rotary in the People's Republic of China. The original Rotary organization in China had begun in the City of Shanghai in 1919 and the last Rotary Club was terminated on mainland China in 1952. (Dr. Allen describes the 1950 closure of the Chungking Rotary Club in Chapter 12.) A similar R.I. workshop was held in Vienna in 1993 to extend Rotary to central and eastern Europe, and there are now clubs in Russia.

Although at present there are no Rotary clubs in the P.R.C., Rotary is recognized there for its service activities through the Rotary Foundation, which has contributed polio vaccine and funds for a vaccine production plant in the city of Kunming. The People's Government has also received Rotary exchange teams focussing on international education and understanding. However, other R.I. humanitarian aid there is not well known.

Before Rotary can return to China, first to Guangzhou (Canton) and then Shanghai or Beijing, R.I. intends to work at telling the Chinese the true story of Rotary—as a cultural, not political, association—and to use flexibility and patience in its approach. R.I. will need assurance from the People's government that clubs would be able to function freely, meet regularly, fulfil R.I. financial obligations and carry out their educational and health care service projects. The Rotarians of Hong Kong have a particular interest in seeing progress in the near future, as the P.R.C. resumes sovereignty over the British colony on July 1, 1997.

While it is natural to hope for closer ties with China in coming years, it is also wise to be cautious. In 1981, Ruby Wong told Dr. Allen she feared future controls and suppression, in spite of the lull at the time. In 1989 the Chinese army swept into Tiananmen Square in Beijing, where thousands of students were demonstrating for freedom and democracy, and ruthlessly massacred many people and imprisoned many more. As long as the Government can turn on its own people and suppress their will to be free, it will be difficult to "forget the bad and remember only the good."

Dr. Allen certainly remembered the good, but he did not forget the bad. Over the years he wrote letters to the People's Government in Beijing requesting a pardon for the charges made against him. It is regrettable that he never received this pardon before his death. He felt no rancour toward those who had accused him and imprisoned him. He always felt these people only did so for fear of the consequences to themselves and their families if they refused. He realized that although they respected him and many were his friends, they lived under a new regime so suspicious of the motives of all foreigners that it was prepared to use any means to discredit and ultimately remove them from China. His Chinese friends and associates did what they felt they had to do, and Dr. Allen understood. As Rev. Jean Baker of Christ United Church in Lyn, Ontario (where the Allens retired), said at his funeral, "He had a long love affair with China and the Chinese people."

Dr. Allen was always eager to talk about his China experiences. In his later years, whether it was with family, friends, medical associates or fellow members of his church, the Brockville Stamp Club or the Prescott Rotary Club, he had a rapt audience any time he recalled his year in prison or reminisced about his twenty years as a missionary doctor. He spoke in a slow, deliberate way, relying on his amazing memory to make his stories come alive. One morning in August 1979, when he and Win were celebrating their fiftieth wedding anniversary, he was surrounded by all his grandchildren and kept them completely absorbed for several hours as he related anecdotes and answered questions. On another occasion, early in 1981, when he was visiting Stanhope, Quebec, following the birth of his second great-granddaughter, his granddaughter's husband, David Hortop, asked him, "What was it like—to be in prison?" That question opened up a flood of reminiscences which absorbed the gathered group for a complete evening.

Many other instances could be related when people wanted to hear about China from his point of view. He always obliged his listeners and their response usually was: "You should put all this in a book!" *Trial of Faith* is the result of the encouragement of his many friends and his large extended family. Those who have worked to publish it posthumously hope it is a book of which he would have been very proud.

Appendix A

Court Judgment

THE TRANSLATED text of the judgment handed to Dr. A. Stewart Allen on October 15, 1951, by the Chungking City People's Court appears below. (A photograph of the original Chinese document can be found with the other photographs in this book.) While in Hong Kong in January 1952, Dr. Allen had two qualified scholars of Chinese help him translate the document. He needed an accurate translation to submit with his reports to the Board of Overseas Missions of the United Church of Canada and to the Canadian Department of External Affairs in Ottawa. The translation below is one that appears to follow the original document very closely and may be the more accurate of the two. Where there are differences that may be significant, the less formal translation's wording appears in curly brackets {}.

Judgment of the People's Court of Justice,

City of Chungking

Criminal Case No. 2657, of the Year 1951

PROSECUTOR: The Public Prosecution Bureau of the People of the City of Chungking.

DEFENDANT: Liang Tseng-luen (A. Stewart Allen), male, 51, Canadian, residing in the Jen Chi (Canadian Mission) Hospital, Chungking. He was, before his arrest, medical director {superintendent} of the Jen Chi Hospital. Before liberation he was the medical officer of the Consulate of the United States and chairman of the West China Branch of the International Relief Committee, and of the Canadian Red Cross Society, and of Canadian Aid to China.

The defendant, accused by the Public Prosecution Bureau of the City of Chungking for offences committed (1) in hiding and taking unlawful possession of goods and property of the 'puppet' (false) enemy (Kuomintang Government) and (2) in violating the People's Government Income Tax Act, has been arraigned before this court for trial. The trial having now been concluded, this court hereby pronounces judgment as follows.

TEXT: Whereas A. Stewart Allen (Liang Tseng-luen) concealed and took unlawful possession of large quantities of goods of the 'puppet' enemy Government which ought to have been turned over to our People's Government and, furthermore, evaded payment of taxes and duties in violation of the People's Government Income Tax Act, this court hereby sentences him to be expelled (deported) from the territories of the People's Republic of China.

Besides being required to make retroactive payment of the evaded taxation of $636,984 J.M.P. (U.S. $21.23), he is fined $2,707,182 J.M.P. (U.S. $90.24) for his attempt to defraud the People's Government.

The court will also order the return for confiscation of the one hundred and seventy cases of drugs and medicines of which the accused took unlawful possession from the 'puppet' government. (The above forcibly seized and held drugs, amounting to 170 cases of the "false" enemy government, we have traced and retrieved.)

THE FACTS: The accused, Liang Tseng-luen, came to China in 1929. He came to Chungking as superintendent of the Jen Chi Hospital in 1938. On the eve of the liberation of this city the accused conducted meetings in secret to take unlawful possession of and find ways and means of dividing and distributing the drugs and medicines kept in Chungking by the Joint Committee for Rural Reconstruction, set up by the Puppet Executive Yuan (Office of the Executive Ministry). In consequence, the entire lot of drugs and medicines—350 cases—was completely divided, with nothing remaining. Liang Tseng-luen himself took fifty per cent, namely 170 cases, of the said drugs.

After the liberation of the city, the accused continued to distribute the remaining drugs and medicines and continued to conceal them and, in defiance of court order, refused to surrender them.

In February of 1950 this offender took drugs and medicine of the Jen Chi Hospital, such as vitamins and glucose, and sold them privately, obtaining $6,647,000 J.M.P. (U.S. $221.57). He kept this transaction secret and issued no receipts for money received, thereby evading the stamp duty (sales tax) of $19,941 J.M.P. (U.S. $0.67), the temporary business tax (merchandise tax) of $398,820 J.M.P. (U.S. $13.29), and the local surtax (supplementary tax) of $59,823 J.M.P. (U.S. $1.99). Early in March of the same year he sold fifty pounds of glucose powder to the Jen Ngai Tang (Catholic Hospital) for $2,200,000 J.M.P. (U.S. $80.00), and again evaded the stamp duty (sales tax) of $6,600 J.M.P. (U.S. $0.22), the temporary business tax (merchandise tax) of $132,000 J.M.P. (U.S. $4.40), and the local surtax (supplementary tax) of $19,800 J.M.P. (U.S. $0.66).

Thus he had, in all, unlawfully evaded taxes and duties in the amount of $636,984 J.M.P. (U.S. $21.23). It was for this that our Public Safety Bureau (Police Department) had him arrested for indictment.

THE REASONS: The accusations against the accused were made by all staff and workers of the Jen Chi Hospital and all the teachers and students of the hospital's school of nursing. These accusations were thoroughly investigated by the Public Safety Bureau (Police Department) and were found to be absolutely well-founded and true. *During his trial at this court, the accused also admitted that all the offences he was accused of were true. It is therefore beyond a doubt that the accused is guilty of the offences of which he is accused.* (The other translation of the document words the sentences between asterisks as follows: The accused confessed without concealment in the assembly hall of the Hospital. The facts of the crimes are already established beyond doubt.)[1]

(The investigations prove) The 'puppet' executive of the Yuan's committee of the Joint Committee on Rural Reconstruction was a reactionary agency of the reactionary Kuomintang, conspiring with the American imperialists to enslave the Chinese people. The drugs and medicines left over in Chungking by the above-mentioned committee should therefore be listed as property of the puppet enemy and taken over by our People's Government. After the city was liberated the Military Commission of Chungking issued a proclamation (its first order) announcing the time limit within which such supplies belonging to the 'false' enemy government should be handed over. The accused completely ignored the order and, in defiance of law and command, continued to divide, distribute and conceal the above-mentioned goods and property, which he refused to surrender.

Besides this, he held in contempt the tax laws of the country and evaded tax payment.

Acts and conduct such as related above constitute serious detriments to the interest and welfare of the Chinese people, and perpetrators of these are transgressors and breakers of the law and should be corrected and punished accordingly.

Hence, apart from

[1] demanding the return of the entire 170 cases of drugs and medicines according to the law, and

---

1 Dr. Allen confessed to *nothing* during the accusation meeting in the hospital nursing school's auditorium: he was not permitted to say one word the entire time.

[2] ordering him to pay retroactively taxes and/or duties amounting to $636,984 J.M.P., under the temporary by-laws, Article 7, Section 1, Subsection 8, Item 19, and the temporary regulation pertaining to merchandise tax, Section 5, Column 2, Item 11, and

[3] to pay fines amounting to a total of $2,707,182, which is made up of a sum ten times the amount of the evaded stamp tax, four times the evaded temporary business tax and four times the evaded local surtax,

this Court has ordered the accused to be expelled from the national territory of the People's Republic of China.

Summing up what has been said in the foregoing, the Judgment, as per details given in the TEXT above, has been pronounced.

*Criminal Court of the People's Court of Justice
of the City of Chungking*

*Judge: Chen Kwang-han
Clerk: Hu Ke-chi
Dated: October 15, 1951*

If the judgment is not adhered to, within ten days after receiving this decision a copy of the appeal should be given to this court for forwarding to the highest People's Court of the South West District.

(End of translation)

Dr. Allen wrote a long report to his superiors, detailing the facts relating to the charge that he concealed medical supplies. That report appears in Appendix B.

Here, however, follows a brief description of the facts concerning the charge that he evaded sales tax. It appears to have formed part of another report he sent to the Canadian government and the United Church.

Respecting medicines said to have been "taken from the hospital," these two sales were cleared through the stockroom and drugroom in the usual way. Both places have complete records of the transactions. The first sale took place before the publication of tax regulations; the second after publication for one day only in the official government paper. One staff member especially appointed to scan papers daily for announcements affecting the hospital failed to do his duty and we did not know of the regulation until two weeks after the sale was made. These two transactions during a three-month period of almost daily transactions were overlooked in April at the time of checking by taxation officers, since they were kept in a special Building Account kept in my hands and separate from the general hospital accounts which passed through the accounting office. These medicines were not part of the regular hospital stocks being gifted by Canadian Aid to China and the proceeds were to be placed toward the erection of a new outpatient clinic to replace that bombed out by the Japanese in 1940. There was no irregularity as this method was suggested and approved by the general business manager of the hospital.

Respecting the sales tax due, it should be noted that similar medicines used by the hospital, which transferred its receipts to the building fund through the accounting office, at no time in the year 1950 paid either the temporary merchandise tax or the local supplementary tax, but sales tax only. This amounted to $26,541 J.M.P. (U.S. $0.89) for both sales. In clearing payment of the sales tax in the first three months of the year, a difficulty arose over the separation of taxable and non-taxable receipts, since these had not been completely separated as stated in the tax regulations. Therefore a flat sum of $9,000,000 J.M.P. (U.S. $300) was agreed upon as a reasonable settlement. As I stated to the Police Department, even if these two items had been remembered at the time, I would have neglected to report them because of the nature of the settlement in April, since the sum of 89 cents was insignificant in a sum of U.S. $300.

These two matters were brought before the Police Department and acknowledged by me on November 1, 1950. I was requested to prepare a statement and report two weeks thence. All discussions were conducted in an amicable atmosphere. When we appeared to present our report and suggested punishment for these two [tax] irregularities, we were informed of a delay and that we would be asked to report when our presence was desired.

Although these two official accusations [in the final court judgment] may have appeared among those made by the staff and students at [my] big Accusation Meeting held in the hospital, the statement made in the previous paragraph shows that this fact is entirely incidental. The Accusation Meeting, which lasted four hours while I was kept in a kneeling position, was of the usual type which has become so familiar to all who know Communist China today, and had to do mainly with attempts to prove [my] special connections with the former government, spying activities, mistreatment of patients, American imperialistic connections, making anti-government statements etc. I was told that I was taken into custody because of the political elements in the charges. I then [at the Accusation Meeting] had no opportunity to say even one word in defence, nor did I make any confession whatever on any of the charges made from the beginning to the end of the meeting. Two days later I was placed in solitary confinement and held for eight months while the charges laid by the meeting were being investigated. On August 27th, 1951 I was transferred to the common court prison and tried the following day. Judgement was handed down on October 15, 1951. This judgement shows none of the charges made against me at the Accusation Meeting for which I was taken into custody, except for one oblique reference to the fact that among my other responsibilities I acted before "liberation" as medical officer of the American Consulate. Released from prison on October 23, 1951, I still remained under house detention until all personal and hospital business matters were cleared, following which I was escorted to the Hong Kong border on December 28, 1951, one year and eight days after being placed in confinement.

Appendix B

Medical Supplies Issue

FOLLOWING is a statement Dr. Allen prepared and presented to his superiors, the United Church of Canada and the Department of External Affairs, Ottawa, following his release from China. Comments and phrases within square brackets are taken from other letters and reports he wrote on this issue; they are added to clarify or expand on points in the original report.

The drugs I am supposed to have seized, concealed and refused to turn over were the residual supplies of the E.C.A. (Economic Cooperative Administration [in Washington, D.C.]), which were being distributed *at their request* by the Joint Committee of Rural Reconstruction to all government and private institutions, Chinese and foreign, which were capable of using them.

These supplies had been asked for jointly by the National Health Department of the previous government at Nanking for their institutions, and by the International Relief Committee of China, with headquarters in Shanghai, for non-government institutions including mission hospitals. With the exception of this distribution made by J.C.R.R. all previous supplies from E.C.A. for hospital use had been distributed by a committee composed of representatives of both the above parties. At no time had any such medical supplies been in the keeping of any branch of the Government Administration. As chairman of the International Relief Committee, West China Branch, and because Shanghai was now "liberated," and the committee in Shanghai was no longer able to operate in the still "unliberated" West, I was requested by J.C.R.R. and E.C.A. loaned personnel [Americans] to head up a special committee to complete the distribution of the remaining supplies. In the name of the committee I received these supplies [at Peipeh, near Chungking] on November 15,

1949, on a written [witnessed] agreement to make fifty-fifty distribution to government and non-government institutions.

[Not part of his report to his superiors, but apropos here is his own reaction to receiving these surplus supplies. It was clearly stated in his letter dated November 15, 1949, to Rev. A. Lloyd Smith and the Session of Dominion-Douglas Church, Westmount, Quebec:

> I have just come from a situation in the city which makes one disgusted. The E.C.A. group refused to listen to all advice that could be offered to them regarding suggestions for the distribution of their supplies (which we already had made plans to do). They dropped the committee set to assist it. Now with trouble (the imminent arrival of the Communist armies) not more than a short distance away they fly to Chungking to ask me to pull them out of their stew. They of course all want to leave China, so this morning I received notice that about seventy miles away there is about $200,000 worth of unallocated medical supplies. Would I take charge of a committee to handle the case, taking the whole lot into custody tomorrow, if you please, for they are all off on Friday? (Today is Monday.) There was nothing to do but accept . . . . The general idea is to take it, do what one can in continuing the distribution, and if the balance is lost by inability to deliver it, well, it's for China anyway. It is annoying (to come at this time) when I should be with my own staff to keep the dampers down a little on fear, for they are not too happy about the imminent change, and of course have little idea of what is coming. *A.S.A.*]

The division was made in committee on November 17th. The portion allocated to mission hospitals was removed by Catholic and Protestant representatives and taken to their respective headquarters. [Rev. F. Olin Stockwell and Dr. Yu Enmei, both of the Kuan Ren (American Methodist) Hospital in Chungking, and I distributed the supplies for the Protestant group; Brother Pretat took those for the Catholics.] Because of the imminent fall of Chungking, the government representatives on the committee had no facilities to make the distribution and I, therefore, arranged to take responsibility for the safety of their portion during the "liberation" period. I arranged personally for suitable protection for them. [These supplies were left in a Canadian Mission Business Agency go-down, or storeroom, in Peipeh, about seventy miles by road from Chungking. As chairman of the committee, I arranged with Mayor Lu of that city for him to give full protection of these supplies until he could ultimately turn them over to the authorities.]

Chungking was "liberated" on December 1, 1949. On or about December 5th I went in person to the Military Control Commission [which was] in charge of the city to report the matter. I was refused audience on the grounds that I was a foreigner and that they had not yet set up a Foreign Affairs Bureau to deal with business connected with Occidentals. It was suggested that if there was any urgent business to transact a Chinese be sent to present the matter.

The vice-chairman of our International Relief Committee, a Chinese doctor [Dr. C. C. Chen, superintendent of the government's Central Hospital in Chungking], was approached and asked to act for me. I have his letter under date of December 8, 1949, in which he agreed to act and stated, "I have got in touch with the authorities . . . and in a few days I may, with them, visit Peipeh and decide what is to be done with the fifty percent of the medical supplies for government institutions."

During the following week it was decided that the Military Control Commission should be provided with full details of the transaction made with J.C.R.R., this to be made in writing. This would serve not only to give them full information, but also to guard against possible repercussions should the matter not be reported in writing. The secretary of our committee sent this letter to our vice-chairman on December 15, 1949, for presentation to the proper authorities. The letter was in both Chinese and English. On December 16th the vice-chairman replied: "A group of officers of the Military Control Commission are to visit us tomorrow morning. I will discuss matters with them in person."

On December 20th he wrote, in a final letter, "I have just returned from Peipeh where the supplies were handed over in total to Mr. Chang, the representative of the Military Control Commission, who went with me. He sealed off the room and gave the key to Mr. Han [the warehouse keeper appointed by the committee]. Further developments will depend on the decision of the Military Commission. For the time being we do not have to do anything more." The commission took almost immediate action, checked and removed the supplies from Peipeh without undue delay.

After several months had passed and no official instructions were received by us, and the supplies for the government in Peipeh had all long been checked and removed, we decided that we might now complete the distribution of the fifty percent which had been allocated for mission hospitals. This distribution was made between April and August 1950. The 170 cases which the judgment accuses me of having taken were that portion of the supplies which were earmarked for all the hospitals of the United Church of Canada in Szechuan, the West China Union University Hospital, and the Red Cross Hospital in Chungking. A proportional distribution was made.

No action was taken by the authorities until [August 1950 when], without warning, representatives of the Foreign Affairs Bureau of the Public Safety Department [in Chungking] came to question us about these supplies. They acted as though the matter had only just come to their notice, though it was well known in other government circles that these supplies had passed through the hands of the committee. [They informed me that one hundred per cent of the supplies in fact belonged to the People's Republic of China. They requested return of those supplies that had passed through the hands of the I.R.C.] At once we placed in their hands complete documents and all information concerning the receipt and distribution of these supplies. It was then that we learned the statement we had sent to our vice-chairman for presentation on December 15, 1949, had apparently not been handed to the Military Control Commission. A copy of this statement was placed in the hands of the Foreign Affairs Department. This naturally raised in our minds the question why our representative had seemingly failed to act as requested.

In spite of all explanations, the authorities insisted that all supplies, including the fifty percent allocated to mission hospitals, were the property of the government. Their claim was that all supplies from E.C.A. in China had been given to the former government (a fact we never have been able to confirm) and therefore were the property of the new government. They insisted that final responsibility for the recovery of all distributed supplies must rest on my shoulders. I gave all assistance freely to them in their recovery. [In deference to their wishes, I supplied the Bureau with lists of hospitals to which the supplies had gone. We sent instructions to each hospital asking that any remaining supplies be returned to the accredited persons acting for the Bureau. This transaction was completed to our satisfaction and that of the Bureau in an atmosphere which was friendly and non-controversial.] What was not taken into consideration was that *all agreements made prior to the setting up of the new government did not come under the jurisdiction of the new government*. This point was affirmed repeatedly, both by the investigators of the Political Section and by the court. On this basis the supplies clearly belonged to the mission hospitals to whom they were given.

All the above facts, previously prepared in English and Chinese, were placed in the hands of the Political Section of the Public Safety Department. The Foreign Affairs Bureau of the same department also was given all the original documents. The Political Section was the department that prepared the charge preferred against Dr. Allen. The judge also, at the time of the trial, had all these facts in hand and there was no possibility of any misunderstanding because of language differences or difficulties. Yet, as can be seen by looking at the Court Judgment, in Appendix A, the alleged misappropriation of these medical supplies was one of the two offences of which Dr. Allen was found guilty.

Both Olin Stockwell and Brother Pretat ended up in the same prison as Dr. Allen. Charges made against them may initially have included their role in the distribution of the medical supplies, but their official judgments did not include reference to the issue. According to Foster Stockwell, Olin's son, who wrote to Margaret Williamson in 1994:

> When [Olin] was arrested, the charge against him was one of mishandling the finances for the [American Methodist Hospital in Chungking, but] it later turned out that one of the employees . . . had absconded with [those] funds. . . . The thief was subsequently arrested and jailed, which proved an embarrassment to the authorities in regard to the jailing of my father. They had to change the charge against him from one of mishandling funds to that of being a 'cultural imperialist.' In the case of my father, I don't think that the medical supplies from the E.C.A. had much, if anything, to do with his arrest or imprisonment.

All three men were eventually released, but Dr. Yu Enmei fared much worse. Margaret Williamson researched her story and wrote the following summary:

> Dr. Yu Enmei was arrested in 1951 and spent twenty-seven years in prison, accused of conspiring with imperialists to divide and transport medical supplies. Labelled a counter-revolutionary, she became a prisoner of the lowest status and had no civil rights. She was in solitary confinement from 1951 to 1952 and from 1969 to 1970. She was kept in a totally darkened cell, slept on water-soaked boards, was given plain corn bread to eat for years, had no drinking water and no toilet provision and only mosquitoes and rats as companions. In 1956 she tried to commit suicide by drowning in a pond, but she was rescued. Throughout this ordeal, her faith sustained her. After her release from prison in 1979, she appealed to the Beijing government for a pardon and enlisted the aid of people such as Rev. Olin Stockwell and Dr. Allen, who wrote a letter to then Vice-Premier Deng Hsiao-ping on her behalf. In 1980 she was proclaimed innocent of the crimes of which she had been accused. In 1981, she visited the United States at the invitation of Harvard University School of Medicine and gave lectures while updating her knowledge and visiting other hospitals. Her friends and relatives encouraged her to stay, but she returned to China to help educate and rehabilitate handicapped children in Chengdu. Appointed to the Political Consultative Council, she lived in an apartment complex reserved for retired high cadre members and translated and interpreted new medical information at the Provincial Health Department. Her latter years were lived comfortably and she died in Chengdu in 1994 at the age of 92.

Appendix C

The "Christian Manifesto"

I N MAY 1950, Communist-influenced leaders of the Christian church in China met with Chou En-lai, premier and foreign minister of the People's Republic of China, and other Government representatives to discuss the need to remove foreign influences from the church, as well as the methods that should be used. The resultant document, called the "Christian Manifesto," caused great consternation among foreign missionaries in China.

This appendix has four parts: a letter sent to all Christian leaders in China in May 1950; a draft of the "Christian Manifesto" written the same month and distributed for comment to Christian leaders; the final version of the manifesto as it appeared in September 1950; and a separate statement issued by the Chinese Anglican church, which presented that church's approach to achieving independence from foreign control in the new China.

In Chapter 9 of this book, Dr. Allen describes how the "Christian Manifesto" came up in the investigation of his case in 1951. He states that he knew of the contents of the final version but had not seen it in print before his arrest and imprisonment. He saw it in detail only after his deportation, and although he notes that the final document takes a more moderate tone than the draft, he still finds it objectionable. For one thing, he does not like to see the Government given control of the church. For another, he objects to the assumption that all missionaries who come from countries deemed "imperialistic" by the Communist Chinese must themselves be "imperialists." He admires the Christian churches in China that had the courage to write their own manifestos, and he tells his investigators he believed the United Church in China would do the same.

The documents quoted below are exact copies of English translations of the original Chinese documents. How accurately they reflect the original is not known. For instance, the translator appears to have been uncertain about the wording in the last paragraph of Section III, Part B of the first document.

Report on the Conference of Christian Leaders with Premier Chou En Lai in Peking, May 1950

Digest of Letter to "All Christian Leaders in China, from some Christian Leaders who met with Government representatives in Peking, May 2, 6, and 13, 1950."

I. Mr. Wu Yao-tsung, YMCA Editorial Secretary; Miss Teng Yui-tsz, General Secretary YWCA; Mr. Ts'ui Hsien-hsiang (?), General Secretary, Church of Christ in China; Mr. Ai Nien-san, a Lutheran Christian met on the dates mentioned above, together with Premier Chou En Lai and others from Peking and Tientsin. There were from thirty to forty in the group, some Officials and some Christian Leaders.

II. Considerations. How shall the Church go forward?

(a) The Church must support the "Kung T'ung Kang Ling," (Common Political Platform) the "New Agreement Basic Principles" promulgated last year.

(b) The Church must accept the leadership of the Government.

(c) The Church must work together harmoniously with the Government.

In all this, the Church must struggle for independence, democracy, peace, the unification and prosperity of China.

III. A. Basic Methods. (Most important)

(a) The Christian Church must use her utmost strength to eradicate completely all imperialism ([literally,] erase all imperialistic thoughts).

(b) It must use effective education and propaganda methods to give the Christians a clear understanding of the part played by the imperialism of America, using the Church to cloak these nefarious imperialistic methods.

(c) Use the Christian Three-Self Principles: Self Government, Self Support, and Self Propagation, thus attaining their goal of Revival.

(d) Avoid the old feudal system, and all capitalistic practices.

(e) Practice self-criticism and act in accordance with this criticism.

(f) Educate all Christians to know these things clearly and to support enthusiastically the land-division.

B. Practical Methods.

(a) As a principle, use no foreign personnel. And on this point, consult with the officials.

(b) As a principle, use no foreign funds. On this point Church leaders should consult with the officials.

(c) Church activities should be confined to their routine work, such as scheduled services and meetings, the selecting and training of suitable leaders, and the improving of the work. In addition to this, there is the important work of opposing the feudal system, capitalism, etc., and pushing forward such work as education of the masses, labor, good literature, music, understand the present time, Medical Social Service, care and raising of infants.

(d) A question was asked by the Fan Wen T'an as to what should be done when any Church property is used by force. The answer was that the Christian group involved should report this to the local officials, and that they would consider it.

Christian activities in the Church should be confined to routine matters, as Sunday services, Prayer-meetings, Church schools, Bible classes, Vestry (or Church) meetings. Beyond these, all other activities must (or should?) cease (?) during the period of the Land-division.

DRAFT

A Manifesto on the Direction of the Work of Chinese Christianity from Now On.

In general: Chinese Christianity is thoroughly in favour of the joint principles promulgated by the People's Political Conference of last year; accepts the guidance of the government; and cooperates fully with the government in the struggle for Chinese independence, democracy, peace, unity, and prosperity.

Fundamental Policies:

(1) The Christian religion should make the utmost effort to eliminate the strength and influence of imperialism in the Church; should use effective educational means and propaganda to make the people in the Church see clearly how Christianity in the past was allied with imperialism and what crimes were committed in China by the same. *The Church should*

be on guard against imperialism, especially the American type which utilizes religion to nurture reactionary forces and plots.[1] The Church also should join the peace movement. Besides anti-imperialism, the Church should be opposed to feudalism and capitalism and educate her members so that they support whole-heartedly the Government policy of land reform.

(2) The Christian Church should use effective means to cultivate the spirit of patriotism and democracy, self-respect, and self-confidence among her members. Within the shortest time she should be self-governing, self-supporting, and self-propagating. At the same time she should practice self-criticism, and in all her work there should be a re-examination, simplification, and frugality so that a reformed Christianity will be produced.

Practical Ways:

(1) In principle Christian bodies should not employ foreigners. How to carry it out is by consultation with the government.

(2) In principle Christian bodies should not accept foreign financial aid. To carry this out they have to consult with the government.

(3) In religious work the Churches should emphasize henceforth a deeper understanding of the essence of Christianity, a greater fellowship among themselves, the training of leaders, and the reform of Church government. In other phases of work the Churches should emphasize anti-feudalism, anti-imperialism, and anti-capitalism. They should promote production, social games, literacy, political education, medical and health work, child welfare, etc.

(4) Local problems of the Churches. When Churches are occupied they should report to the local and Central Government for decision by the Government.

(5) During the period of land reform, Church activities should be temporarily suspended, except the routine work of Sunday services, prayer meetings, Sunday schools, Bible classes, and vestry meetings.

(Drafted by Bishop Kiang, Dr. T.C. Chao, Y.T. Wu, Cora Deng, Y.C. Tu, H.H. Tsui, L.M.Liu, N.S. Ai, to be signed by others and to be published in Chinese newspapers in June.)

---

1 Italics are Dr. Allen's.

(CHRISTIAN MANIFESTO)

*(As it appeared in final publication in the Peking Press
on September 20, 1950)*

"The Task of the Chinese Christian Movement in National Reconstruction in China"

Protestant Christianity[2] has been introduced to China for more than one hundred and forty years. During this period, it has made a not unworthy contribution to Chinese society. *Nevertheless, and this was most unfortunate, not long after Christianity's coming to China, imperialism started its activities here; and since the principal groups of missionaries who brought Christianity to China all came themselves from these imperialistic countries, Christianity, consciously or unconsciously, directly or indirectly, became related with imperialism. Now that the Chinese revolution has achieved victory, these imperialistic countries will not rest passively content in face of this unprecedented historical fact in China. They will certainly seek to contrive by every means the destruction of what has actually been achieved. They may also make use of Christianity to forward their plot of stirring up internal dissension, and creating reactionary forces in this country.*[3] It is our purpose in publishing the following Statement to heighten our vigilance against imperialism, to make known the clear political stand of Christians in New China, to hasten the building of a Chinese Church whose affairs are managed by the Chinese themselves, and to indicate the responsibilities which should be taken up by Christians throughout the whole country in national reconstruction in New China. We desire to call upon all Christians in the country to exert their best efforts in putting into effect the principles herein presented.

<u>The Task in General</u>

Christian Churches and organizations in China give thoroughgoing support to the "Common Political Platform," and under the leadership of

---

2 Chi-tu Chiao, 'Christ Religion' as opposed to Tien Chu Chiao, 'Heavenly Lord Religion' or Roman Catholicism. *A.S.A.*

3 Italics are Dr. Allen's.

the Government[4] oppose imperialism, feudalism, and bureaucratic capitalism, and take part in the effort to build an independent, democratic, peaceable, unified, prosperous and powerful New China.

Fundamental Aims

(1) Christian Churches and organizations in China should exert their utmost efforts, and employ effective methods, to make people in the Churches everywhere recognize clearly the evils which have been wrought in China by imperialism, recognize the fact that in the past imperialism has made use of Christianity, purge imperialistic influences from within Christianity itself; and be vigilant against imperialism, especially American imperialism, in its plot to use religion in fostering the growth of reactionary forces. At the same time, they should call upon them to participate in the movement opposing war and upholding peace, and teach them thoroughly to understand and support the Government's policy of agrarian reform.

(2) Christian Churches and organizations in China should take effective measures to cultivate a patriotic and democratic spirit among their adherents in general, as well as a psychology of self-respect and self-reliance. The movement for autonomy, self-support, and self-propagation hitherto promoted in the Chinese Church has already attained a measure of success. This movement from now onwards should complete its tasks within the shortest possible period. At the same time, self-criticism should be advocated, all forms of Christian activity re-examined and readjusted, and thoroughgoing austerity measures adopted, so as to achieve the goals of a reformation in the Church.

Concrete Methods

(1) All Christian Churches and organizations in China which are still relying upon foreign personnel and financial aid should work out concrete plans to realize within the shortest possible time their objective of self-reliance and rejuvenation.

(2) From now onwards, as regards their religious work, Christian Churches and organizations should lay emphasis upon a deeper under-

---

4 This phrase, "under the leadership of the Government," is of paramount importance, since nothing can succeed under communism except it be under, and following, such leadership. This phrase seldom, if ever, is absent from any document where relationships between people and government are concerned. *A.S.A.*

standing of the nature of Christianity itself, closer fellowship and unity among the various denominations, the cultivation of better leadership personnel, and reform in systems of Church organization. As regards their more general work, they should emphasize anti-imperialistic, anti-feudalistic, and anti-bureaucratic-capitalistic education, together with such forms of service to the people as productive labour, the teaching of an understanding of the New Era, cultural and recreational activities, literacy education, medical and public health work, and care of children.

(Signed by 40 Church leaders and approved by 1500 other signatories.)

A Pastoral Letter to Fellow-Christians of the Chung Hua Sheng Kung Hui. (Anglican [Church])

Greetings of sympathy and respect from the Standing Committee of General Synod of Chung Hua Sheng Kung Hui, and the House of Bishops, jointly meeting in conference in Shanghai, on this fifth day of July, 1950, to fellow-believers in the Lord, throughout the country.

At this conference, we have thoroughly discussed questions relating to the ways in which the Church should show itself able to take its due place in this new era. In order to help Christians throughout the country to pay attention together to these matters, we are specially listing below the more important results of our deliberations:

(1) We acknowledge that the Church is not only unable to compromise with imperialism, feudalism, or bureaucratic capitalism, but takes issue with them as being fundamentally in opposition to the faith of the Church. The Church has ever regarded alliance with power and prestige, and the exploitation of the common people, as a contradiction to the spirit of Christ, Who Himself never compromised with power or prestige, and Whose apostles' teachings on these subjects are recorded in Holy Scripture at too many places to enumerate.

(2) By its faith in God as the Ruler of the Universe, Who sent His Holy Son into the world because of His love for all men everywhere, Christianity is actually engaged in bringing freedom to those who are oppressed. We therefore greatly rejoice in the liberation which has come to the people of our nation, and with the utmost sincerity uphold that freedom of religious faith which is guaranteed in the "Common Political Principles".

(3) Our Church has already made real achievements along the lines of becoming self-governing, self-supporting, and self-propagating; we are

now determined along with all our fellow-Christians to press forward together to achievement of our goal, within the shortest possible time.

(4) Within the Church, there have been in the past black sheep, who have disregarded the tenets of the Church and rebelled against Christ; but their actions have been those of a small number of individuals, who cannot be held to represent the whole Church; their sins, moreover, have been abhorred by the Church itself. From now onwards, we must therefore redouble our efforts to make pervasive throughout every part of the Church's life the spirit of holiness and Catholicity, which are distinctive characteristics of the Church.

(5) The things which our Church must henceforth promote in a positive way are, on the one hand, an emphasis on cultivation of the spiritual life, religious education, and the fostering of Christian personality, and home life; and on the other hand, an emphasis on productive labour and the service of society.

(6) Christ is the Prince of Peace, and our Church has therefore in all the past history stood for the promotion of peace. We are opposed to every form of weapon which cruelly slaughters human beings.

Finally, in order to strengthen our Church, and to prepare ourselves to overcome difficulties, we propose that starting from now on, for the next year, all Christians throughout the country use a few minutes at noon every day in mutual prayer, thus constantly reminding ourselves of our common mission and responsibilities. As to the concrete tasks to be undertaken by the Church from now on, and the deepening of our apprehension of the Faith, our Church is already engaged upon preparation of a series of Church Study handbooks to be distributed later.

Issued by the Standing Committee of General Synod of the C.H.S.K.H. and the House of Bishops, July 5, 1950.

Index

This index lists names of most people found in the book. It is not a subject index. It lists only a few other proper names of places or organizations. Names in photo legends are not indexed. Note that the Chinese surname always appears before the given name. If the name has been anglicized, eg. John Chang, a comma appears after the surname in the index.